CW00689137

Growing up in

'Lederhosen'

Steven J Burt

Memories of growing up on a newly built council housing estate in the sixties; a small west country village on a hill, surrounded by fields, woods, river and canal in the valley below.

A village where kids could roam freely and do pretty much as they pleased.

This is a chronicle of childhood friendships, feuds, and escapades and also the unusual quirks of growing up with an English dad and a German mum.

Written as recalled my book is dedicated to all the Winsley kids of the sixties especially my lifelong friend Jeff whose amazing recollection of events contributed greatly to the content.

Former members of the JKC gang, the families on our estate, friends from my years at Nelson Haden Boys School and our time living in North Bradley.

And of course to my own family past and present.

Growing up in

'Lederhosen'

First published in 2015
by Steven John Burt

No part of this work may be reproduced, stored or copied in any format, including digital, without the express permission of the publisher in writing

© Steven John Burt

ISBN 978-0-9570538-2-3 (book)
ISBN 978-0-9570538-3-0 (ebook)

Published by Chapel Rank Publications

About the author

The author, as this book will explain, grew up in a small West Country village during the sixties.

With a German mum and English dad life was at times confusing but never boring.

Although well-mannered and polite Steven was not the best behaved kid on block, and soon began to flash on the radar of the local village policeman. No matter how harsh the punishment misbehavior persisted and school results plummeted; parents despaired.

John and Else's rising concerns were brought to a halt when their now fourteen year old wayward son came home from school one evening and announced he was leaving home to become a boy soldier in the Royal Engineers.

From that moment life changed. Two years as a Junior Leader Royal Engineer stationed in Dover; followed by four years in Germany defending the free west from the Soviet hordes posed in readiness behind the 'Iron Curtain', and two active service tours on the streets of Northern Ireland, changed Steven from boy to man.

The years that followed his time in the army were interesting, and exciting, with jobs in the oil industry and the world of International Marine Tourism; the latter taking him all over the world through numerous contracts and adventures.

Steven eventually married in 2010 and settled in Norfolk where he works in a variety of management roles.

Now approaching retirement he hopes to fulfill a final ambition to live a few years in the country of his mother's birth which he dearly loves, Germany, and eventually return to retire in West Wiltshire.

Chapters

Prologue

From those days of toddling round our gardens to the present, Jeff is still my best mate; we phone each other up once every couple of weeks; we laugh and joke about football or anything else that's been the news topic of the day.

When I manage to escape my adopted Norfolk and visit the West Country for a weekend to see Jeff and his wife Sue, we'll drive over to visit Pat and Maurice, Jeff's mum and dad in Winsley, the small country village where he, I, and our brothers grew up and went to school.

After a bite to eat and a chat Jeff and I will wander to the 'Seven Stars' for a pint. The village pub that's stood for many hundreds of years; the pub where generations of Hosey's, Sartain's and Burt's, my ancestors, have stood and drunk after a hard day's work or a game of bowls.

We never go directly to the pub; inevitably we will wander through the old part of the village pointing out places and remembering stuff we got up to as kids. Looking for Slow-worms on the allotment wall, ringing the twist bell on Mrs Allen's front door and running away, jumping on the back step of the 'Mothers Pride 'bread van for a ride round the village, or going to old man Scadden on Saturday morning for a hideous saucepan haircut.

It was a time between 1960 and 1970 when kids could run free in the woods and fields without fear of being abducted; a time when we could walk to Bradford-on-Avon and be offered a lift home by a neighbour in a passing car, or ride our bikes for miles only returning home as dusk fell.

Our village stands on top of a hill; a peninsular of land jutting out into the Avon valley.

The railway, John Rennie's Kennet and Avon Canal, and the River Avon, run side by side in a big semi-circle through the valley below.

I can still recall the sound of trains chugging their way through the valley as I lay in my bed as a child.

On leaving our house in Winsley we could walk in any direction, though fields and on footpaths to Conkwell, Turleigh, Murhill and Avoncliff; a different walk for every day of the year.

As a family we would walk to Conkwell through Inwoods, then over the common to Farleigh Wick. We did this almost every other Sunday afternoon to have tea with my auntie Dart; a round trip of at least five miles.

Our playground as kids stretched for miles, and within that

1

playground we had everything we could desire; acres of woods in which to play, trees to climb, caves to explore, the old workmen's punt on the canal, and the river to fish and swim in.

The parents of a couple of friends owned dairy farms where we could rig Tarzan swings from the rafters in the barn, or build castles from the small rectangular bales of straw as they were then; fortifications preceding the stubble fights that would inevitably end in one child running home in tears. But the tears soon dried, and any telling-off rarely lasted long; it was an idyllic childhood.

As we walk round the quiet pretty old part of the village on our way to the pub we both agree; the village has an aura.

Winsley is a special village and we grew up in a special moment in time.

Jeff & Steve in the front room of 17 St Nicholas Close
1958

A bit of family history 'The Burt's, Hosey's& Sartain's'

I was born in 1956. My mum comes from Dusseldorf in Germany; my dad's a country boy from Winsley, a small village in Wiltshire; the son of Grace and John Burt.

Grace my grandmother was born a Sartain, the daughter of Fred and Annie.

Annie was a Hosey; one of three sisters and a brother. All three families lived either in Monkton Farleigh, Winsley, or in the hamlets of Turleigh and Murhill, half a mile down the hill from Winsley.

Fred in his RFC uniform 1914/15 with Annie and Grace.

John Hosey, the son, was in the Somerset Light Infantry and Dorothy Blackmore (who I'll mention later), told me he was killed in the Second Boer War in the late eighteen hundreds.

Annie was the eldest sister followed by Rosy and Elizabeth.

Annie married Fred Sartain, Fred also served in as a young man in the India campaigns, also with the Somerset Light Infantry.

During the Great War he enlisted again with the Forces and served as an auxiliary in The Royal Flying Corps; he would have been around forty years old at that time. The photo shows him in RFC uniform with my gran Grace and Annie, our 'little granny' as Pete and I called her. Sadly he died in the year I was born.

When Fred was discharged from service after the war he worked as a laborer on the widening of the Warminster Road above Limpley Stoke and also as the Wharf Master on the Kennet-on-Avon Canal dockside at Dundas. The crane he used to unload the barges is still there to this day; gran told me her dad lost the top of his finger in the gear wheels. I still have his army pocket knife and the steel crowbar he carried to work with him every morning while working on the Warminster Road building project.

Fred and Annie had only the one child, Grace our gran, who married John Thomas Burt, her cousin; I'll explain this further on.

I was told by gran that Rosy married a man called Badder. He had something to do with the K&A canal, either working on the wharf or on a barge moving freight along the waterways of Southern England.

Elizabeth went to work in service; she fell pregnant to the gentleman's son and was dismissed with a payoff. She gave birth to a daughter; Dorothy.

Following the birth Elizabeth disappeared and wasn't heard of by her daughter or family for fifty years. She left Dorothy behind with the Hosey family and she was raised by Annie and Fred, also I'm lead to believe by the Dagger family who were neighbours in Murhill; I knew her as auntie Dot and she married Bert Blackmore.

Henry George & Sarah Burt (Sartain) with Grace Matilda outside their house in Murhill around 1911. Six sons and two daughters grew up in this house which stands to this very day.

Unlike the Sartains and Hosey's who had been residents in and around Murhill and Winsley since records began, the Burt family arrived in Turleigh from the Westbury, Warminster area around the early 1800s when another John Burt married to Matilda is recorded as setting up as the village blacksmith in Turleigh; he would be my great, great, granddad. He had two sons and two daughters; the youngest son born in 1860 was Henry George, my great granddad on granddad's side.

Henry married Sarah Sartain who was one of Fred Sartain's sisters. This is how my gran and granddad Burt ended up being married cousins.

John Thomas, my granddad was one of five brothers and two sisters born from Henry and Sarah.

William, Arthur, Fred, and Lesley, were the other four brothers; Grace-Matilda and Dorothy, or auntie Dart as we called her were the sisters.

I know four of the brothers fought in the First World War and returned because I knew them as a child. A miracle really when you look back at the film footage of the 'Great War' and the trenches.

William was also known as Robert (his second Christian name); he and my granddad courted two girls working in service and eventually married them. John married Grace my gran and Robert married Amy, they had a daughter Ada.

Amy came from Swindon and their marriage would link the Burt family into a huge clan in Swindon; the Adams and the Cockells. Robert and Amy lived in Bradford-on-Avon until Robert died; Amy then returned to Swindon living till death in Manchester Road, just down from 'The Town' football ground.

Fredrick Burt married and had two children, a daughter called Freda who married an Irishman with the surname 'Cosgrave'; 'Paddy' as he was known in the family, I'm sure this was his nickname, his real Christian name I never knew and a son called Henry. Uncle Fred had the shop in Turleigh and I believe Freda and Paddy took it over when Fred retired. My aunt and uncle had a little daughter called Maureen.

Auntie Darts house in Farleigh Wick, The porch and wall are new additions.

Maureen died when she was around seven years old; I was always led to believe this was in a car accident. Following Maureen's death Freda and Paddy moved from the bungalow in which they now lived in Turleigh Hill to Kendell in the north of the country. We believe this to be because her Brother Henry had settled there. Henry had spent time there with his parents before the outbreak of war in 1914. At this point our family lost touch with them.

Arthur also lived in Turleigh; he was known as Archie, married and had a son (Arthur) Cyril; Cyril lived in Winsley with his wife Betty. Betty suffered badly with depression and they never had children. Cyril was a great bloke who I'll mention again later on.

Lesley is recorded as being in the house in Murhill for the Census of 1911. But I can find no trace of him after that, however he would have been of age to fight with his brothers in the Great War and may have lost his life on the Western Front.

Grace Matilda disappears after the 1911 census but then she could have been away working in service or married and moved from the house in Murhill and taken her husband's name by the time the 1921 census came round; only persons present in the house at the time, were, and still are recorded on the census.

Dorothy or 'Dart' as she was known to all, was the eldest of the brothers and sisters; she married a miner from Wales, their surname was Smith and they had three daughters, Dorothy, Connie and Joy and two sons, Bert and Horace in Farleigh Wick.

Both brothers went off to war, the Second World War this time.

Bert joined the Royal Engineers; he fought at the siege of Tobruk and was involved in all the campaigns in North Africa and probably Italy as well. He fell in love with a local North African girl but his parents were horrified by the thought of him marrying an Arab girl and forbade the union. He finished the relationship as his parents had asked but never had another woman in his life, never married or had kids. He lived with his mum until he died of a stroke in the mid-seventies; very sad.

I remember him as a lovely gentle man who took great pleasure in knowing that I had followed in his footsteps by joining the Royal Engineers.

I would visit him when 'on leave' from the army and talk to him about the stuff I got up to, my intentions of training as a 'Heavy Plant Operator', the same job role he'd carried out in North Africa during the war.

Horace served with the Wiltshire Regiment. He married and had two daughters roughly the same ages as Pete and me. They lived somewhere near Melksham.

Then there were daughters Connie, Dorothy, (nickname Shush) and Joy. Connie married during the Second World War and had a daughter Ann, a second cousin who was bridesmaid for my mum; Connie's husband was killed during the conflict.

Joy and Shush remained unmarried and lived together in the house in Farleigh Wick until the end of their days.

Finally John and Grace Burt, my gran and granddad, had a daughter Susan and a son Denis John, my dad, or John as everyone called him; he didn't like the name Denis.

Sadly my auntie Susan died when she was around five years old so my dad grew up an only child.

A bit of family history 'The Hopp's'

My mum arrived in England a few years after the war. The eldest of two brothers and two sisters, she came from Düsseldorf in Germany.

My Grandfathers family (Opa) had their roots in Konigsberg East Prussia, the German enclave within Poland which is now part of modern day Poland. Opa's parents moved to Dusseldorf before he was born, however a big family remained in East Prussia throughout the war.

My Grandmothers father was French, from Montpellier on the Mediterranean coast, he met and married a German girl and moved to her home city of Dusseldorf. He set up a thriving brickworks in Lorick a suburb of the city on the south side of the Rhine; when the First World War started he fought for Germany, but in a noncombat role. My Oma was born and had three sisters; then my great grandmother Barbier died and my great grandfather

Mum and Opa next to the river Rhine Dusseldorf before coming to England in 1949.

remarried. They still had the brickworks at the onset of WW2. But it was destroyed in the bombing.

My German granddad fought in the Second World War as a Military Engineer Officer; he served in Norway, Normandy and on the Russian front. He was captured in Odessa on the Black Sea right at the end of the war and kept prisoner for a long time after hostilities had ended. He was repatriated to the west in 1949.

When the bombing of the industrial Ruhr area of Germany became so bad that to stay would have meant almost certain death. The authorities evacuated the family from Dusseldorf to a small village in Pomerania in the east which is also now part of Poland, Glowitz near Stolp (now renamed in Polish Słupsk) on the Baltic coast.

Pomerania remained a quiet backwater until the tide of war on the Eastern front turned and the Russians advanced pushing German troops back toward their own borders.

The advancing Russians pushed westward and soon occupied the village of Glowitz.

Many women, mum included, were rounded up and marched east for slave labour in Russia. During the march eastward into Poland mum escaped with another girl Ruth; they done this by hiding in a couple of storage containers in a barn while resting overnight in a derelict farm. They remained hidden long after the remainder of the column continued on its journey. This was an incredibly brave step to take as discovery would have meant a bullet in the head at the side of the road.

Over the course of weeks and with great care they returned cross-country on foot back to Glowitz where the rest of the family were still living under Russian occupation.

Following the random executions and deportation of work-age women from the village, many dwellings were left empty. My Oma took the children and occupied a vacant house on the edge of the village where they struggled to survive while keeping as far away as possible from the occupying troops and praying my mum would eventually return.

My Oma's prayers were answered and by a miracle my mother did return. To avoid the possibility of recapture my Oma kept mum in hiding both by day and night, in a pigeon loft above a barn.

Within weeks of mum getting back to the family, Polish troops replaced Russian troops in the surrounding area; this part of Germany had been gifted to Poland by the allied leaders in Potsdam.

However, brutality under the Poles was no less severe than under the Russians and it would be only a matter of weeks before the Poles would forcibly remove all Germans from Pomerania. Those putting up resistance would be shot out of hand; although at the time this was unknown to the German population that remained.

My grandmother made a decision that probably saved the lives of the whole family.

The fighting had passed them by. Although the battle for Berlin still raged the end of the war was only days away. She decided that to remain where they were was more dangerous than trying to find their way back to Dusseldorf in the west and so an epic journey began on foot; the family of five struggling to get back to their home city over eight hundred miles away while the last pockets of war raged around them.

Eventually, after bypassing the centre of Berlin to the south, they made it through the Russian front and into the American lines at Helmstadt, and from there back to Düsseldorf.

The city at the end of the war was unrecognisable. Their street along with most of the city was almost completely flattened; their block of flats, by a miracle, was one of only a few left standing.

When they entered their flat for the first time in four years they discovered four orphan children who had taken up residence and managed to survive.

My gran adopted the four waifs until they could be cared for properly by the authorities, and with my mum endeavored to keep the family from starvation.

Being almost fluent in English she got a job with the British occupying forces as an interpreter, working as a personal assistant to a Captain Svenson

The British servicemen were kind and gave her food, cigarettes and other odds and ends; these she traded at night on the black-market in bars and backstreets for the essential everyday items needed to survive. Very slowly over the course of time things got better.

Captain Svenson asked my mum if she would like to go to England, to his small West Country village of Winsley, and work as a nanny for his children.

By living for a time among an English community mum hoped to improve her English even further; so she jumped at the chance.

After introducing Captain Svenson to my grandparents and satisfying their concerns on her safety and welfare mum left for England.

This was 1949 and my Opa had only been released from captivity by the Russians a couple of months earlier.

During those first months following the end of the war Oma found

Captain Svenson's house where mum first lived on coming to England

9

out through the International Red Cross that my grandfather was alive; after a while he was able to correspond with the family as negotiations moved slowly between the western powers and the Russians for the release of remaining German POWs (prisoners of war).

The Russians were using his skills as an architect/engineer in their own rebuilding program so were reluctant to release him but, at the same time this probably saved his life as German soldiers with no skills were sent to dig salt in Siberia and thousands disappeared into the tundra never to be heard of again.

I have only just scratched the surface of my mum's war years. Her story on its own has filled a book which she has published both in paperback and electronically on Kindle; *Innocence Lost* is an incredibly good read.

At the time mum started working in Winsley my dad was doing his National Service in the RAF; coincidentally he was stationed in Germany at RAF Gutersloh.

One day while home on leave he spotted my mum in the village pushing her charges in a pushchair. He told his mate, 'that's the girl I'm going to marry.' And he did.

The rest of the story

Late forties early fifties Britain was still under rationing, times were hard, money was short.

Mum was German. While working for the Svenson's she was enclosed within that family, but making a life outside of that protective environment was not easy for a German woman; after five years of war she was still viewed by some as the enemy.

Mum left Svenson's to train as a nurse at the Bradford-on-Avon district hospital, she moved into the nurses accommodation and she and dad became engaged. Mum continued to work as a nurse until they moved to Winsley.

Following their wedding mum and dad moved to rented rooms in Trowbridge but this was far from ideal, a newly married couple living in 'digs'. Mum was sure the landlady was trying to get into dads boxers so within a short space of time they moved to a small and basic cottage in Ashley Road, Bradford-on-Avon, and applied for a newly built council house in Winsley.

In 1955 they were offered a new two bedroom house on the council estate being built in the village, and so moved into 17 Saint Nicholas Close.

Shortly after moving I was born; three years later along came my brother Pete.

The council estate was not bad as community housing goes. Today almost every house on the estate has been sold off as a private residence and after the normal 'now it's mine' type of customisation, extensions, garages, and conservatories, etc., you would never know they had been local authority dwellings.

Mum and Dad preparing me for my first swimming lesson in our pond following my Christening party at 17 St Nicholas Close summer 1956.

'The estate', as we called it was separated from the old village by the Church, the Churchyard, and the allotment. To go to one of the two village shops you had to walk up Vinegar Path, so named, rumor has it, because at some point in history somebody had dropped and broken a bottle of vinegar on the path and the name had stuck. Another route to the old village was to walk down Dane Rise to the Turleigh main cross roads then up the hill past the police house and into the old village past the school. The aerial photo on the previous page shows the school centre right, the church centre, with the churchyard hidden behind the trees in the middle left of the photo. Behind the trees are the bungalows of Nicholas Close and the lower part of Poston Way; in the far distance you can see the 'new estate' as we called it, which began being built in the mid-sixties.

We kids would walk up the hill past the police house to get to the playing field which sat on top of the hill next to the war memorial. We had heaps of fun in that playground, which was bordered on one side by a small Copse of 'Poplar' trees and on the other by a high sandstone wall; the playing field contained a see-saw a huge slide and two swings. We would mess around on the play equipment and do the most dangerous things under the banner of playing; our parents would have died if they had known what we got up to in that playing field. Sadly the parish council sold the land to a builder called Bevan sometime around 1965 and he built a house on it. He had a son Michael around my age who was not very popular; the blame lay squarely on his shoulders that our field had disappeared and consequently he got it in the neck quite often at school.

Our two-bedroom house in St Nicholas Close was set back off the road on a footpath that joined the Close to Poston Way.

Jeff my mate and the first of the four White brothers lived two doors away further down the path. He was six months behind me in age; we were set to be life-long friends.

My gran and granddad had also obtained council accommodation on the estate. They moved from a beautiful cottage in Chapel Rank in the old village, first to a flat in Dane Rise, then, when Fred Sartain died and little granny moved in with them, to a two bedroom bungalow round the corner from us in King Alfred Way. Annie Sartain known to Pete and I as 'Little Granny 'would sit in a corner of the kitchen all day long with the dog Trudy lying on her feet; Trudy was a very old dog, a Labrador Collie cross and belonged to my great gran and granddad. When I turned up, either with mum and dad or when I was older on my own, gran would plonk me on a chair beside her and I would chatter away while drinking a glass of Corona cherryade.

Lederhosen and wellies...
Look out world here I come!

There were very few cars in the village at that time. Dad had a motorbike, a BSA, which would be kept against the wall at the back of the house; even at three years old I would love to sit on the motor bike and hold on to the handle bars.

Mum hadn't yet started work and wouldn't until I started school in 1961. Most mums at that time were at home.

The first car dad and mum owned was a Ford Thames van they bought in 1959. Mum called it Belinda. Dad went to Alfred Chatfield who had the scrapyard over in Southwick near Trowbridge and bought windows and seats from a couple of old wrecks. Cutting holes in the side of the van he fitted the windows and also the seats; job done, we now had an early sixties version of a people carrier.

Mum sewed a canvas canopy that fitted over the back doors and turned our people carrier into what could easily have been the first camper van; dad's ingenuity knew no bounds.

I remember only one holiday in that van, at Woolacombe Bay on the North Devon coast. Pete and I would sleep in the back of the van with mum and dad on camp beds in the awning.

Opa, Oma and me at Weston 1959.

Dad also had a pushbike with a small seat bolted to the crossbar for me to sit on. I would be perched there as happy as Larry while dad whizzed round the lanes of Conkwell. No helmet, bare legs waving back and forth. People would be mortified today and call dad irresponsible for taking his son unprotected against an accident on that bike. I suppose he was; but in the late fifties nobody did any different.

Belinda was sold and another car bought. We were setting the scene for the next fifty years. Dad's love of motorcars and the constant changes were always met with excitement by Pete and me and with a resigned sigh by mum. When dad sat quietly looking through the 'cars for sale' section of the 'Wiltshire Times' we all knew what was coming.

With the next car, a Ford Popular, came the start of the family venture into camping proper.

Mum and dad bought our first tent from 'Tommy Best's' army surplus store in Bath. Best's was set up in an old Nissen hut somewhere around the back of the Theatre Royal, an Aladdin's cave of ex-military hardware. To me, a trip to Bath had to incorporate a trip to Best's. I would beg dad to take me down there so I could look through the mountains of ex-this and ex-that, the shop sold -tents, webbing, boots, knifes, cooking equipment, you name it Tommy Best's sold it.

When I was around nine years old dad bought me an ex-British army jungle knife from Best's; a machete about 24" long in a khaki canvas sheath.

This jungle knife would be strapped to my waist when we went to Murhill woods to play army's, and also contributed to the felling of many a 'Guy Fawkes' bonfire 'centre-pole.'

The tent we bought from 'Best's 'was a minuscule sized thing in

14

which we would all sleep crammed together on our treks across Germany and France.

The tent was made from parachute material and when it rained we had to be careful not to touch the sides. If you did, the rain would just pour in. I could never work out why that happened and consequently had to touch just to watch the effect.

Sometimes my German granddad and gran would accompany us on these camping trips and I have vivid recollections of the family having an early morning wash in a cattle trough in the corner of some French field or German forest glade. Mum bent over the primus stove pumping the handle like mad building up the pressure in the cylinder so we could cook breakfast, while dad wandered round in a string vest smoking.

Mum spent most of the holiday with her fringe and eyebrows singed to a grey frizz where the stove had back-fired in her face; this was a normal event prior to today's modern outdoor cooking and no one worried, it was just par for the course.

Oma and mum cooking breakfast in a field in Northern France 1963. The tall cylindrical object is a ex-military food flask, no doubt purchased from Tommy Best's.

After our camping expeditions were over we would return to my grandparents' house in Mulheim, where I, maybe not so much Pete, would feel just as at home as in my village in England.

Prior to our summer holidays we would spend weeks planning. We would load the car and the roof rack for our three weeks abroad in Germany, France, Austria, or Switzerland. Mum and dad would buy Pete and I some new clothes and toys and we would be given spending money to change into German Deutschmarks either on the boat or as we crossed the border into Germany.

We would leave in the early hours of the morning to catch the 6am ferry to Calais.

The night before we left dad would make up a bed in the back of the car with a board to cover the rear foot-well. Around 11pm Pete and I would be put to bed in the back of the car while mum and dad locked up the house, had a parting word with gran and away we went. To begin with Pete and I would find it hard to sleep; the excitement would get to us.

15

But after a few miles we would nod-off to be woken by mum as we approached Dover.

It was a long journey in those days. There were no motorways; we traveled along the A4 to Reading, then took a sweeping route round the south of London, Guildford, East Grinstead, Ashford and on to Dover.

This was a six or seven hour trip with stops along the way at transport cafés. No 'Little Chefs' or 'Happy Eater's', just grimy steam boxes for truck drivers serving big chipped mugs of tea with a plate of egg, chips and beans.

A few years later when the M4 was being constructed we would change our route and use the London South Circular Road, coming off the Chiswick flyover and joining the A205.
This was a real higgledy-piggledy route meandering through Kingston, Wandsworth and Lewisham before finally hitting the A2 at Bexley.

Mum, Pete and I had to keep a sharp look out for road signs that were hung in trees or drawn in the oddest places on the road, or on the side of bus shelters and shops. As I got older I was allowed to ride in the front with dad and guide him around London. Mum could never remember her right from her left and this would cause major rows in the car. She was only too happy to hand the navigation over to me.

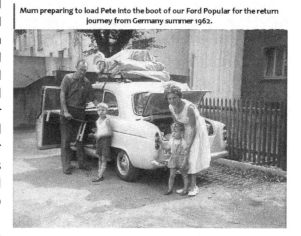

Mum preparing to load Pete into the boot of our Ford Popular for the return journey from Germany summer 1962.

I would continue to use this road prior to the M25 being constructed right up to 1977 when I was posted in the army to Maidstone and Chatham in Kent; the sign posting never improved.

We would arrive at Dover around 5am. Mum would wake us and we would play the game of who'll be the first to see the sea. We would drive through Whitfield, where in 1971 I would end up serving the first two years of my army career as a boy soldier.

Depending on our route to Dover we would either come down Whitfield hill and along the main street to the sea front. Turn left to the Eastern Docks. Or arrive along the cliff tops from Folkestone and drive the length of the promenade.

After checking through customs we would sit patiently in rows in the car for boarding.

One by one the cars would be guided on. I remember the excitement of the clang clang as we went over the metal ramp between the dock and the boat. Driving into the hull of the ferry, sometimes on the bottom deck and sometimes having to go up the steep ramp to the upper car deck wondering if our old car would make it.

Then, armed with coats hats and cameras we would leave the car, doors for some reason had to be left unlocked, and dash for the best seats.

The crossing was short, only three hours and again we would be back in the car heading east for the German border.

We would arrive around two or three in the afternoon and there would be my German granddad, pacing up and down and driving the border police crazy while waiting for his daughter, his English son-in-law and his two grandsons. He was such a lovely man and although he loved Pete and me equally, I really was his favorite.

Opa and Oma's flat in Mulhiem. The ground floor three windows to the left of the single door. It was lovely inside and very spacious.

I suppose it was because I came first by three years and I fitted the mould of the little German boy. My genetic pool had come mainly from my mum's side of the family. I took after my uncle Ralf in appearance. I had the blonde hair and Germanic looks. Don't get me wrong, Pete was a good looking boy as well, but taking after the 'Burt' side of the family genetically, he did look more the English kid.

Also I had been back and forward across the English Channel to my grandparent's house since I was born.

Opa had often taken me as a small child down to the pub to sit on his knee and drink the froth of his beer while he chatted to his friends. I had grown up embracing the German as well as English way of life. I was at home with the lifestyle and language. I had a German friend, a boy my age who lived in the top floor flat. Gerhart, I would play with him in the large back garden of the flats and go out and play with other kids in the streets. Sometimes I ended up in a fight if things got a bit heated playing football or some other game and the kids would chant , 'Englander, gehen sie nach hausa.' (English boy go home). Then the fists would fly. I don't think I ever lost. Funny really, at home in England I was the German boy. When in Germany I was always the English boy. But I felt equally at home in both places.

I knew my way around the area where Opa and Oma lived as well as I did my own village in Wiltshire. I would go and buy stuff from the shops talking quite easily in German, and knew my way into the centre of town through the back streets. I even knew which tram to catch for the journey home, the one that stopped directly outside my Oma's flat. Sunday afternoons it would be my job to collect the cream from the cake shop. I would take a liter jug from Oma and walk to the 'Backerei' to collect the thick whipped cream for the cake or flan Oma had spent the morning baking.

Marlene, Hans-Dieter, mum and Ralf in Mulhiem 1970.

Mum had two brothers and a Sister; Ralf, Dieter and Marlene. Marlene was the youngest and she would briefly pop by while we were staying but I can't remember seeing that much of her until she married Gerhard (ending with a 'd' not a 't') and had two children of her own Elke and Horst my cousins. Then she seemed to come back into the life of the family. They lived in Geltendorf a small village in Bavaria where we'll have a fantastic winter holiday with them in the late sixties which I'll come to later on.

Dieter was the eldest of the two brothers. He was married to Doris and had a stepdaughter Brigitte. He and Doris also had a daughter of their own, Gabby an incredibly pretty girl. The family would, as the years went by, endure turbulent times and sadness; with Gabby having a breakdown and Brigitte passing away very unexpectedly in her late twenties.

Ralf the younger brother was my favorite uncle the difference in our ages was not great, only about eighteen years. He loved his beer and fun and I always looked forward to seeing him. He married a much older woman who came from Munich, Stephie, but they never had kids. They seemed happy in their own way but I always thought it sad my uncle never married someone closer to his own age and had children.

He and his friend Karl came to visit us in Winsley a couple of times while we lived there.

He had a late fifties Opel Rekord which could do 100kph, he would drive Jeff, Bern, Pete and me from Bradford up through Belcombe getting faster and faster while the gang of us watched the speedometer, cheering as it hit the hundred. Of course we didn't know this was only 70mph, as far as we were concerned it was a hundred, faster than we were ever likely to go in Maurice or dad's car.

Diving from the barge mooring poles into the Ruhr. Ralf and me in the summer of 1971

When we visited Germany in the summer Ralf would take me down to the river Ruhr to swim. Here he taught me to high dive using the huge barge mooring poles as a diving platform. I had no fear in launching myself off these four meter poles that could vary in height up to two meters depending on the river flow.

Ralf died of a massive heart attack in 1979 he wasn't even forty years old. I was gutted; he was a great uncle and friend.

The months and years passed slowly in St Nicholas Close. My brother was born in 1959; Pat and Maurice had Jeffery in August 1956 and then Bernard in 1958.

Dad worked in the Avon rubber factory in Bradford-on-Avon as did my grandfather. Gran worked in Turleigh cleaning for Mrs Smith, a lady who lived in a house that had been converted from the old water mill.

When I started school mum found herself a job; she worked as the village Post lady and walked miles every morning; starting very early she had to be at the Post Office to sort the mail at 6.30am.

During the week Peter and I would be dressed, fed and sent off to school by dad, who would arrive home after the 10pm-6am night shift at the factory.

If dad was on a 6-2, that's six in the morning till two in the afternoon, then Pete and I would be taken over to gran's where we would have breakfast and then I would toddle off to school at 9am.

I started school after Easter 1961 at five years old. There were no preschools then or child minders. You were at home with mum or gran. Most mums didn't work in the early sixties but ours' would be the

A child's birthday party on the estate around 1960. Jeff second left, me far right both front row.

exception to the rule with her job as the village Post lady.

The day I started school, the new intake day, mum took me to the school gates. I was in Miss Norris 'class, a class of about twenty kids in a porta-classroom. We kids would spend the next six years together working our way up through the classes till we moved on to secondary or grammar school education.

Who else was in my first class? To name a few, Paul Orchard, Steven and Richard Bowles, Phil Mayell, Christopher Eskdale, David Bird, Chris Strickland, Sue Mayell and Norma Cottle. Sarah Beale and her brother Simon, Sally Beal and Robert; one with an 'e' and one without. And one pretty little girl of my age, Angela Holt.

Angela; the girl who as the next ten years went by would be my girlfriend; right up to the time we moved from Winsley to North Bradley the other side of Trowbridge, and even after the family move, and my leaving home for the army I would still hold a candle for Angie.

We kids weren't all the same age; it couldn't work like that in a village school because of the limited number of children; but we were all within a year or eighteen months of each other.

Angela had started school in the January and by the time I arrived at the Easter term she had already settled in.

Just like today all the mums would gather at the school after seeing their little ones through the gates. Some mums would be crying, which of course would start their children crying; all very upsetting on the first day of school. Again at three in the afternoon, there would be the mums, once more waiting to take the children home. This went on for a couple of days, maybe a week and then life settled down. Kids soon learnt to find their own way home. A small Victorian school in the middle of a country village didn't in the early sixties warrant a school run by car. Even the kids coming from Murhill or out on the Bradford Road would walk to school.

Angela's mum, Violet, was a lovely lady. But life was not easy for her family. Her husband Jack was a truck driver who spent a great deal of time away from home.

It seemed as if every time Jack came home he put his wife in the family way; they almost had a football team. Myrna, Linda, Judy, John, Mavis, Malcolm, Angela and Kevin, and all the girls were stunners. I remember sitting with Jeff on the step of his Drum watching Judy & Linda swinging their hips down the path in miniskirts while our eyes popped out of our heads, we were only around tenor eleven years old at the time.

There were no child credits in those days; you got a small child allowance from the government and that was probably only for the first one or two kids. Today large families would be getting a small fortune in tax credits, but not in 1960;any of the large families on our estate must have found it hard financially, heaven only knows how they all fed and clothed their clans but they did, people pulled together to help each other get by.

After the first couple of days at school mum no longer took me along. In the morning there was a knock at the door and there stood little Angela; my escort to school.

Angela was older than me, her birthday being in January. I think the 5th or the 15th. Angela having started school in the January term was an old hand in Miss Norris' class. Violet and my mum had agreed that for the time being Angela would walk with me to school.

Angela and I were firm friends right from that moment.

At play time we would play football and other kid's games in the play-ground, the girls at the front of the school, the boys at the back.

The school is now the village social club and I sometimes walk through the playground when I'm down that way; when I look round it seems so small. Those two playgrounds at the time seemed so big.

I tried to recollect what the facilities were like and failing had to ask Jeff 'The Oracle' who seems to remember all. I quote his letter to me…

We had two WCs and a long urinal. The WCs were enclosed by wooden dark green doors. The inside walls were rough stone thick with whitewash. The urinal was painted black and was wide enough for about 3 of us. There was a small window that was always left open to let out the

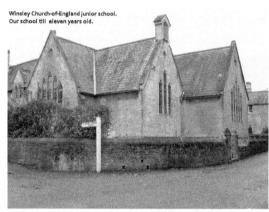

Winsley Church-of-England junior school.
Our school till eleven years old.

smell -it always smelt of stale urine and was always freezing cold.

Outside was a black vent pipe that we used to hold onto and everybody had to try and pull each other off. Whoever pulled the person away from the pipe - it was then their turn to hang-on.

Next to the WC building was a very small stone hut with a locked latch.

This was the PE hut - we kept the large coconut mats and small oval mats for PE on the hard playground, the balls and hoops.

I remember this hut as in our last year Angela and I were games-monitors and we would sneak in there and lay on the mats holding hands and chatting on the pretext of 'tidying-up'. (SB).

There was also a vaulting horse (which we hardly ever used); also the team shields for sports-day.

Next to this was the Coke bunker which was fronted by a small breeze block wall about 3 blocks high. When it was nearly empty I used it to try and set off live rifle bullets that Pete (your brother) had brought back from the south coast army ranges; I would do this by dropping a breeze block on them. The Coke nuts were used for turtle stoves - one in each class Mrs Haynes used to light them at about 7.30 each morning. In the winter we thawed out the milk on these stoves and also when nobody was looking melted wax crayons on the top. What a memory!

22

The infants were schooled in the porta-cabin to the side of the boys' playground; still there to this day. The juniors and the seniors were in the main building; old and Victorian it had windows so high up the wall you couldn't see outside, wooden floors, worn shiny from hundreds of feet, including my dad's, my granddad's, and my great granddad's. No central heating; as Jeff says pot-belly stoves with Coke, that had to be filled a few times during the course of a day.

Even though we only had a small village school we did have a school football team. Being a small school meant that the team had to be made up of all ages; although in truth most of the kids were ten or eleven years old. The boys without exception aspired to be in the team and competition for a place was intense; girls were not even considered.

We grew up with football. Just like being able to swim, I can't remember not kicking a ball; dad must have got me out kicking a football at two years old.

Winsley infants portacabin and boys play ground.
Apart from the two hand rails exactly as it was in the early 60s.

Each kid in the village had the team they supported. Jeff supported Everton, Kevin - Manchester United, Chris Strickland (Sticky) - Chelsea.
I was a Manchester City supporter; a great team in the sixties, with names like Tony Book, Colin Bell and Francis Lee.

Dad was a mad keen Bristol Rovers fan and would go every Saturday afternoon when they played at home. As I got older five, six years old, I would go with him. In those days the grounds were, but for a small area, all standing. The men would bring a couple of bottles of brown ale or IPA to the match in the pockets of their long drab coats. Then instead of going to the toilet they would quite openly pee in the empty beer bottle and stand it down on the terraces. I remember being really shocked when I first saw this around six years old. Dad said I shouldn't tell mum, she would be horrified and wouldn't let me go with him again.

Every year we had a new head boy and head girl at school; we also had a games captain for the boys and a games captain for the girls. Both games captains were also captains of either the football team for the boys or the 'Rounders' team for the girls. I never aspired to being head boy, more than anything I wanted to be the captain of the school football team.

Classes at junior school covered the basic subjects, English, math's, history, and basic geography; we also had lessons in art and nature studies. Both those subjects I found interesting but school never came easy to me. I could never hold my concentration and being left handed I was constantly being nagged for untidiness in my handwriting as my left hand dragged over the written page.

My interests lay far beyond the confines of a village school. Even at six years old I wanted to know what was over that next hill. My future as a restless soul was preordained; inherited no doubt from my mum's side of the family who all had the travelling bug.

Memories of my time in the classroom seem to be of constantly being told-off for lack of concentration; stargazing as they called it or fidgeting.

At that time of my life it seemed I was not academic at all. My skills lay in other areas. Even at that young age I had a sharp mind and I could use my initiative. My skills lay in the use of my hands and feet. I was an outside boy. In the countryside or on the football field I was at home; definitely not in the classroom. I found school very difficult and if I went to junior school in today's world I would probably be deemed as requiring some kind of special needs!

In truth I had a very short attention span which remains with me till this very day. I find it impossible to sit still for very long. It doesn't matter if I'm at home on the couch, at work at my desk, or in a training classroom, I can't help it; after twenty or thirty minutes I must get up and go outside for a walk around, it only needs to be for a minute or so and I'm fine for another twenty or thirty minutes.

My gran used to tell people I suffered with St Vitus Dance. Look that up on the Web if you will! I'm sure that was a definition for lots of kids like me who suffered from a short attention span; their grannies telling all and sundry their grandsons or granddaughters had St Vitus Dance...

Still I suppose back then people never knew the true meaning of St Vitus Dance or what it was. It's a side effect of rheumatic fever... I've never had rheumatic fever!

As I got older, and I mean into my early twenties, it became more and more obvious to me that I suffered from some kind of, what is now referred to as 'hyperactivity disorder' and knew I had to make an effort to control it; into adulthood I have, but it does take a conscious effort.

But during those school years 'Stop fidgeting! 'Must have been shouted at me twenty times a day.

Anyway… dad would spend hours with me teaching me how to run with a football at my feet, how to tackle, trap, and dribble. Football terminology that I don't think even exists today. Football was as natural as walking or talking and I was good at it.

Every evening we kids would be on the green kicking a ball about; or in the playground during school breaks; I was working my way toward a place on the team.

At Christmas the kids would put on a school show for the parents. I remember being in three different productions, one being just a general play; I was only around six years old, and in Miss Norris' class. We all sung as a choir; apparently my voice was so flat and over-powering (at six!) that I was moved to the back and told to mime. In another year I was given the part of a soldier. I was happy with this as I already had it down as a reserve occupation. However during the numerous practices I was told I looked to stern… right?

I needed to be a smiling soldier.

Well, no matter how I tried I couldn't change my stern appearance so I was removed from the ranks and ended up doing something inside a cardboard box. (*With hindsight they probably just stuck me in the box to get me out of the way!*).

Can you believe it? It would never happen today.

Told to mime one year then hidden in a box the next. Psychologically I must be as strong as an ox, remember I was only very young, probably around six or seven years old, but I managed to keep my head together. (Others of course may not agree).

Then in the last year of juniors I remember doing the nativity. This was held in the church just prior to the Christmas holiday break. It was just at the point when the church was having heating installed but it wasn't yet completed; it was so cold in the church people could barely see through the fog created by their breath.

In this production I was head Shepherd with Stephen Little and Alan Kettlety. Jeff of course was Joseph with Janice Forsyth as Mary (Head Boy and Head Girl) Angela was the Angel Gabriel. Down floated Angie from the Church pulpit in a halo of light and frozen breath and I fluffed my lines; this of course caused Angela (appropriate name for the part) to look at me blankly. Of course her lines had been memorised off the back of mine so it all went to pot. Once again I got ear-ache from everyone including my girlfriend.

Sports days would be held once a year; parents were invited and competitiveness was actively encouraged; cups and certificates could be won. Events for the younger kids consisted of the egg and spoon race, wheelbarrow race, the sack race and the three-legged race. For the older kids the 100 yards the 400 yards (or once round the field); high jump, long jump, triple jump and the slow bicycle race.

Finally you would have the mum's race; which to everyone's annoyance my very athletic mum won every year to the point where she was too embarrassed to compete.

Then a couple of weeks later the winners of the school events went on to represent the village in the zone sports. These were the area sports where all the local schools came together to challenge each other; a place in these games usually only came in the last year or two at the school and it was a real honour to take part.

Monday afternoons were swimming afternoons, we would get on a coach from the village garage and be delivered to the local baths in Bradford-on-Avon.

They were old marble and tiled Victorian baths. Public baths, 'Slipper baths' I think they were called. As well as a swimming pool, people who never had a bath in their own home could come down to the public baths for a scrub.

A whole row of these bathtubs were for hire in private cubicles. Some in the men's changing area and others in the ladies.

Intricate cast iron rusty painted pillars standing on worn slabs held up the roof which I believe was glass; the walls were covered with old cracked ceramic tiles.

Sadly their days were numbered; within a decade these ancient baths were to be replaced with modern new facilities. Indiscriminately they would be ripped apart without a thought to historical value and a modern library erected in their place.

Swimming lessons for me were an enjoyable break from the classroom; I loved the water and swam very well.

Even though the baths were old the waters were warm and it beat sitting in a classroom doing Mathematics or English.

The first taste of male bonding would be in the communal changing rooms of these swimming baths. In this one open room with benches

26

round the sides and hooks on the wall we were obliged to expose our thin naked bodies to each other. Some kids were very shy and this usually resulted in them being picked on and bullied. Looking back now I feel sorry for the one or two boys who would have

A school swimming sports day at the old Bradford-on-Avon Baths

their towel ripped from them by a group of laughing taunting children while trying to protect their privates from view. I won't refer to these boys by name, but I am sure the effect must have had a life-long impact on them.

After swimming we would board the bus for the return trip to Winsley. Angela insisted she became travel sick on the coach and had to sit in the front seat. An argument for this prime spot would erupt between the girls on a weekly basis, but Angie would win the day, coming from a big family as she did she knew how to look after herself and was not to be messed with. The boys dashed for the back; it was always the gang leaders who sat on the back seat; pecking order decreed where you sat on the bus.

Slowly a group evolved that were, apart from the odd argument or two throughout the years, to remain good friends. As well as Pete and I in St Nicholas Close there also lived Jeff, Bern, Trevor Pryor and John Phelps who were slightly older, Johnny Gibbs. Gibbo as he was meanly nicknamed was a lanky lad who frankly looked malnourished; one of four brothers and sisters brought up by Pam their mum. I can't remember a dad being around.

Pam had been in the army during the war and though a kindly woman she struck an imposing straight backed figure when she walked through the village. She always had a cigarette hanging out the side of her mouth and a plume of smoke following her up the road like a steam engine.

Johnny was picked-on both in and out of school. I don't really know why, when kids are in a pack they pick on the most vulnerable, and possibly John came over that way. His main defense was throwing stones. He had this extraordinary ability to throw for what seemed like hundreds of yards, Jeff maintained he should join the army he would excel at throwing hand-grenades. He did join up and it really changed his life; he had a long and very successful army career and on leaving the army started his own business.

The bottom of Nicholas Close. The Gibbs house on the left, auntie Connie's bungalow on the right and our house to the right of the tree.

Gibbo could also run like the wind and many a time he would be chased up the path to his front door where he would stop, hurl abuse at his tormentors and start throwing stones which we would all take delight in dodging, laughing and egging him on further hoping that the stones would hit one of the few cars parked in the street and really drop him in the muck.

During one such fracas John threw a stone that almost took my brother's eye out. Blood poured from my brother's wounded head and suddenly all us kids realized what John had done. He turned and ran for home with me hot on his heels. He was fast and had a head start of 50 yards but my blood was up and I caught him just before his mum opened the front door. I was still laying into him as Pam pulled him into the house.

John had an older brother Francis and two sisters, Mary and Katherine. Jonathan and Christopher Eskdale were two brothers living at the top of the road; their parents rarely let them out to play; they were (as we thought at the time) slightly stuck up. My mum thought them marvellous as they were the only two kids to come to my birthday party and eat slowly and chew their food, instead of snatching, grabbing and stuffing the food down as fast as possible. They had good manners the same as our parents were determine to instill in Pete and me. *Good manners was an expression I grew up with constantly; it was an expression of the time which you rarely hear used today; more's the pity.*

The girls up our end of the estate were Janet, Carol and Susan Pryor, Trevor's sisters; Helen and Eileen Gingell, Hilary Phelps and Norma Cottle. There were two other sisters called Serle. Barbara, their mum, was Jeff's mum's sister. Next door to them lived another lass who I believe suffered a chronic heart condition, Nichola Say.

Down the footpath in Poston Way lived Paul and Peter Orchard both great football players. Kevin, Angela, and Malcolm Holt; round the corner lived Gary, Jane and Lynn Hancock, who had a very dishy young mum Wendy who all the older lads would comment on.

Outside of the block of council houses was a string of private bungalows running up Dane Rise and half way down King Alfred Way. In these lived a few other kids; Sticky, the double of Mick Jagger lived opposite Michael Gardner, my second cousin, Ruth Godfrey, who would be involved in a future arson incident with my brother and a car accident that was written into my future; Christopher and Sabrina Hill. Christopher was another kid who got duffed up on a regular basis; mainly by me. I could never stand him and we regularly got into a scrap with Chris running home crying. If my mum got to hear of it I would be made to go round and knock on the door of the Hill's house and apologize; something I hated doing; or alarmingly on occasion Mrs Hill would turn up on our door step complaining how I treated her son. Mum would be really angry and would use this as an excuse not to let me watch 'Combat' or 'The Desert Rats' on the TV; both of which were weekly WW2 war series which she detested. It would be a case of 'get up those wooden stairs and stay in your room till your father gets home.' A phrase I'd hear hundreds of times as I grew up.

Sabrina, although not a striking beauty at juniors blossomed into a very attractive girl when she started at Trowbridge High School and later during my time at Nelson Haden I really fancied her; too bad she was a couple of years older than me. That makes a whole heap of difference during school years. I didn't get a second glance.

At the top of King Alfred Way opposite the Hill's lived David Bird; Jeff, Christine, Diane, Sue, and Phil Mayell and the Forsyth kids, Stewart, Janise, Alistair, Rosemary, and Kirstin.

Leaving the estate on the edge of the village near the garage lived Alan Kettlety our school team goal keeper.

In the general store named the Wheatsheaf lived Stephen and Wendy Little. Sarah and Robert Beal lived in my great great-grandparents' house in Murhill half a mile down the hill from Winsley old village; they also had a younger sister whose name escapes

A Viewer's Companion to the WWII TV Series (revised)

COMBAT!

By
Jo Davidsmeyer

Foreword by

me, Deena I think? I remember our dinner lady hitting her over the head with the jam ladle one lunch time; spiteful old witch. Poor kid, her head was matted with the stuff.

Simon, Sarah, Annabelle and Jennifer Beale lived in the farm on the Bradford road. The Bowels brothers Stephen, Richard and Jeff lived in Home Farm up the lane toward Conkwell and the Penna's Richard and Robin lived next door to my Uncle Fred in Turleigh. Richard was a nice lad but was slightly what we now call autistic and suffered terribly from epileptic fits. He was in our class at school and we had to be made aware of how to cope with him if he went into a spasm. A steep learning curve when you're only five or six years old.

One spring when the river was in flood, Bernard, Richard and I went with Ross Daniels our Cub Scout leader and local farmer, to the lower pastures below Murhill to dismantle a mobile milking unit and at the same time bring the cows to higher ground. Ross and a helper worked at dismantling the unit while Bernard, Richard, and I took the cows the mile back to the farm. When we got there we found Richard was missing.

An hour later Ross turned up with the milking unit, but still no Richard; when we went back to find him he was wandering aimlessly around without knowing where he was. Poor lad he must have had one of his turns along the way and passed out.

Of course there were many more children on the estate; the names I have mentioned were only within my age range but most had older or younger brothers and sisters such as Michael Cottle and Jimmy Phelps and in the village as a whole there where others who went to private school, or were taken to other village schools. But the names I have listed tended to be a gang of the same age group that would stay together as the years went by and whose names would come up the most frequently. Although I mention some of these kids in a derogatory manner, these were my child or adolescent feelings at the time, not how I see them now as an adult. My dislike of Chris Hill disappeared when I got into my late teens and John or as I call him Gibbo joined the army and as I said earlier had a long successful career, retired and started his own removal business. Kids are cruel and establishing your natural place in the peer group hierarchy can be vicious.

It's probably the same in most villages; there's always the one girl who is well endowed and very liberal with her affections. We had one of these and she kept the boys entertained as we got older. I can't leave her out of the story as she plays an important part in village life (of course she does!) but I haven't the heart to give her away by name so I will refer to her when I need to as Miss X.

In 1963 we had a very hard winter. It snowed for what seemed like weeks and weeks. The school closed due to frozen pipes and toilets and we all had to stay at home. Mum working for the Post Office had a real rough time of it trudging for miles through the snow to deliver letters. Pete and I would spend this time with gran over at nineteen or down the path at Pat White's house. The temperature was way below minus and stayed that way day after day.

Those weeks away from school during the big chill were great. The roads were cleared by bucket loader and the pavements were piled high with snow in which we made fortifications and attacked each other with snowballs.

The snow lasted well into spring then it was back to school again.

During that hard winter and spring of 1963 I had my seventh birthday and moved out of the infant porta-classroom and into the main school building. The teachers at this time were Mrs Carr, who looked after the infants when Miss Norris left; Mr Williams who'd taken over from Mrs Corrigal, and Ms Wayman the head mistress.

Mrs Carr didn't like me at all. The Rounders bat had flown out of my hand one day while I was on the batting spot and hit her in the chest. She went down in great pain like a sack of spuds. All the girls created a real song and dance while she lay moaning on the ground. It wasn't done deliberately and I went over and apologized. She snapped my head off, said I did it on purpose and I had to sit the game out on the sidelines.

It was very petty and not the type of behavior a teacher should indulge in. How she thought for one minute I could have done it on purpose I don't know. She reported the incident to Mr Williams my form teacher. He called me in and after my explanation still didn't believe me to be innocent.

I didn't stand a chance at the school, neither Carr or Williams, who became headmaster after Ms Wayman retired, liked me and in a small county school if your face doesn't fit you're on a hiding to nothing.

Anyone who has seen children through the first years of school will have a view on which is better, the bigger schools or the small Victorian village schools. I would choose the bigger school for a child of mine every time.

Gone are most of the very small Victorian style village schools and I don't believe that's such a bad thing.

Throughout my time under Williams he let his personal feelings toward me, a small boy, dictate his actions and overrule his professional impartiality and integrity as a teacher. He would constantly call me in front of the class and deliberately show me up because I couldn't spell a word or do a mathematical problem, or I got blamed for every unexplained incident that took place. Ok I was no angel I'll admit, but his singling me out as an individual did nothing to improve my schooling. I was old enough to know what he was doing and did my best to shrug it off but at the same time, as young as I was I couldn't help but built up huge resentment and dislike for him.

I suppose the first big shock in my young life that I can remember came in September 1962. The news arrived by red motorcycle; a telegram from Germany that my Opa, had died. The red motorcycle was part of the Post Office information delivery system before the advent of everyday telephones. A person in a foreign country with news, good or bad would go to their local Post Office and a telegraph would be sent to the Post Office in the country they wished to contact. The message would then be printed from the telegraph system and given to the dispatch rider; the bloke on the red motorbike in leather helmet and 'Biggles' type goggles who would deliver it to your front door. From the moment that first red

Oma and Opa in their flat Christmas 1960

motorbike arrived at our front door I had an inbuilt dread of the bloke on the red bike; in fact I think everyone did.

When anyone saw the bike coming through the village they'd stop and watch where it went; it was nearly always the bearer of bad news not good and you knew someone would be in tears after the bloke on the red bike kick-started the engine and left.

When I left home I told mum, never to send me a telegram unless it was the last-resort, because even in the army the telegram bearers of bad news would appear.

In 1975 when in the Army in Germany I was hospitalised with pneumonia mum sent me a telegram to say my uncle Ralf was coming to see me; she could've just phoned, but no it was a telegram.

I lay in my hospital bed in Munster and never opened it; I was just struck with dread at what it might say, and it ended up in the bottom of my pack and I forgot about it; consequently when he turned up in Munster I'd already been discharged back to my unit in Osnabruck.

Anyway back to the death of my Opa...mum was distraught; she had spent the last thirteen years in England and had only seen her father on our annual holidays to Germany.

My Opa had suffered terribly in captivity under the Russians and wasn't released until 1949. On his release and return to Dusseldorf he was very ill.

However he continued to work as an architect for the city council from a drawing office at home; sadly for our family in Germany and England he never recovered from the ill treatment by the Russians and the conditions in the camps. When he died he was still a relatively young man.

Pete and me in our back garden.
17 St Nicholas Close summer 63.

The day he died we had only just returned to Winsley from our summer holiday in Germany; we knew when we left from Mulheim that my grandfather was very ill but his death coming so close to our return was awful news for mum and financially we were unable to go back for Opa's funeral.

But as his eldest grandchild and his favorite I'm glad I was old enough to remember him and pass on my memories to my brother and younger German cousins.

In Nicholas Close we lived next door to an old lady, Mrs Mizzen. I don't really remember talking to her much. I just remember her being dressed in black and banging on our downstairs dining room window from her adjoining window with a walking stick or a broom whenever she wanted to borrow some milk, sugar, or she needed some other help from my mum.

I remember mum saying that the only time the old bat would talk to her was when she wanted something. She'd pass mum in the street without so much as a hello.

I have photos of Pete and me playing in the back garden, me kicking a ball around and the tent in which we slept on summer's evenings. It was a regular thing for the football to end up in someone else's garden, or through our, or Mrs Mizzen's window. Replacing panes of glass was a common occurrence for dad and the cost was supposedly deducted from our holiday money. Pete and I were forever walking up to 'Manning's' the builders merchants in the old village to collect the new panes of glass and putty.

Winsley village hall and bowling green.

Our garden backed onto an old nursery; derelict greenhouse frames protruded forlornly from the tall grass and nettles. Jeff and I could sneak through the hedge at the bottom of our gardens and play among the frames. In the mid-sixties the land was sold and new bungalows were built on the site. One of these bungalows would be bought by Mr and Mrs Mitchard whose daughter Susan, would, twenty years into the future, marry Jeff.

Dad played cricket for Winsley and granddad played bowls. I often went with granddad to the bowls club which was the pride of the village. I would sit on the seats at the pub end of the green while the old pipe smoking men tried to get their bowl as close to the Jack (the little white ball) as possible. Then after half an hour I would be bored and drift off home. I can see granddad now in his white trousers, cap and blue jacket; leather bowling bag in hand and his pipe clamped between his teeth, walking with me hand in hand past the allotments up Vinegar Path to the old village. He didn't talk much, a quiet man who I'm sure like many of his era was quietly suffering from what is now known as PTSD (Post Traumatic Stress Disorder) a legacy of the horrors he witnessed in the Machine Gun Corp as a soldier in the trenches of the Great War.

The old veterans of the trenches were all quiet men who would sit together over a pipe and a pint in 'The Seven Stars' never saying much and playing shove ha'penny or dominos. To this day I have his 'Great War' medals and they have pride of place in our front room display cabinet.

He was a very good bowls player and played for the village team, winning quite a few trophies over the years.

I went a couple of times to the cricket with dad but I didn't enjoy it and I think dad gave it up quite early in the sixties.

I was spoiled by my gran. There was no doubt her and granddad loved Peter and I of equal measure, but I was the favorite at nineteen (our name for gran's house).At home it was Pete; he was quiet and well behaved; he did as he was told and ate everything on his plate; unlike me.

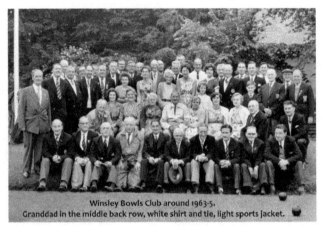

Winsley Bowls Club around 1963-5.
Granddad in the middle back row, white shirt and tie, light sports jacket.

I was a picky eater and remained so until I went to Dover as a boy soldier in 1971. The army soon changed my eating habits. Also I was unruly and answered back. I was always in trouble in my own home but in gran's eyes I could commit murder and be innocent; I always won the sympathy vote at gran's.

Food would be dished up in our house and then the battle would begin. I hated cooked vegetables; raw vegetables were fine, carrots, cauliflower, cabbage, I would eat them all raw but not cooked. My parents would insist that they be eaten and I would be told 'you sit there till they are gone'… and I would.

I was stubborn; pig-headed dad called me. It was not uncommon for me to be at the table long after every other member of the family was sat down in the front room. Sometimes the dog would sneak under the table and I could smuggle food down to her. But even dogs don't really enjoy peas or boiled carrot sticks. The other trick was to hide the food on a ledge on the underside of the table and dispose of it later. This worked ok as long as the leaves of the old fifties style table were extended; the problem arose if we ate with the table not extended or the leaves were pushed in as soon as the meal finished. Either there was no ledge to store the food on, or the food ended up being shunted onto the floor and all hell would be let loose. The general trend would be that I sat for an hour after everyone else had taken up position in front of the TV and then mum would come in take away the plate and I was told to get up those wooden stairs and don't come back down.

I even got taken to the doctor regarding my inability to eat greens. What was the deal? I ate fruit and I ate the vegetables raw, just put it on my plate raw, it's the far healthier option.

But no, in our house everyone ate the same and clean plates were the rule.

Gran and granddad's place, nineteen, was a two bedroom bungalow on a corner plot; a very nice retirement bungalow with a lovely big garden at the front and rear. When you went

Gran and granddads bungalow 19 King Alfred Way.
Photo taken 2014

through the front door the sitting room with a huge bay window was off to the left with the bedrooms off to the right. You went straight ahead down the hallway to the kitchen. In the hallway on the right was a small dresser. A few ornaments sat on the top. One of these was a little brass bell and under it gran would put and old octagonal sided three-penny piece; a Joey as it was called then. I was told I could only lift the bell and take the Joey if I was on my own. When we moved to Poston Way the three pence became a sixpence, (a tanner) and as I left gran's I would lift the bell and slip the tanner into my hand. Those few pennies, an insignificant amount of money now were a fortune then. I loved it at my gran's and would never go by the house without calling in and sit in the kitchen with a glass of Corona and a slice of cake; Jamaica ginger, our granddads favorite.

On a Saturday I would be taken by gran or both gran and auntie Dot to Bath on the bus. This was a lovely day out; we'd get the bus outside the Seven Stars in the village and with luck the front seat on the top deck would be free. The bus would then slowly make its way down Winsley Hill and along the Warminster Road into Bath. The view through the front window of the bus was terrific and looking out as we went down the steep hill into Limpley Stoke was almost scary.

In Bath we get off at Grand Parade and walk through the beautifully ornate old covered market, then across the road through the corridor to Milsom Street. Here was a big four-storey shop called 'Jolly's'; it's still there to this day but now it's a 'House of Fraser'. What I loved about this old family shop was the lifts and the vacuum system for moving money. The former were rattily old things, but very ornate with a lift operator in a peaked cap and the latter, the vacuum system, as a little boy had me fascinated. Had I been allowed, I think I'd have stood for hours watching the sales assistants firing money through the vacuum pipes. It wasn't as if you could see anything, you just knew that the money was whizzing around the shop in the pipes. The trap would open and you could hear the sound of compressed air; then the money capsule would be put inside and the trap door closed; you could hear this whoosh as the capsule shot up the pipe. To a five or six year old this was great stuff. Eventually we would make our way back to the bus but before we got there a visit to the chip shop was written in stone. This was not just any chip shop; this was 'Evans'. The finest fish & chips in Bath. It was in Abbey Gate street (may still

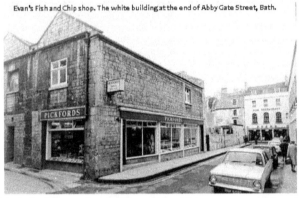
Evan's Fish and Chip shop. The white building at the end of Abby Gate Street, Bath.

be there) and you could sit inside and eat off a plate. This was a real treat; by the time we got there I would be hungry and as you turned the corner from the main thoroughfare the smell of the fish and chips hit you. Standing in the steamy queue I would be hopping from one foot to the other in anticipation.

We would sit and wait with a bottle of 'Tizer' for our food to arrive, pile on the salt and vinegar and then satisfied walk back to the bus station and catch the 48 bus home; which a couple of years up the road would become the 264.

Gran was very popular with all my friends as they were always made welcome and across the years they would come to her house with me; the village kids, sitting eating biscuits, laughing and chatting and even during my years in the army, friends like Les Dixon and Davey Hopwood would travel back to the West Country with me for a weekend at gran's. After I left the army I would try to visit on a monthly basis from Norfolk. Her second bedroom always had two single beds made up for whoever came with me, Pete, friends and girlfriends over the years, Julia, Debby and Corrine had been made welcome and stayed the night at my gran's.

At the weekend the ice-cream van would come round the estate, 'Mr Whippy'. The bell would ring and the tune would play and we would go running out with our money. The ice cream man always had a box of sweets on the van, four-a-penny fruit salads or mojo's, and he would throw a couple of handfuls out on the green and us kids would scrabble round for them. This horrified mum so Pete and I would not be allowed to get involved. At six years old that really annoyed me and I could never understand why Pete and I always had to be different. Dress, behaviour, time for bed, we always seemed to be out of step with the other kids.

Poor mum, I know now she really had a problem with living on a council estate. It wasn't that she thought she was a cut above the other mum's on the estate; it was just the relaxed way life was viewed.

Mum grew up in a very strictly regulated German society and probably considered that this was the correct way for her own children to be raised.

She could never see that this didn't work on a council estate. Like the Eskdale's you either had to be in or out and sadly they were out; kids who are different or act differently are either picked on, expelled from the group completely, or just end up being solitary kids with no friends.

Once or twice a week the pig man from Bowel's farm would come round. A row of bins were left on the green and household slops were taken out and scrapped into the bins. This was common practice until some form of government legislation banned it in the mid-sixties.

We never had much rubbish; vegetable waste would go in the pig bin or be buried in the bottom of the garden. Cardboard, wood or paper would also be burned. Glass would be kept for some other use such as pickling or taken back to the shop for a refund. Plastic was unheard of. The refuse

A village delivery van of the 60s

collection was called the dustbin day and was just a small lorry with a rear cover and 3 sliding panels.

We had two shops; the general store was called 'The Wheatsheaf' and the Post Office owned by Mrs Evens; this was the place mum would go every morning at 6am to sort the Post and start her mail round.

Gran bought everything from Mrs Evens shop, she had a shopping book where all items were recorded this would be tallied up once a week and paid for in a lump.

'The Wheatsheaf' was also an off-license owned by Stephen and Wendy Little's mum and dad. 'The Wheatsheaf' sold most things many from bulk bags, weighed out in scales on the counter. The house next door to Little's shop was the house of my great gran and granddad, Fred and Annie Sartain. They moved up the hill from Murhill to Winsley village when they got married. This was probably considered a good move as they had a water pump in their own garden and the shops were literally next door, unlike living in Murhill.

When Fred died little granny moved in with gran at King Alfred Way and the house stood empty for years. Who owned it I never knew but it certainly wasn't owned by our family.

Other produce arrived in the village by traveling shop which was a van or big truck with steps into the back where the ladies of the estate would queue to buy fresh vegetables, meat, or fish. They would all turn up on different days but the same day every week. There was no supermarket to go to, the closest fish, meat, or veg shop being a bus ride to Bradford-on-Avon. These delivery vans would travel daily around all the villages and it was a good little earner until the advent of the supermarkets and more homes had two cars.

The sixties and early seventies saw massive changes in the way life was lived. I believe the first supermarket close to us opened in Trowbridge; 'Sainsbury' next to town bridge in 1970.

Another mobile delivery was the fish and chip van; this would turn up around 6pm on a Friday and park in Poston Way. The queue would be 50 yards down the street. We occasionally had fish and chips from the van but in truth they were pretty poor quality. The fat never got hot enough to brown the spuds and you would end up with pale coloured chips that had been boiled in oil rather than deep fried. Also they always seemed to contain bits of grit where the spuds hadn't been washed properly.

If mum and dad decided we'd have a fish super it would be bought and brought home by dad after work. The fish and chips tasted much better from the chipper in Bradford-on-Avon.

Dad always ran on about opening a fish and chip shop in Winsley; it was a bit of a standing joke in the family. A fish and chip shop or a scrap yard... sadly he never did either.

On Sundays dad would give me half a glass of 'Mackeson 'with my Sunday lunch. This was a black beer, a Stout or Porter as it's called. I had a real taste for beer. I would drink it and then sleep all Sunday afternoon. I'm sure this was done deliberately so mum and dad could go to bed for a Sunday afternoon romp. Apparently it was quite the norm for young married couples to grab a couple of hours in the sack while the kids were at Sunday school. Probably the only reason we were sent to Sunday school.

I started Sunday school at the same time I started Winsley Primary, around five years old. I hated it. It was two hours on a Sunday afternoon. It was held in the Church between two and four-o-clock and was taken by Vicar Hill and his little wife who I remember looking like Minnie Caldwell from early episodes of Coronation Street. None of my friends went; Jeff, Bern, Kev...no chance.

In fact I wonder if they shipped kids in from another village because I don't remember any child being there that I knew.

To get out of going or to be sent home I would take our family dog; a Golden Retriever called Bruno. He would faithfully follow me into the Church and lay down in a pew; inevitably he would be spotted and I would be made to take him home; silly really he was a very gentle and quiet dog, he would have quite contentedly lain down in the Church and gone to sleep until our religious education finished and it was time for me to go home.

Me at 3 years old with Bruno.

This went on until Vicar Hill caught on to my scam; rather than pack me off home with my dog he put Bruno outside in the church entrance hall where he lay waiting for me to finish my religious instruction. Then I would walk home my faithful friend by my side.

Some Sunday mornings I had to go to church with my gran. I was completely lost at these events never knowing when to sit, kneel, or stand

40

and losing track of the service. Fortunately it was not that often I had to go. I think my parents realized quite early that I was a child who would make up my own mind on things; draw my own conclusions and decide what I wanted or didn't want to believe. Religion was one of these subjects. I would quiz and question my gran on the Bible and religion in general and listen to her answers with astonishment before overloading her with questions. Gran was a firm believer, as was my auntie Dot and throughout my growing up years I enjoyed talking to both of them about religion and hearing them explain and answer my child like questions on the miracles and how we all got here. We had then and over the years that followed many enjoyable discussions.

The one Church service I would willingly go to with mum and gran, or perhaps gran and Dot was the Harvest Thanksgiving service. The church was always full of people for this end of harvest celebration and it really was a lovely occasion. The church would be decorated with help from the kids in the junior school with food baskets, flowers, and corn-sheaves and the hymns that were sung were traditional harvest hymns. I seem to remember the Harvest Thanksgiving service to be held on a Saturday evening in mid-October?
No doubt I'll be corrected on that if my memory has not served me well.

Headstrong would probably be an understatement for me; I was a horror and would get into mischief constantly pushing everything to the limit.

Dad returned from Germany one summer with a box of Underberg, very strong liquor that is supposed to aid digestion after a meal. I heard him talking to mum about these small bottles of digestive and my curiosity was aroused.

He put the box of twenty miniature bottles in the bottom of his wardrobe. My curiosity got the better of me and I told Jeff about them. We sneaked into my parents' bedroom to pinch a bottle and try the stuff. With him skeptically watching me I took a mouthful; it was ghastly! Not far removed from cough medicine. I rolled round on the floor coughing and spluttering after showing-off by drinking this in front of my friend.

Jeff just sat there and watched.

It's little wonder that Jeff was reluctant to get involved with my alcohol experiment; no doubt he'd had a severe finger wagging from Pat following the last escapade of copying the young Steve Burt when he ended up having a marble removed from his nose. This was not full sized marble I hasten to add, but a small round ball from child's game which in this day and age would be banned as being dangerous for young children...just goes to show doesn't it.

Jeff and I had been playing with these marbles on our front room floor when I had the idea of firing them out of my nostril. It worked with me... not with Jeff; I probably have a nose better suited to firing glass projectiles...

Mum ended up taking him in the car to A&E to have the offending glass sphere removed. I was not flavour of the month with either parent. In the long term this probably turned out to be a blessing for Jeff as he became wary of my ideas and unlike me and a couple of others on the estate never appeared on the Winsley law enforcement 'Most Wanted' list.

Dad also collected old pennies which he kept in a glass topped box. Every now and again I would pinch one or two to buy bubble gum up the shop. One day I remember dad questioning me as to whether I had taken any. It would be the obvious thing to count and record them but as a child this didn't occur to me. I swore blind I never had any. But from that moment on I never pinched another one.

Other events came and went on an annual basis. In the summer the whole village would go by coach to Weston-Super-Mare, or Weston-Super-Mud as we kids called it. That would be the Sunday school outing; parents and children alike would dress in our best clothes and board the bus (charabanc) for a village day out.

One year the outing was a few days before mum's birthday. Dad gave Pete and me five shillings (25p) each to spend at Weston but also told us that with the money we had to buy mum a

Our village outing to Weston 1959. Oma in the white coat with me holding her hand.

birthday pressie... We spent the lot, I hasten to add this was no small amount of money at the time; Pete gave all his money to the 'Donkey man' and spent all day going up and down the beach. I don't know what I did with mine but needless to say dad was not amused when we got home broke and empty handed.

When Pete or I had a birthday mum would put on a large spread and invite most of the kids on the estate who would devour the food like a pack of locusts. Poor mum she could never get her head around what she considered the misbehaviour of the other children; Pete and I were subjected to the most rigorous discipline. No talking at table, no playing out on Sundays, hankies in our pockets and hand washing before meals. Talking it over with friends I was baffled to find out that most other kids never went through these strict regimes; half a century on, the majority turned out ok with good jobs and stable families and never went through the set routines Pete and I did.

From the mid-sixties the 'Beatles'- John, Paul, Ringo, and George were in their heyday and every child wanted to be a pop star. We would make drum kits out of cardboard boxes and guitars out of shaped card pinned to a piece of wood. We would set up our pretend 'Gig' on the green outside John Phelps and Norma Cottle's house and bang our drums and sing songs from the Stones, Kinks, or Beatles while crowds of other kids sat round listening and joining in.

At that time we probably would have jumped at the chance to have guitar lessons or lessons in playing the drums. But those types of educational extras were way above what everyday people could afford; unlike today where extra-curricular activity is common place. It probably never entered the heads of our parents that we could be encouraged in that direction, and possibly make a career from music.

But on the other hand we ran free and our parents hardly ever interfered with our play.

In the autumn we could climb either the Horse Chestnut tree in Bowel's field for 'conkers,' or the tree at the bottom of Vinegar Path.

In summer make forts from hay bales after harvest, ride our bikes for miles around the lanes or play armies for hours in Murhill woods.

The footpath from the cricket field to Avoncliff was lined on one side by cherry plum trees, a wild growing mini type of plum. When these ripened in late summer the trees would be laden with the fruit to the point where the branches almost broke. We would go and collect bags of them for home-made jam and while doing so stuff ourselves to the point of being sick.

Tree climbing, playing armies along with trolleys were just a few of our child occupations.

Trees were there to climb and we would climb them to the topmost branches, which creaked and groaned under our weight. I can honestly not remember one of my friends ever falling from a tree. The thought of falling, or the limbs that supported us snapping, never entered our heads, with an inbuilt intuition like moneys we would jump and swing from branch to flimsy branch, each boy trying to outdo the other.

One of the finest trees to climb in the whole village was in the grounds of the Hartman house. A big Victorian house that bordered the playing field at the top of the hill by the war memorial, the gardens stretched right down the hill to the old vicarage and the road to Turleigh. Right there on the crossroads it stands to this day, although having been chopped back pretty ruthlessly it is a shadow of its former glory. It was the biggest and highest Beech tree in the village, with a branch that swept down to ground level so us kids could literally step on and run straight up the broad limb to the main trunk. I've noticed recently that the tree has lost this huge lower limb we used to run up, probably the weight of the limb just became too great.

The Hartman's had a son Robert, who was our age, but he didn't go to our school; he went to school in Bath. But we befriended him and consequently this allowed us to play in his enormous garden and better still climb his tree. The Hartman's had a dog called 'Jason;' a ferocious Great Dane; this dog stayed firmly locked in the house while us kids played in the garden but occasionally Mrs Hartman would call out to us that the dog will be out in five minutes.

We would run in terror to the tree and climb up to a safe height like our lives depended on it, which they probably did. Then we would wait for the drum of huge feet as the hound of the Baskerville roared into the clearing beneath us. Snarling and barking it would hurl itself at the trunk trying to get to us. God forbid if one of us had not been quick enough to make the safety zone or worse still fell from the tree while this dog was loose in the grounds. God only knows what would have happened to Robert's parents if one of us had been mauled by that animal.

Hartman's Beech tree on the Turleigh cross roads. The big branch that we ran up from ground level is missing; but this is a winter photo and in the summer in leaf it still looks majestic.

The wooded slopes that border the Avon valley sides below our village stretch away from just outside Bradford-on-Avon all the way to Bathford. Belcombe, Turleigh, Murhill, Conkwell, Warleigh, then into Bathford; they no longer stretch unbroken, but in places are still grouped in abundance.

Centuries ago these woods were far larger then today; The name Winsley is thought to have derived from the name Wineslega; Lega or Leah, meaning a clearing in a woodland; which is probably where and how the first settlement of Winsley began. As the settlement grew into a village more woodland was cleared for arable crops, until eventually we are left with the present day woods and fields.

The woods may have diminished considerably over the centuries but around Winsley in nineteen sixty there were plenty of woods to keep us kids happy for hours and our favorite woods were on the hillside surrounding the small hamlet of Murhill.

The serious pastimes of playing armies, or cowboys and Indians would take place in Murhill woods.

The woods started on the edge of Murhill and reached right down to the canal and swept around the side of the valley as far as Winsley Hill.

The woods were probably owned by the Sanatorium, or as we called it locally the Chest Hospital; this magnificent building built in the first few years of the nineteen hundreds to cure lung problems of the rich, stood on the edge of Winsley Hill looking out over the valley below.

There are two areas of woodland with a small road dissecting the upper and lower woods.

The woodland on the hospital side of the road had a maze of pathways meandering through it and old photographs show nurses pushing patients through the lush vegetation in wheelchairs. Many soldiers came here during The Great War to recover from gas poisoning in the trenches.

A very early 20th century ariel photo of Winsley chest hospital (the Sanatorium).

My gran worked in the hospital during The Great War as an auxiliary helping to look after the war wounded; she met a young officer who was recovering in the hospital and over the course of time they grew very close. He was a son of the owners of 'Fry's' chocolate factory in Bristol. Of course this crossing of the social divide was completely frowned on, in fact worse than frowned on, people would be horrified, this just didn't happen. My great grandfather found out and immediately took my gran from the hospital and forbade her to contact the lad again; very sad.

By 1960 the paths through the wood had long become neglected and overgrown with the large variety of fern and almost tropical vegetation that would have been planted very early on in the construction.

As less maintenance took place on these woodland paths, plants grew unchecked and produced dark dank tunnels overhanging the pathways, which suited our games of jungle warfare ideally.

High cliffs, the left over workings of a sandstone quarry, ran around the edge of the top woods and at the lower face were caves and tunnels which it was said ran all the way to Bradford-on-Avon. We would pinch matches and candles from our parents and crawl into these moist holes, the roof hanging with hundreds of bats, trying to find the collective bravery to see how far we could get. Inevitably we would give up and go back to the tunnel entrance, sit down and plan another adventure.

We would play our army games to our heart's content, crawling quietly through the lush undergrowth, one group stalking another. It was always the British against the Germans. I was never that comfortable with the choice of enemy as I was well aware that I was half German with German family and friends. So when I was involved I would try and swing it that the enemy was Japanese. We all had bits of wood fashioned into guns and these would be kept in the shed or under the bed to be dragged out when a new war game began. No kids anywhere in the world had Murhill woods; Murhill woods were special. They were full of everything kids could want; the caves, tunnels, cliffs, and odd shaped man made stone platforms that incited heated debate over origin and age.

The woods on the lower side of the road were named by us, 'Corragal woods' because our school teacher Mrs Corragal lived in one of the houses bordering the edge; although we called them after our teacher I believe these woods were owned by the Marshall family.

These lower woods were full of majestic beech trees and hidden glades that filled in the autumn with millions of fallen leaves, so deep we could bury ourselves beneath them, and there were also many remains of dry stone walls that took you from one section of woodland to another. We knew our way around these woods with our eyes shut. Below the woods on the other side of the canal, meadowland ran on a steep slope to the River Avon in the valley.

My gran told me that in her childhood strawberries had been grown on these slopes, picked and sent by barge to Southampton for the Ocean Liners.

In the middle of Murhill a high wall surrounded the large manor house of Henry Marshall; beside the lower wall of the property a very steep track runs down to the canal; this track was the trolley road where goods were brought from the canal to the hospital perched on the hill way above. It's highly likely that the canal also brought the materials that built the hospital.

At the turn of the century the canals were the equivalent of the motorways of England and they were used for the transportation of every type of

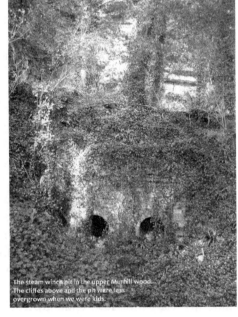

The steam winch pit in the upper Murhill wood. The cliffes above and the pit were less overgrown when we were kids.

produce to all corners of the country; the heyday of the canals came to a slow end during the early decades of the twentieth century as railway transport took over.

The trolley road was far too steep for horses to pull the carts directly upward; at least as far as the road level. Steel rails were laid in the paving on which the cars ran. The cars were loaded from the barges then pulled up from the canal by steam winch.

From the roadway dissecting the two tracks, the second stage upward to the hospital is slightly easier and it may have been possible to finish the journey by horse drawn cart. I doubt anyone is alive now who knows the answer to the question but my forefathers and mothers living in Murhill would have known. Sadly it's too late to get the answer.

I found the article below on the Bradford-on-Avon website.

The quarry was known as 'The Engine Quarry' because there was a steam-powered stone-cutting saw installed there. From there, blocks of stone were lowered by a steeply-inclined tramway to a wharf on the bank of the Kennet & Avon Canal.

The location of the steam house can still be seen at the bottom of the track leading from the hospital down to the road; it is set back among the trees, a large square man made pit with two tunnels going in under the cliffs. This is very overgrown now and people have chucked their rubbish into it, also the walls have partially collapsed, but when we were kids it was still in quite good condition. The photo on the previous page shows the entrance to the tunnels with the quarry face behind.

Half way down the trolley road opposite Marshall's wall a path goes off to the right leading to a row of cottages. There were three individual cottages and at one time these were occupied by the Sartain and Hosey families. This is where a whole clan of my relations grew up and inter-married. Simple one up one down workers' cottages then, now probably all knocked into one and worth a million.

The Burt, Hosey and Sartain families all lived in Murhill during the late eighteen hundreds, a real family Mafia.

Annie Sartain worked in service for the Brinckman's in Murhill house. Christiane Brinckman the daughter married Sir Hugo Marshall so when Grace my gran was born she too was known to the Brinckman's and the Marshalls and went to work for them when Fred took her away from her job in the hospital. I believe at this time Sir Hugo and Lady Marshall had moved into Murhill House. *Sir Hugo Marshall was the last colonial governor of Western Nigeria. He was invested as a Knight Commander, Order of the British Empire (K.B.E.).*

This familiarity with the Marshall family was passed down through the generations from my gran to my dad and to me. When I was in the village or in Murhill and Lady Marshall would meet me I was always incredibly polite; she would stand and talk to me for ages asking about the wellbeing of our family. I remember her as a lovely lady and after our conversation and her departure I always felt ten feet tall having had her attention. Friends who were with me would move away and wait while I conducted this adult conversation with one of the prominent elders of the village, then I would be ribbed about my politeness. But I do remember the issue of the Marshalls as being the one thing my gran was strict with me about. She would always say to me 'Steven if you meet Lady or Sir Hugo Marshall in the village you give them the time of day and ask after them, they've watched you grow up and I want them to see you've been brought up with manners.' Manners were still important in the sixties; although only too often I was badly behaved, manners and being polite were never areas where I let my parents down.

The photo gives some idea of how the woodland surrounded our village. Conkwell woods are in the foreground. The strip of woodland wrapping round the top right hand corner is actually just as deep only it's on the other side of the hill sloping away from the photographer toward Avoncliff. If the camera panned ninety degrees to the right then Murhill woods would look just the same as Conkwell woods. The woodland furthest on the right is actually Westwood woods on the other side of the valley. The little white mark on the far left hand side center is Conkwell...phuh!, that was a difficult explanation, I hope it makes sense.

In 1963 my great grandmother Annie Sartain died. Little granny was ninety five when she passed away. She died quietly in her sleep from old age; a long life span was common on the Hosey, Sartain side of the family. Her death was very sad she was a lovely old lady. However every cloud as they say, has a silver lining and it was my good fortune to inherit her wheelchair.

Now this may seem an odd thing to say, but her wheelchair was unlike the big wheeled chairs of today.

Her chair had thick solid axels and four strong wheels roughly 300mm in diameter and dad used the wheels to build Pete and me a trolley; with these small, strong wheels it was built to last and fast.

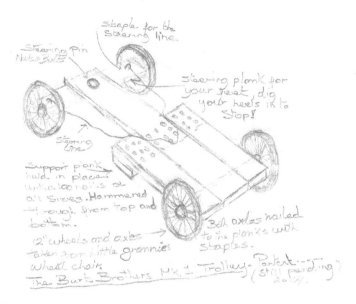

Bernard reminded me of a story involving him and our trolley that nearly cost him his life... or could have crippled him for life. A trolley would be knocked together with whatever wood nails and bolts could be found in your dad's shed. I was lucky; dad had heaps of tools, nails, bolts, and washers so the trolley ended up looking like my sketch. It had no brake; you had to press down with the sole of your shoe on the steering plate and dig your heels into the road; however at the point of improvised braking it became very difficult to steer, remember the driver was only controlling the vehicle by baling twine and you probably only owned a pair of wellies and one pair of shoes, which, if you damaged during the course of 'Play' would get you, if you were lucky, a cuff round the ear from dad or a sting across the back of the legs from mum; or if you were really unlucky and your parents had had a bad day a whack with anything that came to hand, which was par for the course. (Where was Childline or Esther RantzenI ask)?

So the first thing you thought of... yes, protect the heels on your shoes.

Bern and I had meandered up through the village on the trolley taking it in turns to steer and push, till we got to the Wheatsheaf. Gran had given me a bag of red peanuts in their shells and we'd slowly munched our way through the bag leaving a trail a mile long till we got to the top of Murhill.

'Where shall we go next? 'Asked Bern.

'How about going down the woods?' I replied.

Bern was easy going, it was ok by him, so across the road we went, him steering and me sitting with my back to his, pushing us along.

Murhill is steep and long; that's Steep and Long with a capital S & L.

If descending this hill on a push bike you would keep your brakes on the whole way down. The Trolley let me remind you had no brakes. As we went down past our football field and the back gate to the Sutcliffe School the trolley began to speed up.

'Slow us down' said Bern.

'No, you slow us down; dig your heels in.' I said.

'I can't,' shot back Bern, 'I can't brake and steer, slow us down.' His voice had gone up a couple of octaves.

I jumped off...

'Steer into the verge Bern,' I shouted... But it was too late.

'Oh God I can't stop! Helpppppppppppp'.......... were the last words I heard from my friend as he disappeared round the bend.

Let me describe the hill -it was not dissimilar to a dry ski slope in its angle of descent; however it was only the width of a modern day 4x4 and went through two severe drop zones over a half mile before hitting an undulating section and arriving at the T-junction with Winsley Hill. An uncontrolled descent of this hill by any form of wheeled transport should be classified as a suicidal undertaking.

Bern's scream faded into the distance...

When I caught up with him, he'd come to a stop in front of Mr Shrecker's driveway, 200 yards from the junction having covered a total distance of close to a mile.

When I got to him he was still sitting on the trolley looking a bit shell-shocked. If this had been an Olympic event he'd have won Gold.

Good old Bernie.

We discussed his heroic survival as we slowly pulled the trolley back up Winsley Hill; heels of shoes intact.

Many of the other kids had a trolley but their wheels came mainly from discarded children's prams or pushchairs. These types of wheels from prams or pushchairs tended to be big and thin and prone to buckling if you cornered too fast.

Winsley village hall front entrance 2014, still very much the same.

Most prams would be obtained through the jumble sale, an event that was held in the village hall three or four times a year and awaited with anticipation by everyone young and old. I suppose the modern day car boot sale has replaced the village jumble, but back in the fifties and sixties the village jumble sale was a way, when times were hard, of providing working and playing clothes for dad and the kids. We didn't live in a disposable world everything was used, passed down or passed on to families next door. Clothes cost money and money was hard earned; abundant disposable income was a luxury most families didn't have. Make do and mend was a common expression of the time. Who today darns socks? Hardly anyone I should think, yet in the sixties it was still common practice.

My first pair of jeans came from the jumble, mum bought them and when she gave them to me to try on I found they were women's jeans with extra girth in the hip area, no zipper and buttons up the side. Another battle ensued. There was no way in the world I was going to wear them.

Mum said she'd buy a zip, remove the side buttons, sew up the opening and put the zip in the front. Thank God the project died a death... I probably reported my mum to gran and she fought my corner again.

My first pair of jeans I bought myself from my paper round earnings in North Bradley.

Levi original 501s with buttons; they cost £3.75 a pair and took me weeks of hard saving to afford. This was after an embarrassing episode concerning a pair of brown elephant cord trousers which I shall come to later on.

The jumbles would start on the dot of two-o-clock on a Saturday afternoon and a queue would be patiently waiting for the doors to open. When they did there was a mad scramble similar to the January sales or getting a seat on Easy-Jet but no one ever beat Mrs Forsyth to the door, she must have camped there overnight, she was always first in the queue.

We kids would come back with all sorts; Jeff bought a pair of snow shoes that he couldn't wait to try out in the winter; he pushed them under his bed looking forward to the day he could try them out on Turleigh Downs; however Pat, while clearing up the boys bedroom found them and threw them out, much to Jeff's annoyance.

I had a set of golf clubs and two piano accordions at home. They would clutter up my bedroom until mum had enough and then they would end up in the loft or back in the jumble again for someone else to buy. By rights I should have been a football star who played golf and the piano accordion. I really don't know where I went wrong.

A less strenuous child occupation was marbles. Every child had a bag of marbles and the favourite place to play was outside the Phelps' house. We had a great pitch and a crowd of kids would gather for a big game. Stakes were high and if you weren't on form you could lose your complete collection in an afternoon. Swapping marbles was an art form and the size, lines, colors and air bubbles inside were a guide to the values of the glass balls. The swapping or trading of marbles was carried out in a very serious and grown up manner. A big marble could be worth up to ten small ones and you never played with them; they were your status, they showed how good you were at the game, and were a form of currency that you swapped for the standard playing marbles if you lost them all in a match.

To try and replenish marble stock a player who was wiped clean would offer to swap one of his big marbles for five, six, maybe even ten small ones.

So if you were good you won matches collecting small marbles and then swapped them on for big ones.

Paper 'Comics' were another great love, just like the different first division football teams we all had our choice of 'Comic'- Eagle, Hornet, Hotspur, Valiant or Victor for the ten plus age group; Beano and Dandy for the younger kids. Also kid's football related papers like 'Shoot' and 'Score'. These would be delivered or bought in town on a Saturday and then swapped between us during the week. Never thrown away, piles of comics would accumulate under the bed until mum lost patience and either threw them out or made us bundle them up to go in the shed or loft. One of mum's common expressions and I'm sure it wasn't just my mum was, 'What on earth do you want to keep those for?' This question would be met with either a blank look or some mumbled incomprehensible answer before you slid quickly out of earshot.

Every November we would build a bonfire for the Guy Fawkes night celebration and once the fire was going have sausages and baked potatoes cooked in the hot embers while watching the fireworks.

While living at St Nicholas Close we did this either in our back garden or round at the White's. The families would take turns. This went on until mum formed the Cub Scout group then she and Ross Daniels who jointly helped her with the Cubs decided to hold a community Guy Fawkes for the Cub Group. Eventually this turned into a village bonfire organized by our group of village kids and was kept going until we all started work in the early seventies. The younger kids coming behind Jeff, Sticky and I, sadly, never kept the tradition going. More on the bonfire building later...

Guy Fawkes night would come and go then came Christmas.

Christmases in our house were celebrated in a mix of the German and the English, or looking back on it now, just mum's own idea of how it should be carried out.

We were never allowed to see the tree until Christmas morning. Every house in the village would have their tree up two or three weeks before but not the Burt's. Nothing was on display until the big day.

Mum and dad would decorate the tree on the night of Christmas Eve and in the morning Pete and I had to dress in our best clothes, and wait at the top of the stairs till mum had sorted out all the presents and the breakfast. Then she would ring a bell and we would dutifully tramp down to the front room.

Looking back as an adult I can see no sense in the way my mum regimented Christmas. It wasn't really even a German Christmas; they at least open the presents on Christmas Eve. While Christmas trees twinkled in the windows of all the houses in the street up to three weeks before the day; Pete and I had to sit without a tree or decorations right up till Christmas morning, then go through some bizarre ritual before we were allowed to open our presents.

While other kids were finding stockings at the bottom of their bed and running down stairs to rip paper from packages, Pete and I were stood waiting for a bell to ring allowing us to go down stairs, washed, hair combed and in our best clothes I might add and then had to sing carols under the tree and eat breakfast before we were allowed at our presents. I don't quite know what planet our parents where on. Christmas is a time of fun. When little kids should be able to dash excitedly around wide eyed and with chocolate all round their mouths. If they are too full to eat a roast dinner, what the hell does it matter? Enjoy! Regimentation will come later in life and all too soon.

Please don't misunderstand me; mum and dad went to a great deal of trouble to make Christmas special for Pete and I; our presents were lovely and dad's ability to work with wood and his hands meant we had some lovely presents made exclusively by him.

One year dad made me a 'Fort'. It was a work of art, with turrets and a drawbridge that worked from a little handle on the side. It measured around three feet square and stood roughly two feet high. I manned the fort with plastic soldiers and field artillery pieces from 'Corgi' that fired matchsticks.

Another year he made Pete a 'Garage' with a car park on the roof and a lift worked by a little handle to take the cars up and down as well as a ramp and petrol pumps on the forecourt. These were wonderful models built and painted with love and care. I wonder where on earth they went to. I would give anything to get them back.

No, Pete and I did have very happy Christmases; but we grow up; when I was small I didn't mind the peculiar way our family went about Christmas, it didn't really register, but as I got to that realisation point, around nine and ten years old when you find out there is no fat bearded fellow from the North Pole coming down your chimney, but you carry on the charade for your younger brother's sake; that was the point I began to wish our Christmases were like other people's in the street.

When it came to holidays, there's no doubt we were two very fortunate kids. I had seen most of Western Europe by the time I was fourteen years old. This made me incredibly worldly as a child and gave me confidence into adulthood that put me miles in front of others of my age; my brother and I had seen and done what the majority of adults at the time had not experienced in the way of European travel and culture.

But oh, how at times I wished I could do what my mates were doing; a week at Butlins holiday camp, just once that's all; playing in swimming pools, riding donkeys on the beach and having a whale of a time in the adventure playground. Just the once Pete and I would have liked to do something everybody else was doing and the same applied to Christmas; after all we were in England not Germany; at least that's how Pete and I saw it.

Life went on while we were in Germany on holiday; child alliances were made and broken; plans were formed and if you weren't there, you weren't in.

In the summer of 1965 once again we were off to Germany, this time gran and granddad came along. It was a lovely holiday and

I practice the art of right handed drinking while my parents discuss who will pick up the bill. Germany 1965 with gran and granddad.

the first holiday either of my grandparents had taken outside England let alone the UK; both of them had a great time although travelling with six of us in the car was not the most comfortable long distance journey we ever did.

On returning to Winsley after the three weeks in Germany, a knock soon came on the door and there stood Jeff, Kev, and Sticky asking if I was coming out to play in their new gang.

'What new gang?' I asked.

'The JKC gang; stands for Jeff, Kev, and Chris gang,' I was told.

'Well what about me?' I asked.

'Well you were on holiday when we formed it so it's our initials that make up the name of the gang and are on the flag.' I was told by all three of them in an off-hand manner.

'And no you can't add your initials it wouldn't sound right.'

So, due to the fact I had spent three weeks in Germany, regardless of the fact it was against my will, my initials were never included in the gang logo. Regardless of providing the first aid kit that was carried by Pete everywhere we went, our dog, which became the gang's mascot and protector, bill-hooks, machete, and other lethal equipment that would not have looked out of place on medieval battlefield, plus the material for the flag; I was destined to remain nothing but a secondary gang member.

A bitter snub the psychological impact of which I carry to this day. (I am of course joking).

The other embarrassing thing I had to put up with, although I laugh about it now, was wearing German leather pants, 'Lederhosen'; the type you always see the German kids wearing in films.

Hence the name of this book of memories 'Growing up in Lederhosen'.

I did really grow up in these German leather pants. They were very comfortable and incredibly durable and looking back I know that wearing them was second nature to me; in fact I own a pair to this very day and still find them great hard wearing shorts... but oh dear they did create some fiery situations for me while growing up. They're fine if you live in Germany and all the kids are wearing them, but completely out of place on a sixties council estate in the West of England.

Oma looks on as I try to convince my brother that bare-back mountain goat riding is as easy as donkey's on the beach at Weston and its free. Austria 1964

I had worn them since the day I could walk; so the other kids in the village had got used to seeing Pete and me wearing them and it never raised a comment; it wasn't really anything out of the ordinary.

But wearing them outside my own village was an entirely different matter; then came the inevitable 'mickey-take' that needed to be nipped in the bud; growing up in Lederhosen I had to know how to use my fists.

Another great advantage with Lederhosen, they came in very handy when dad gave my backside a tanning, something that happened on quite a regular basis; the leather took the sting out of his thrashing and oddly my dad never seemed to cotton-on to this, I'd howl and shed crocodile tears but in truth I never felt a thing.

When I heard the words, 'get up those stairs and stay in your room till your father gets home.' I knew I needed to change into my leather shorts...

In the summer of 1963 Jeff's mum and dad moved from their house in Nicholas Close down to Poston Way.

It wasn't long before my mum and dad also arranged a Poston Way house swap. These houses were three bedroom; bigger than the two bedroom houses in Nicholas Close; they also bordered the road whereas our house in St Nicholas Close was down the footpath.

Our house, 2 Poston Way. The gateway where dad ripped out the hedge, the annex between the shed and house, the green and the garages where we played square-bash are still exactly the same. The only addition in thirty five years is the tree.

Dad arranged a move to number two on the end of a row of four with a big garden. We swapped with Mrs Harper, Mrs Forsyth's mother who being on her own only needed a two bedroom house.

Next door to us lived the Hansford family who had two children Linda and Robin, but neither of these kids ever came out to play.

Next to the Hansford's on the other side of The Drum (a tunnel, which led to the back garden of the two middle houses and so called because of the drum like noise your feet made when walking through it) lived the Holts and my girlfriend Angela.

I would sit next to Angela at school and she like me was very good at sport. Unlike me, she was pretty good at the other subjects as well and some evenings she would come round to our house and help me with my homework.

We were around eight years old now and firm friends.

Girlfriends weren't discussed or admitted to, but quite a few kids had their favorite girl or boy at school; chalking hearts on the pavement around the estate was common with the initials of your fancy inside; SB loves AH or the other way round; these childish scribbles drove mum nuts when she saw them while delivering the Post, especially if they appeared outside our gate and a couple of times I was made to go out with a bucket of water and wash it away; even though I pleaded my innocence. It would have been one of the girls, Angie, Ruth, Sue Mayell or Sue Prior… it could've been any one of my friends; a typical type of practical joke.

But it wasn't just chalk hearts on the pavement, all over Murhill woods names, initials, and hearts would be carved into the bark of Beech trees, I've recently walked through the woods and looked at the trees, Angie and my initials are still visible on one giant tree to this very day as are many other kids.

At night after we had been put to bed we would sneak to the window and chat to each other for ages. Pete and I slept in the front of the house with mum and dad's big bedroom in the back. So after being put to bed I would watch the clock and at 9.30pm tiptoe into mum's bedroom, open the window and wait for Angela to appear. If she or I couldn't get there we'd get a wet piece of paper and put it on the open window to show we had been. We called these clandestine meetings, 'half past nine paper on the window'.

When our parents called us in from after school play we would whisper this line to each other before disappearing indoors; very romantic for kids so young.

Once during our time at Winsley Juniors a very attractive newcomer arrived at the school and in the short term came between Angela and I; that girl was Perry Jane Shrecker.

Perry Jane was our age and one of four kids with two older sisters Cherry and Honey and a younger brother Guy.

The Shreckers had moved into a bungalow in Murhill. I can't remember now if both or one of the parents came from the Middle East, maybe they didn't, but all three kids had a dark olive skinned complexion and were very attractive.

I fell for Perry Jane the moment she arrived in our class and it caused a bitter break up between Angela and me.

I would visit Perry Jane's house and family in Murhill. But as nice as Perry Jane was she was very reserved; I was used by now to having a peck and a hug from Angela and hoped for the same from Perry Jane, but that would not be happening with this girl.

One day after school, Angela who had a pretty vicious temper when she got going, let rip at Perry Jane. She didn't for one minute believe Perry would retaliate and for that matter neither did I; but she got that wrong big time!

This was the first time I had ever seen two girls fighting, let alone as it seemed over me.

I'll give Perry Jane top marks for trying. Angela was a real hard nut; she had grown up in a big family; scrapping was not something she worried about. She would take on any of the boys in the village and in some cases send them running. Perry on the other hand came from a very well-to-do family. Certainly not council estate kids like us. Fighting was not really etched into her upbringing. But she fought back with tooth and nail, an impressive display, which ended with teachers pulling them apart at more or less a draw.

But which of these two girls would continue to be my girlfriend?

It went to Angela... had to really.

Life at school quietened down and went back to normal side by side at the same desk and at night half past nine paper on the window.

Mum decided that I should start going to Cub Scouts. She had spoken to Mrs Strickland and found out that Chris was going to the Cubs in Bradford-on-Avon, run by Mrs Green who with her husband owned the cycle shop in town; Jeff reminded me we were called the 1st Bradford-on Avon Lord Fitzmaurice's Own; sounds like a Military Regiment doesn't it.

The Bradford-on-Avon Cub group was based in the old Trinity school next to the Trinity Church near the river.

The following Thursday evening mum took both Chris and I in the car and enrolled me.

It didn't take long before Pat asked if Jeff could join us, and so the three of us went off on the bus to Cubs; after Cubs we would walk to the chipper on Silver street at the bottom of White Hill and buy a penny worth of chips; this was a penny from our three penny bus fare money from Town Bridge. Having spent a penny we then had to walk to the next 'Fare Stage' stop (a stop where the price increases) where it would only cost us tuppence for the bus, this would be at the top of Masons Hill, a couple of hundred yards up the hill from the chipper.

As summer drew to a close and the evening's drew in mum ended up doing the Cub Scout run in the car. She would then stay and help out, taking us home at the end of the evening.

This didn't last long.

Mum started making enquiries about starting a Cub Pack in Winsley. We had our own village hall but for some reason the parish council wouldn't let mum use it.

Eventually she found two other helpers. Gillian Strickland, Sticky's elder sister and Ross Daniels the farmer from Turleigh.

We ended up in Turleigh village hall. Most of the kids in the village joined including Pete and I.

In total there were around twenty children and on any night there would be at least fourteen at a minimum.

The Cup pack got involved with loads of things. As well as the annual Guy Fawkes bonfire we carried out the once a year Bob-a-Job. This exploitation of youth labour lasted for a couple of weeks in the spring and during this time a Cub would have a sheet of paper headed with names, addresses, amount, and date. The idea was to go door knocking and do jobs for a 'Bob' (the slang name for a shilling in pre-decimal currency). I don't believe any of us liked doing this mainly for two reasons. Firstly we had to do door knocking in uniform and secondly we never got to keep the money which had to be handed over for the group funds. The jobs we carried out for people varied from window cleaning, weeding the garden, mowing the lawn, or just simply taking the bin to the end of the drive. Some people were very kind and slipped us an extra tanner (sixpence) off the sheet and others exploited us terribly by keeping us for hours on end and still only paying us a Bob. We collectively made note of these houses and wouldn't go there. However the people concerned would collar mum while she was on the Post round and ask why one of us Cubs hadn't been to see them. Inevitably I would be the one to knock at the door and do four hours of forced labour. These houses were also the houses who never gave mum a 'Tip' at Christmas so she should have just ignored them instead of trying to keep them sweet.

On completion of the chore or chores a 'Job Done' sticker would be handed over to the occupier to put in the window.

We also went carol singing at Christmas, although the attendance figures were pretty low; I don't ever remember Jeff and Bern turning out for carols, but of course Pete and I had to go as did Sticky, as his sister was one of the pack helpers. We would trudge round the village churning out 'The Holly & The Ivy', 'Good King Wenceslas' and

others until we finally arrived at our last house; what was then Colonel Walker's house, big, very old, and set back off the lane between the Post Office and the Wheatsheaf; the old Colonel would open the door and listen to a couple of carols before inviting us all inside for drinks. Ross would get a 'Port', mum a 'Sherry' and the rest of us would be given a drop of 'Egg-nog', a yellow substance that to this day I still haven't a clue what's in it. But it was a good evening and always raised a tidy sum for our group.

All in all the Cubs was good fun and looking back I really don't know how, at times, mum put up with the bad behavior. After an outing to the American museum in Bath we were walking back along the canal and

Dundas aqueduct. Photo taken from below the canal shows the ledge that I would casually walk around.

Bernard and I disappeared. I had found my way onto the outside ledge of the Dundas Aqueduct at Limpley Stoke. Seventy five or more feet above the river and railway line I was strolling casually along the two-foot wide decorative rim. A trick I did many times in the past, but without my parents being there or their knowledge. My mum had kittens and from that moment banned me from Cubs. When I stopped going other kids stopped going in protest, so mum had to reinstate me. What a horror! Mind you it wasn't all the kids who were badly behaved it was a select group. Most were quite good. The photo shows Dundas Aqueduct, the two foot rim and the river below.

On Saturdays and in the school holidays to earn some extra pocket money I would help mum deliver the Post; on a few occasions Angela would come along as well.

Angela and I would do the long deliveries; down the hill through Murhill to the Toop's house alongside the canal at Elbow bridge. The Toop's were a family of Dutch ancestry whose daughter also attended our school. I believe Toop's house, Elbow cottage, was originally a canal side tavern.

A mile to the bottom and a mile back up; half the journey was on a slippery uneven mud footpath with trees and brambles on either side. No Post-delivery person today would entertain doing such a trip on a Quad-Bike let alone on foot. As well as the Toop's, mum had to deliver to the Trussler's; again on the canal but at the other end of Murhill at the bottom of the trolley road. It was a hell of a Post round and she was grateful for a pair of young helpers in Angela and I.

We were now around eight years old and it was generally accepted by our gang of kids that Angie and I were now boyfriend and girlfriend.

We played out together, we sat next to each other at school, we just did stuff together. It was just something that happened from those very early years of her walking me to Miss Norris' class at school.

Green Lane Turleigh.
Photo taken from the entrance
of Ross Daniels farm. Photo 2013

One summer's afternoon I asked Angela if she would like to come round mine. My parents weren't home at the time but I made a pot of tea and with a plate of biscuits I sat with her in the back garden of our house and had a picnic. Another afternoon after school we decided instead of going straight home we'd go for a walk; we walked through the old village past the Manor to the cricket field then down the footpath to the farm track leading around the hill from Turleigh to Elbow bridge.

Turning left we headed back toward Turleigh village, down Green Lane above Ross Daniels' farmyard and back up the hill past the Trows.

This is a lovely cool spot covered by overhanging copper beech trees where an underground stream merges from the hillside, a place where it is said locally the Anglo Saxons and Romans came to get their water.

We walked back up the road through the woods to our village; we held hands and every time a car came we would quickly and guiltily let go of each other.

Half way up the hill I gave her a kiss. It was a kiss on the lips, it was the first kiss I had ever given a girl on the lips and as odd as it may seem, even when I think of it now all these years later I can feel the moment, the touch of her lips, smell her almost black chestnut colored hair and remember the touch of her hand on mine; it has stayed with me all my life.

As young as we were at the time Angela was my girlfriend; two kids in a small village who were fond of each other from a very early age; life changed our destined pathways, had I not gone to a different secondary school it's quite likely the bond between us would have remained, who knows.

When I look back now I see the changes in my younger life over which I had no control; my parents insistence that I go to secondary school in Trowbridge rather than the catchment area school of Trinity in Bradford-on-Avon. That in itself wasn't so bad, as I at least remained living in my village. But then came the move to North Bradley in summer 1970 and the eventual move to Norfolk in summer 1971.

To this day I believe that final move to Norfolk was not in the family's best interest. It cut the ties with our extended family in Swindon; it cut the ties with dad's mates, those who he went to football with and others from Marcos where he worked from1967 to 1971;the friends with whom he would work on all sorts of projects at the weekends.

Mum had an overriding desire to leave Winsley and when Marcos was going through a rough patch and dad was worried about his job, leaving Wiltshire altogether for a fresh start somewhere else in the country was not a big concern to mum.

After all England was only an adopted country and Wiltshire an adopted county; there were no strong ties for her.

We moved to the East of the country but I know my dad was never really happy living in East Anglia he always talked about moving back down; maybe not to Winsley but somewhere in West Wiltshire.

The saddest thing for me was leaving gran in Wiltshire. Our moving to Norfolk broke my gran's heart; as far gran was concerned it may as well have been the other side of the world. She came from an age where families stuck together and lived close by each other. It brings tears to my eyes even now thinking about it.

It took me years to accept Norfolk as home and throughout my army career my parents almost had to pay me to come and see them; my preference was always to board the train westward from Paddington to Bath Spa and go to stay with my wonderful gran in Winsley.

I enjoyed living in Poston Way. The house and garden were bigger than Nicholas Close as well as being closer to Jeff, Bern, Kev, and Angie.

No sooner had we arrived then dad started to make his inevitable changes.

He tied a rope to the back of the car and pulled a big lump of the hedge out by the roots. He wanted to make a drive and parking space off the road. The council guy who came round to collect the rent, Mr Francis, went ballistic! Dad didn't care, the hedge was gone and we set-to building a drive.

Dad couldn't help but make changes to everything. A natural at carpentry and anything DIY he would want to improve his house. The fact that the house belonged to the council and not him made not an iota of difference to dad.

In Nicholas Close he built a massive brick and stone pond in the garden and then enclosed the alleyway between the garden shed-come-coalhouse and the main building. He knocked down the internal wall between the dining room and the living room with no thought to the structural integrity of the house. Then he started all over again in Poston Way.

The front garden was on a steep slope but dad shored it all up, got hard core from somewhere, and set about making a raised driveway with a pit in the middle so he could get underneath and service the car. A mammoth task all done by hand. It was still there a few years ago and used by Moggie Clift who took our house over after we left for North Bradley in the summer of 1970.

We'd had a few dogs since Bruno our wonderful Golden Retriever died in the summer of 1963.

Dad brought home a big Alsatian we named Shane, but he was just too big and boisterous around the house so we arranged for him to go to the Swindon Police Force; then came a little Border Collie/Alsatian cross we named Nipper who was given away to a farmer because he was just completely hyper and needed far more exercise then we could provide for him.

But one evening dad came home with a small Alsatian bitch puppy that was in a sorry state.

This puppy we called Gina. She was the runt of the litter and was going to be put down by her owner.

Dad had taken pity on her and brought her home suffering from some kind of mange. All her fur had fallen out and she was in a sorry state. Over a period of time with the help of two very strange old ladies who owned a pet shop next to the Cathedral in Bath we nursed her back to health and she became a very special pet in the home. She would lay by the gate with her nose just on the edge of the path but never once would she venture over. The mascot for the JKC Gang, she went everywhere with Pete and I a gentle obedient animal and a loving companion. It was Gina who would crawl under the table at meal times to take my unwanted food.

I suffered terribly with tonsillitis as a child and lost many days from school. I would stay at home in bed and Gina would be curled up on the eiderdown at my feet. At night when the living room door was shut and mum and dad were watching TV I would sneak downstairs and open the kitchen door, then skipping quickly back to bed I would tap the covers with the palm of my hand and Gina would come quietly up the stairs as if knowing she mustn't be heard and bounce onto the bed, curl up on my feet and go to sleep.

Mum believed chamomile tea would cure every ailment and fed it to me by the gallon when I was ill. I hated the stuff, just the smell of it turned my stomach over but Gina loved it.

It would be left in a cup and saucer by my bed with strict instructions that I should drink it while it was hot, I would mumble my consent but as soon as mum had disappeared down stairs I would tip the tea into the saucer and my faithful four legged companion would get rid of every last drop. Mum never found out.

The funny thing about Gina was she never barked. It wasn't until I came home on my first leave from the army in October 1971 that she barked for the first time. By then she must have been at least six years old, it was very strange. She lived to a ripe old age passing away in 1978 around twelve years old, very old for a German Shepherd.

The tonsillitis got worse as I got older.

I spent more and more time away from school and eating was painful, but Doctor Thomas our GP refused to send me to have them taken out, he ridiculously said he didn't believe in it.

Mum despaired, I was having one week in four away from school, possibly even more. My health and schooling were suffering, I wasn't eating and my normal happy disposition had deserted me.

Eventually in desperation mum took me to see an elderly gentleman, an Ear, Nose, and Throat specialist who lived just across the road from the bowling green in the old village. Dr Bembridge knew me well from chats I'd had with him while helping mum on her mail delivery.

He would always speak and I was polite and chatty. He told mum he didn't mind us going to him for help and so I was taken to his house in the village for him to examine the back of my throat.

Dr Bembridge was horrified at what he found. My tonsils had all but rotted away with infection; it was no wonder my health had deteriorated so dramatically.

The old doctor still had his contacts, in no time I was admitted to St Martin's hospital in Bath (Combe Down) and what was left of the tonsils were taken away. After a few days of jelly and ice cream (the food of the time for post tonsil removal) my throat felt better and I wanted to go home, I was a child in a male ward of roughly twenty grown men. Dad came to visit me one night and I begged him to take me home; not only did I hate being there, but 'Man from Uncle' was on the TV that night, a spy series that I never missed. Dad went to ask the Sister but she condescendingly said 'Absolutely not.'

This got right up dad's nose so he promptly chucked my clothes into my bag, picked me up in my PJs and took me to the car and home. The Sister created merry hell but this cut no ice with dad.

I went home a new child. The change in me was dramatic; I started eating again and my ruddy good health returned. I was back on track.

Generally the doctor's service was very good; our GP, Dr Thomas shared a lovely surgery with Dr Barnett on the corner where Woolly Street meets the Holt Road. If you needed an appointment you went down to the surgery and saw one of the doctors, if you required a home visit a doctor came to your house, you didn't have to worry or argue with a receptionist or a practice manager, it just happened; it was a lovely simple time and things worked in a lovely simple manner.

Our dentist was Mr Brown on the Trowbridge road opposite

Fitzmaurice Grammer School, his surgery equipment was medieval, his electric drill was only one step removed in speed from the early foot-pedal operated drills, a patient could almost count the revolutions by eye!

But he was kind to kids and I wasn't frightened to go and have work done by him. There was no six monthly routine for check-ups as there are today, but mum would take us at least once a year. Mr Brown had no X-ray machine, he'd inspect our teeth visually and tap them, asking if they hurt or watching to see our reflexes. Pronounced sound we'd go home for another year or till a niggle cropped up.

However an incident while in Germany put the fear of dentists in me that has lasted to this very day, we were at Oma's for three weeks when I began to suffer terribly with toothache.

I was taken to a dentist two doors down from Oma's flat; the bloke was a bloody butcher he drilled and filled five or more of my teeth in one go. No anesthetic; they almost had to strap me to the chair. It was the most horrendous treatment I've ever experienced and gave me a lifelong dread of the dentist. I don't know why my parents let him do it, my teeth were good, ok maybe one tooth did need a filling, but never five. The swine really enjoyed himself and even now my mum doesn't like me to talk about it, she feels so guilty.

I was in agony all the holiday and crying with pain, when we got back to from Germany the first thing mum did was take me to Mr Brown. He was horrified at the work and had to redo all the fillings.

He did a good job and I never had another filling till I left the army in 1977 when the army dentist renewed all my fillings in a superb pain free procedure. He said I should have them changed as they were getting passed their sell-by-date and asked me when I'd had them done; I told him the story. I didn't want him anywhere near my mouth but he persuaded me and I'm glad I agreed, he was a great dentist and I was very grateful. Some of his military fillings are still going strong in 2014.

Jeff and I started playing footie for the school team when we were around nine years old. It was an honour and I remember vividly Friday sports afternoon walking with the other boys in a line to the Sutcliffe school playing field, a private boarding school on the edge of the village, carrying our boots in our hands so the studs wouldn't damage on the road. We would line up in our respective positions and play a game against each other; I played left wing, Jeff played centre forward. It was a great feeling playing with the older boys and we had a pretty good team. Stephen Little played behind me as 'left half back'. He was also a very good football player and could slot the ball up the wing for me to cross to Jeff in the middle; yep we had a pretty good team regardless of our lack in numbers.

We also played inter-school football against other local villages. The only team we had problems with was Christchurch in Bradford-on-Avon.

Christchurch was a big school by junior standards, probably around 300 pupils at the time. Their choice of boys to play for the football team outnumbered us by four to one. I can't remember ever beating them.

Football was our everyday occupation.

We kids invented a game called 'Square-bash,' a football game of ball passing requiring quick thinking and skill.

In 1968 the council took over a big lump of our garden and built six garages to go with the council houses down our end of the estate.

Mum and dad didn't mind this as the backs of the new garages gave a nice closure to the garden.

Within the tarmac square that was the front of the garages we would pass a ball to each other. The ball couldn't go above head height or pass further than a stretched leg from the person you passed the ball to. You could only touch the ball once, passing it alternately to another person in the square. The ball would move faster and faster until one by one someone would miss-kick the ball or break one of the game rules and be voted out until there was only two left. Then the tempo would rise with the ball being hammered backwards and forwards without hesitation, like boxers in a ring one player would close on the other trying to force a mistake, then a miss-kick or a missed ball and it would be over. It was a great game, which we played for hours on end and it honed our passing skills to perfection.

Now when I enter Dane Rise and drive up past my old house I always feel I would love to turn the clock back and once again play a game of 'Square-bash' on the tarmac in front of those garages.

Above the garages and next to our hedge is a green; here in the evenings we would play at numerous games; we would try balancing on top of the Poston Way road sign or do somersaults over the top of it; see how far we could climb up the steel wire rope that supported the telephone pole, or see how many kids could stand on top of the large brick Post-box outside of Hancock's, which has now been replaced with a small metal one; probably because it had a crack in the brickwork running the whole circumference and the older boys would try to push it over; maybe they eventually succeeded?

We would play football using the telegraph pole and the supporting wire as a goal. If only a few kids were out we'd have two small groups of two or three one defending and one attacking the one goal under the wire and play 15 minutes before swapping and seeing who could get the most goals in that time.

The ball would go everywhere; our garden, Hancock's garden or over the road into the dairy that was owned by the Elliot's. Mrs Elliot would get really annoyed and at times kept the ball even when we politely asked for it back. So we just didn't bother to ask, just ran into the garden and grabbed it. But we were never rude or destructive; just kids at play.

Elliot's delivered the local milk and also sold the most wonderful orange juice in little glass bottles with tin foil tops. It was a treat to get some money from our parents and go to buy a bottle of that lovely orange.

Next to Elliot's dairy were two bungalows then came Mumford's Nursery. This family owned rows and rows of greenhouses where they grew lettuce, tomatoes and cucumbers. If mum needed any salad stuff she would just send Pete or I over the road to get it fresh from the ground or the vine. I remember the most horrendous hail storm one summer; hail stones as big as golf balls that caused colossal damage to property all over the village but the damage at Mumford's was total; I don't think a pane of glass survived.

The nursery was sold off in the early seventies and big expensive houses were built on the plot.

Summer nights when it was warm we would put a tent up in the garden and sleep out. Now and again friends would be invited round and with our sleeping bags we would jam ourselves in the tent like sardines. Jeff, Kevin, Sticky and others, we would laugh and giggle our way to sleep. I remember one night we kept laughing and joking until dad completely lost his temper and at four in the morning he sent Pete and I to our rooms and the others he sent home.

Not wanting to wake their parents they lay down their sleeping bags on the pavement in front of our house and continued with the hilarity. My dad was fuming!

My poor parents…but honestly what did they expect from eight, nine and ten year olds?

Friday night was Library night and after school I would walk to Bradford-on-Avon, generally with Bernard.

Even though I was not that interested in school I loved books and loved reading; when I was six or seven auntie Dot and uncle Bert had given me the first in the series of 'Famous Five' books by Enid Blyton - 'Five On A Treasure Island', the story of

Julian, Dick, Anne and their cousin Georgina with her dog Timmy who get into a big kidnap adventure on an Island.

From that moment I was hooked on the books and used my hard earned pocket money to collect the whole series, around 20 books in all. There is a flower shop in Church Street called Nestons. This was a second hand book shop in the sixties. The used books would sit on a couple of bookcases in the alleyway next to the shop door, and that's where I would go to seek out the latest 'Famous Five' book on our journeys to town.

I have the complete series to this day in a bookcase at home. They beat Harry Potter hands down.

We would walk to Bradford down through Turleigh and Belcombe and then catch the bus back from the town bridge or arrange to meet my dad from work.

If he was on a two-till-six shift, we would walk back up past the Anglo Saxon and Trinity Church to the Masons Arms, a pub on Newtown where we would sit and drink lemonade and talk to the Mynah (the mime) bird that the pub kept in a cage out the front till dad came along and picked us up. The bird would have us in stitches of laughter, as every car that went past would get a shrill whistle. The driver if not a local person would screech to a halt and back up wondering who on earth had tried to flag them down; they'd wind the window down and ask if it was us and look very disbelieving when we said no it was the bird. When the car drove off we would sit cracked up with laughter.

Now and again we would hold a summer Fete in the back garden. Have little stalls like a coconut shy and bobbing apples. Mums would make toffee apples and other homemade sweets for us to sell. It normally took six or seven of us to arrange this and what money we made we kept. Closer friends would help run the stalls; at one such event we put up the tent and borrowed an ornamental green glass ball that my auntie Betty had in her flower garden. Angela dressed up as Gipsy Rose and told fortunes at a penny a go.

I also had a set of hand puppets given to me by Oma. Sometimes a few of us would get together and hold a puppet show from the bottom of dad's car pit in the drive. We would charge a penny to watch and the kids would sit in rows while two of us performed Punch and Judy from inside the pit. These shows were a good little earner when you were only nine years old and it all helped to subsidise our pocket money allowance, which in our house had to be earned. The open pit led to a disaster later on in 1968 when Pete and I forgot to replace the covering boards.

Our friend Simon Beale lived on a dairy farm along the Bradford road. He had three sisters, Sarah a stunning looking girl, older than Simon by a year or so and Annabelle and Judith, both a couple of years younger than their brother.

Simon's mum and dad are a lovely couple of people, who always made their children's friends from the village very welcome.

Going to play at Simon's was always fun. They had a huge barn full of straw bales where on rainy days we could jump and climb about. We would rig a 'Tarzan' rope from the girders in the roof and swing from the uppermost bales fifteen or twenty feet above the ground; when we ran out of energy we'd sit and watch the rain coming down outside.

We would go with Simon's dad and help drive the cows in for milking, making slides in the fresh cow pats along the way. 'What's that' I hear you say? Well as a cow walks along and releases a long stream of muck in its wake, we would smooth it all out over the grass with our boots, take a long run-up and then slide across the top of the brown stained grass. We've had slides up to five yards long made from cowpats; woe betide if you fell over!

Simon's parents had chickens running around all over the farm; they would lay eggs in all the nooks and crannies; we would collect these eggs some that may have been laying there for weeks and take them across the fields to the top of Turleigh Downs, our sledging hill; from here we would hurl them into the valley below, trying to get them to burst against the wall at the bottom of the hill or even better go over the wall into the road beyond.

Across the back of Simon's the fields led down to 'Belcombe'; a quiet area of very posh housing on the outskirts of Bradford-on-Avon. Big houses hidden on one side of the road behind high stonewalls, slowly they petered out into meadows and woodland as you moved in the direction of Turleigh.

The haunted house at Belcome. Now repaired and lived in.

Here was to be found the haunted house.

The old shell of a house had been labelled as haunted long before our generation of kids came along. It stood back 150 yards from the road behind the high sandstone wall. Green meadowland ran steeply down to the building sat in a hollow. Scattered on the hillside were large horse chestnut and beech trees hundreds of years old.

Around the top of the hill woodland and Copse formed a boundary where we would sit in an old slate roofed shed and look down at the ruined house waiting to see the shadow of the black ghost bird that we kids believed lived there.

If it was a bright sunny day and we felt brave we would flit from tree to tree down the hill with our hearts pounding. Sometimes a shadow would black out the tree tops, it was of course a cloud across the sun but we believed it was the ghost bird; or a noise would make our hair stand on end then we would run like mad back up the hillside to hide in the old shed.

Other days we would just play around the shed clambering along the tops of the old walls or trying to balance across the wooden roof joists that still remained. Utter lunacy!

One day Simon, standing above me on a beam, kicked down a slate, which caught me side-on in the middle of my head. It was a miracle it never spilt my skull open like an axe. Nevertheless the damage was horrendous and blood poured from the wound. The kids dragged me to a cow-trough and plunged my head in. The water in the trough turned instantly red. After a few minutes I took my shirt off and wrapped it round my head and we made our way back to Simon's house.

Mrs Beale cleaned the wound up and took me home. The bleeding had stopped but I was in a real mess and not feeling that well. One thing with me though, no matter how big the hole it always seemed to heal really quickly. This would be a godsend in years to come when all types of injuries came my way.

Old Mans Beard... Still covering our hedge where we scrambled along the top.

Simon's dad kept a huge brown bull for breeding, it was a pretty passive animal but Simon would kid us that it was ferocious. One day, braver than usual we walked back to the farm house crossing the centre of the field containing the mighty bull and his harem. I doubt it was in anger but the bull looked up at us and started scuffing the ground. Us kids ran like the wind toward the nearest tree and clambered up; me, the show-off deciding to go higher than the others ended up stuck in the uppermost branches unable to pluck up courage to come down. In the end Simon and the others had to go and get his dad who clambered up the tree to coax me down; a real loss of face in front of Simon's eldest sister.

In the summer we would play on the footpath leading to Elbow from the cricket field.

The hedges that lined the long descending footpath were covered in a thick mat of 'Old-Man's-Beard' a creeping vine that was as strong as rope winding its way through the upper branches. It was called that strange name due to the flowers that covered the runners. They were in thick white bunches just like the beard of Father Christmas.

We would climb up the inside of the hedge and break through the canopy onto the thick outer layer that spread like a carpet over the hedge. Then we would precariously scramble across the top fifteen feet above the ground seeing how far we could get before falling through.

The dead 'old-man's-beard' we would break into small pieces the size of cigars, catch light to the end and try to smoke it. The vine had minute holes running up its length, which let it smolder really well when lit. To inhale the smoke was a killer but we did it nonetheless, coughing and staggering around with our eyes streaming. All good character building stuff when you haven't even reached your teens.

Following the cutting of the wheat or barley in the summer the fields were covered with small square bales of straw waiting to be collected or lifted into large 'stacks'.

The older boys would move these small bales together and build a fort ten feet high; then, divided into two opposing armies we would spend fifteen or twenty minutes making 'stubble bombs'. These were the short left over clumps of wheat or barley left in the ground after the combine harvester and been through and cut the crop; we'd pull them up and compress the earth around the root into a hard ball. Then the deadly stubble fight would begin. You would either be an attacker or a defender on top of the fort. If you were an attacker you never ran out of ammo. The defenders had to wait patiently heads down while bombs rained down on the top of their fort, conserving ammo for the final defense.

At some point the attacking force had to scale the side of your 'rick fortification' to take control; that's when patience paid off, the defending force having conserved their ammo could seriously injure the opposition as they tried to scale the outside of the fort. Kids got injured big time; a big battle could see three or four kids walking home in tears sometimes holding bloody wounds. We also made long tunnels from the straw bales.

The older boys would be in control of building these tunnels that went round in circles in a labyrinth of corridors measuring two foot wide by a foot high. Within these tunnels were cross roads and rooms. We would crawl through these twisty corridors sweating buckets without being able to see a hand in front of our faces. Why..? Well just for the thrill of course.

Then, inevitably the farmer would turn up at the gate and we'd run like the wind and hide-up for all of half an hour and then we would be back at it.

The farmer couldn't win unless he sat there 24/7 and really we didn't do any harm? Well harm did happen but that was still a few years up the road.

Dad had introduced me to fishing when I was around five. This was a few years before the Bath to Bradford-on-Avon section of the Kennet and Avon Canal was finally drained in the early sixties. We still lived at Nicholas Close at that time and early on a Saturday morning he would be out in the garden digging worms; then, loaded with kit, away we would go to the canal at Limpley Stoke.

Looking back it always seemed whenever we went fishing that there was a thick frost on the ground and my toes would be freezing. I can't ever remember it being a sensible time of day, or a day when the sun was shining. I would sit fidgeting and shivering on the towpath while he fished and watch the sun melting ice and the steam rising from Godwin's fields in the valley below the tow-path.

My patience was very thin, it was the attention span thing again and after half an hour without catching anything I would want to go home. My ability to sit and watch a fishing float hasn't improved as the years have gone by; I just don't do it anymore.

The Canal at Winsley Hill Bridge; looking toward Bath Dads fishing spot. Dundas Aquaduct can just be seen through the trees.

Normally dad would end up catching something, a Perch or a Roach; good size fish he would knock on the head and take home for mum to cook. I didn't like fishing that much but I did love the taste of river fish, that muddy strong taste.

As we got older we collected an odd assortment of fishing gear; old bamboo rods a mixture of reels, line, hooks, and floats that we got together through jumble-sales, handed down from our fathers or grandfathers; or swapped and bartered for other junk we had hidden away in our bedrooms.

Sticky had the best gear, his father was right into fishing and Sticky followed in his dad's footsteps. He had all the top notch stuff and a proper fishing seat to keep it in.

By the time we were ten or eleven we were allowed to go off on our own. Our favourite spot was half a mile above the weir in Avoncliff; a field next to the river that ran alongside a wood.

To get there we would lug our gear down though Turleigh, up Green Lane past Ross Daniel's farm and down the track to the lower Avoncliff road; almost a two mile trip. The descent into the

Our Pike fishing spot below the weir in Avoncliffe

valley was the easy bit; it was the return journey that was the killer.

At the bottom of the track we had to scale a wall and cross the railway line before arriving at our preferred fishing location. This I hasten to add was not a designated railway crossing just a normal section of track between Limpley Stoke and Bradford-on-Avon, a hazardous undertaking with the rail line running very close to the wall.

One of us would jump over first; the far side being three or four feet lower than the road, care needed to be taken that you didn't end up on the track. Then the gear would be handed over and finally all of us would cross the line to our fishing place.

Then came the job of setting up the rod, fixing the weights, float and hook and adding the bait, either worms dug from the garden or bread. If Sticky was with us he would have maggots. His father always seemed to have a box of fresh ones in the fridge; gross but true!

If we caught some small Gudgeon or Roach we would persuade Sticky to have a go at Pike fishing below the weir; Sticky was the only one with a rod strong enough to pull in a Pike so we would pack up our spot by the wood and walk along the railway line for half a mile to the station house.

To get to the prime spot below the weir entailed a seriously dangerous trek along the riverbank and a spit of mud to a spot directly below the cascading white weir water and only inches above the rushing torrent of the river.

Now we were between the supports of the old mill, derelict for years. On this small out-crop of muddy bank opposite the 'Cross Guns' pub we would wait for the big one. The noise from the weir was deafening and we had to shout at each other to make ourselves heard. If we were lucky a Pike would take the live bait and we would shout and laugh as Sticky hauled in the fish and we waited with the landing net. Then we would bang it on the head or slit the gills and take it home for the cats; no one ever ate Pike.

After an hour boredom would set in; normally Jeff would become restless first. He wasn't really into fishing either. He'd start mucking about and disturbing everyone else by chucking stuff in the river. A couple of us would wander off and put pennies on the railway line. The old copper pennies would be flattened like paper after the train went over them. They would be flicked of the tracks and we would need to hunt around to find them. Then we would stand against the wall as the trains went by, they weren't the high speed Inter-city trains but none the less they travelled fast and we would have been killed if we had been hit. It was a great sensation to stand against the wall and feel the rush of the wind as the train went past a few feet from your nose.

A very old photo of Avoncliff, probably pre-World War One; it shows the railway tunnel abutment in the foreground and Westwood village on top of the hill in the background.

We would also discuss the possibilities of lying between the tracks and letting the train go over us; a stunt we had all seen on war or western movies.

'Dare you and double dare'; none of us, I hasten to add had the bottle to do this.

However another pastime revolving around the railway was the aqueduct above the weir.

A fantastic piece of architecture the aqueduct carries the canal over the road, river and railway. At the point where the railway passes through the tunnel two massive sandstone abutments in the region of six feet in width go from the road at the top in a steep slope to the railway below.

Climbing over the wall we could slide down these abutments to the ground below. Probably seventy five feet from top to bottom; had we fallen it would have been serious if not fatal. How none of us got hit by a train heaven only knows.

After fishing and other antics we slowly made our way home, up across the field to 'The Chase' picking fruit from the cherry plum trees as we went.

To quickly recount a story my gran would tell me about her childhood antics.

In the early 1900s the local workhouse for the homeless elderly people was in Avoncliff on the Westwood side next to the river. (It's still there now as luxury apartments). When someone passed-away the dead body would be taken by horse and cart into Bradford-on-Avon for burial. The old boy driving the cart would plod along slowly toward Belcombe half asleep on his perch at the front of the wagon. The local boys and girls would hide in the bushes and as the wagon went past a couple of boys would fall in behind the cart and pull one of the bodies off the back. Of course the clop of the horse's hooves and the clatter of the metal banded wheels on the stone road masked any noise and the driver would carry on his merry way to Bradford leaving the body lying in the road; not realizing his missing inventory till he got to the morgue in town.

The kids thought this was hilarious and would do this on random occasions without being caught.

So this was our huge outdoor playground.

From our little village on top of the hill you could go in any direction to find fields, woods and common land.

We had the river where we would fish, or further along toward Bath at Warleigh, where we could swim above the weir. Murhill woods where we would play armies or go caving; walking or riding our bikes to the hamlet of Conkwell where Gibbo fell down the tip; he was potholing with Anthony Colmer and they both got trapped in the pothole and had to be rescued.

Conkwell woods where we would scramble our old bikes on a race track beaten out through the hazelnut trees long before the BMX or mountain bike craze.

Above Conkwell are 'Inwoods' where the narrow lane meanders half a mile through a natural arch of hundreds of hazelnut trees to the common and then swings sharply to the left and drops steeply downhill to Warleigh and on to Bathford. At the end of 'Inwoods' we would climb over the style and follow a footpath that took us across the common land to Farleigh Wick and auntie Dart's house.

To begin with the path is narrow and muddy through clumps of Hazel and Birch, but after a few hundred yards it breaks out onto the common and the going under foot becomes light and soft, walking on short coarse grass and moss.

The view from here is spectacular. Hundreds of feet up above the Avon valley; below us ran the canal, the river and the railway. Away in the distance across the valley you could just make out the start of the buildings that led into Bath through Claverton & Bathampton.

From the other side of the valley, looking back toward Winsley from Brassknocker hill the little hamlet of Conkwell looks as if its tiny cottages have just tumbled down the valley side. In Conkwell village a steep narrow road leads from the top of the hill down past a few straggling houses.

Half way down the narrow road through the quaint little houses is the old village well and beyond that the tarred road runs out into the woods, fields and a footpath. At the bottom of the hill is the expanse of Dundas Water and aqueduct (named after Charles Dundas the first Kennet and Avon Canal Chairman) the terminus where in years gone by the Somerset coal canal joined the Kennet-on-Avon.

'Dundas' looking from 'Brassknocker hill' claverton side of the valley. On the far side, Conkwell village sits in the dip of the tree line.

Here in this big canal basin sits the old wharf warehouse and crane for unloading supplies of all sorts from the barges. The crane my great granddad Fred Sartain operated in the early 1900s for the Great Western Railway who took over the canal from the original operators the Kennet and Avon Canal Company.

As we got older, and by older I mean eleven, twelve, and upwards we could go even further afield. To Farleigh Hungerford to swim in the river or watch the World Championship Motocross racing, or ride to Castle Combe race track to watch touring car or one design racing.

One of our favourite sorties as a gang was visiting the 'Pepper Pot' a Victorian folly on the hills overlooking Bath at Monkton Farleigh. This would be discussed and agreed by a group of us, then we would go to our parents for some money and ask them to make up a lunch pack and off we would go.

Up to 'Inwoods' then down the steep long hill into Warleigh.

We would cross 'Sally-in-the-Wood' road and carry on to Church

Street in Bathford. This had been mainly a downhill stretch, now came the hard work. At this point we were pushing our bikes up the High Street till we came to a turning on the right 'Farleigh Rise'. Here began a staggeringly steep climb for a good half mile till we came to the open space that served as a car park for those wishing to visit the 'Pepper Pot'.

Here we would leave our bikes and take to the tracks for the last half mile to the Folly. The 'Pepper Pot' as we called it stood seventy or more feet high above 'Sally' woods the hills overlooking the whole of the east side of Bath. The view at the time was magnificent, you could on a good day see across Bath to Bristol. This view was from the hill, not from the tower which was boarded up and not accessible to the public.

'Browns Folly' standing on the hill overlooking Bathford and Sally-in-the-wood. Known locally as the 'Pepper Pot'

How dearly we all wanted to get to the top of that tower, but sadly it never happened.

I seem to remember a wall running in front of the tower, the tower itself being on private land behind the wall but the land in front of the wall was 'Common' ground. The area of 'The Common' was soft grass on chalk with very little growth other than a few blackberry bushes; it fell away to the A363 'Sally-in-the-Wood' road, Warleigh, the river, canal and railway in the valley below.

It was peaceful and lovely up there on a sunny day and we would run around playing and then sit and eat our sandwiches; jam, honey, or if you were lucky boiled egg or banana; all washed down with water, or orange squash if we were lucky. There wasn't the mid-boggling array of sandwich filling or fizzy drinks there are today; anyway even if there were, the money wasn't there to buy them.

The last time I visited the spot in 1993 the grassy common had all but disappeared, taken over by encroaching hazel, willow and alder; sadly the view has also been obscured by the encroaching trees.

When we had tired of our games we would set out on the return leg home. Heading back on our circular route through the village of

Monkton Farleigh where we would drink fresh water from the pump in the middle of the village on the corner in front of The Kings Arms pub,(now changed to the ridiculous name of 'The Muddy Duck'; some people just have no sense of history).

The pump has been removed but the metal sign still remains.

It says 'Waste Not Want Not'. I've always remembered that sign and those wise words.

After a rest and a drink it would be back on the bikes down through Farleigh Wick, over the common, back through Inwoods and home; a round trip of 15 miles.

To briefly explain the origin or perceived origin of the odd name 'Sally in the Wood'.

There is more than one tale of how this name came to be.

'Sally in the Wood' is the area of woodland continuing around the valley side from Conkwell and Warleigh. The road running from Bradford-on-Avon through Farliegh Wick and down to Bathford is the A363 a busy 'A' class road.

However a hundred years ago or even less this would have been no more than a cart track similar to the road running next to the river Avon through Warleigh further down the valley.

One story that we know of relates to a Sarah Gibson, baptised at Monkton Farleigh in 1732 and who married a gamekeeper from nearby Warleigh Manor in 1762.Upon his death she was evicted from their cottage. Her family had moved away and she is said to have inhabited a little hut in the nearby woods through which the first road (now the A363) was driven in 1792.

Henry Duncan Skrine of Warleigh Manor, who was a Justice of the Peace and a Deputy Lieutenant of Somerset at the time recalled his childhood memories of Sarah Gibson in which she was accounted a witch.

'Her smoke-dried hut was like an awful cave to us children, and her thin shrill sepulchral voice still rings in my ears. At her death the carpenter who acted as sub-bailiff burned the cottage down, and declared to us children that he saw something on a broomstick go out of the chimney'!(Howells, 2010).

However another tale which is plausible, and this is the version Jeff believes, is the English civil war story. It relates to a skirmish that took place before the Battle of Lansdown in July 1643 when the Roundheads were ambushed by the Royalists. 'General William Waller's troops had made a temporary bridge across the Avon below Claverton, he crossed his troops by it to the Monkton Farleigh side, where they laid an ambush for their opponents. The following day a battle appears to have begun and continued up to Monkton Farleigh and over to Batheaston. The term 'Sally' at that time had the meaning of 'a sudden rush out from a besieged place upon the enemy'.

Of course this could be true... but I don't believe the woodland would necessarily be named after a skirmish.

Other ideas relate to murders, ghosts and girls being knocked down by motor cars... I don't subscribe to those theories either. I like to think of the Sally Gibson story as being the correct account as this is a true tale; Sally really did live in the wood.

Turleigh Downs, our sledging hill.

In the winter when it snowed and it did snow every year, we would drag our sleighs down to Turleigh; 'The Downs' a long very steep hill where we would go up and down all day shrieking, laughing and rolling in the snow as we got colder and colder. Our hand-knitted winter socks and mittens getting wetter and snow-matted until ice formed around the fingertips.

As dusk fell we would drag ourselves home, tired, wet and cold, socks sodden in rubber wellies and feet and hands blue with cold. Knitted gloves and bobble hats stretched to twice their size encrusted with snow. We would get home crying and shuddering where mum would undress us and rub the life back into our frozen limbs with a towel in front of the open fire. Hot chocolate, Cocoa, and a hot bath the woollens would be dried out in front of the fire for the next day's wear. The following morning we would jump out of bed and rush to the window to see if further snow had fallen through the night. Then after breakfast do the whole thing again.

Most sledges at the time were homemade wooden affairs that didn't move that easily over the snow; But Pete and I had a wonderful traditional German sledge given to us by our Opa and Oma it had the curved wooden runners and the metal banding; the real thing. The days we were on 'The Downs' everyone wanted a go on our sleigh, it went like muck-off-a-shovel!

I had a lovely conversation with a lady from Turleigh recently; she told me the hill is still used by the local kids in the winter for sledging. She and her husband can watch them across the valley from their house at the top of Green Lane; it's great to know the tradition continues.

The list to our adventure playground was endless. We were never bored.

Back in the everyday life of 2 Poston Way dad came up with another harebrained scheme. This time it was to keep Geese.

His plan - to buy two young ones and fatten them up in our garden for Christmas. Great idea if you live out in the sticks, but on a council estate...maybe not.

You can't imagine the racket they caused; they were free range; running round and round the garden causing a din that could be heard all over the village.

Poor Gina hated them and she would slink around the garden wearing a muddy pathway under the hedge. Pete and I had a goose each; mine was white and called Donald. Pete had a coloured one he named Jemima. At night we would lock them away in a pen that dad made from a set of old wrought iron gates. Even then they were rarely quiet and getting them into the pen was taking your life in your hands as they hissed, rearing up and flapping their wings at us.

Eventually the noise got too much for the neighbors and Mr Francis the rent man insisted that dad get rid of them.

Dad did no more than knock them on the head; mum cleaned and plucked them and in the pot they went.

Young birds? Who the hell did the farmer think he was kidding? They were as tough as old boots.

I knew Donald had been destined for the pot, but Pete was mortified to think his goose would be eaten.

Mum and dad made me promise not to tell him and Pete was led to believe we had swapped Jemima for a chicken. This story remained in place for years and I think it was only sometime in the nineteen nineties that Pete found out the truth.

After dad had knocked them on the head and mum had drawn and plucked them, all the entrails, head, feet, and guts were buried in the garden. The problem was mum buried them in a plastic bag. A few months later dad asked Jim Burdon who lived across the road in number one if he would like to earn a bit of pocket money by digging our garden.

Jim was a good bloke; he was married with twin girls and another daughter about two years younger. They were not that well off and Jim would do odd-jobbing around the estate for a few extra quid. What he done he done well. His wife always seemed short of the basic foodstuffs in the house and we were forever lending sugar, milk, flour, and other things. Mum didn't mind helping neighbours, it was the done-thing, it was an excepted way of village life.

However Jim had a big veggie garden and grew everything, spuds, cabbage, onions, etc. Mrs Burdon would always drop some veg over the road to our family, so it all balances out in the end.

Jim's two daughters were very bright; they passed their eleven plus exam at Winsley Juniors and went on to the Grammar school in Bradford-on-Avon.

Anyway Jim said he would do the digging and Pete and I watched expectedly. After a few rows had been dug mum came flying out the house and stopped Jim in his tracks.

'Come up the house a moment Mr Burdon would you,' said mum; she would never have dreamt of calling him by his Christian name, it was just not the German way.

It has dawned on mum that Jim, would, at some point dig up the entrails of the Geese and if he looked inside the bag without knowing the contents would not only chuck-up his breakfast over our lawn, but probably let the cat out of the bag that poor Jemima along with Donald had also received dad's hatchet across the back of the neck.

So Jim was aware and sure enough after digging a couple of rows up came the plastic bag with the entrails. Jim knowing what they were left the bag unopened threw it on the path and carried on digging.

When he disappeared for his lunch Pete and I ran down, grabbed the stinking rotting bag and buried it further up the garden.

Once again we watched as Jim returned to his digging and again dug up the bag. We were in stitches. Why we found this so funny I really don't know. But we carried this on right to the top of the garden. I'm sure Jim dug up those bits of goose at least four times over the two days he was in our garden, but Pete never clicked it was Jemima's remains he was continually burying.

The summer of 1966 was a monumental summer. It was the year England won the Football World Cup.

We were on holiday in Germany at the time and dad and I followed England through every game. We did the usual round of visits, all the relations in Dusseldorf, Duisburg and Oma in Mulheim, then with Oma joining us we drove to see her sister-in-law and mother-in-law (another great grandmother) in the pretty little village of Rurberg near the city of Monschau in the German Eifel.

Mia, my Opa's sister was a very wealthy woman. She had married into the German aristocracy before the war and her husband was a senior German officer.

During the fighting on the Russian front he was posted as missing in action.

After hostilities had ended in 1945 she spent years and her inherited fortune trying to find him; she never did.

I loved visiting my aunt and my very upright and imposing

Auntie Mia's bungalow above. The balcony overlooking the lakes. Standing, Mia and Doris. Sitting, Oma and my great grandmother with Gaby in the middle.

great grandmother in their absolutely fantastic house sat on a hillside overlooking a lake and outdoor swimming pool in the valley below. The bungalow set among woodland with a massive sweeping veranda and electronic gates, yes electronic gates in the sixties; that was pretty amazing to Pete and I.

We would meet my cousins Brigitte and Gaby here with my auntie Doris and uncle Dieter. The four of us would go to the pool and take boat trips with our parents for miles across the lakes. It was a lovely place to be.

I went back a few years ago and it was surprisingly unchanged. The boat trips still ran, the swimming pool was still there. A few more houses on the hill around my aunt's place, in fact my aunt's house was dwarfed by some of the new mansions built in the grounds of what was her property.

My great grandmother died in the early seventies, then Mia in the late seventies; the house was sold and now some other family lives there. Change is inevitable, although sad, but great memories from that house and village.

Anyway to continue with the world cup story...

Beyond our wildest dreams England ended up playing Germany in the final and this would happen on our return journey. There was no way dad was going to miss this once in a lifetime game so with plenty of time to spare we stopped in a German pub to watch the match. The pub was in the Ardennes, the mountainous border country between Germany and Belgium. As the hour of kick-off approached the pub began to fill with German men. As a family we sat down to eat lunch in the caravan and half hour before kick-off dad and I made our way into the bar. You could hear a pin drop when dad and I walked in talking English; but seats were graciously found for us in front of the TV and the whistle blew.

At half time dad drank a beer with the locals, while I ran back to the caravan pouring out the result to poor mum, who refused point-blank to venture into the bar.

Full time and the score was 2-2 we were into extra time, dad at the bar for another beer with the locals and again I reported in. Mum was getting agitated, after all we had a ferry to catch at Ostend, but we were going nowhere for at least half an hour.

What a game. I'll never forget it. England taking a third goal which sent the pub into uproar; yes it was! No it wasn't! Dad puffing out his chest and going to the bar for another beer... Ah well it all ended in tears, for once for the Germans.

With seconds to go Hurst volleyed goal number four and those famous words shouted by Kenneth Wolstenholme 'they think it's all over... well it is now!' Of course we didn't hear this as the complete commentary had been in German for us; but I've heard it hundreds of times since and though I'm half German by birth they still sound good every time I hear them.

Final score 4-2 and as dad and I (me in lederhosen I may add) left the pub the German men stood, although rather disgruntled by what they believed to be an unfair goal, with long faces they shook our hands and said auf weidersen.

Wow! What a day that was.

We got back to England where Pete and I still had a couple of weeks of the summer holidays left to kick our heels around the village. That was until mum came home and told me she had got me a job.

Oh yes, at ten years old a full time position in one of the big houses in the old village, working for Mr and Mrs Lavington at 'The Chase', a big late Georgian or early Victorian house opposite the cricket field with fantastic views over the valley

The Chase; the windows face over what was the rose garden and pond. The other frontage looks over the front steps and the lawns down to the haha wall and the Avon valley below. You can just make out the chapel on the far side of the house.

below. The house had its own church, stables and tennis court. A big kitchen garden surrounded by high, perfect, sandstone walls and lawns that roll away in front of the house to a ha-ha wall; from the wall the fields drop sharply to the canal, river, and railway in the valley. The whole place was immaculate and very beautiful.

Oh how I loved that house, and still do.

If, in the years I have left to me I ever win the big one on the lottery I'll knock on the door and offer the present owner whatever they want for it. I would pay whatever it takes to get it.

Mum had arranged with Mrs Lavington that I would work for her during the holidays in her garden and when the holidays finished I would work Saturday's and the summer evenings after school. I would be paid the sum of one shilling and sixpence an hour for my labour's. In present decimal coinage that's 7.5 pence.

The first Saturday morning I donned my old clothes and rode my bike to 'The Chase'. I knocked boldly at the back door. A little old lady wearing an old-fashioned maid's style uniform answered the door; at least she seemed old I suppose she was only about fifty five at the time; this was Winnie.

'Ah, you must be Steven' she said, 'just one moment I will call Mrs Lavington.'

Mrs Lavington came to the door. I remember her as being a very petite woman with fair shoulder length wavy hair. I suppose she would have been around forty at the time.

She asked me in to the time worn kitchen, a kitchen that may not have changed in a hundred years and told Winnie, the maid, to ring for Hazel.

She introduced herself and gave me a glass of homemade lemonade. Within the space of a few minutes Mr Hazel arrived. A nice gent, probably around fifty years old he was Mrs Lavington's gardener and handyman. He also looked after the horses.

Peter Lavington, Christian's husband was a very wealthy man in his own right without the fact he had married the daughter of Wilf Harvey a newspaper magnate and racehorse owner. Wilf Harvey was the chairman of BPCC Purnell at Paulton.

Peter Lavington worked away and during the years I worked for his wife I rarely saw him.

So at 10 years and a few months old I had my first job.

Mrs Lavington told Hazel that I was to be shown round the garden and grounds; so begun my Grand Tour.

The kitchen and outhouses had been built within a kind of sunken courtyard used in the past as laundry rooms, ice room, and storage rooms for smoked meats and jarred preserves. We walked up the steps from this courtyard and along the inner wall of the huge kitchen garden to the potting shed.

Three or four paths ran the length of the garden and each path was bordered on either side by fruit trees trained on wire.

The walls of the kitchen garden are roughly eight feet high. On one side runs the narrow road ending at the cricket field and on the other, the footpath leading from the village hall to Murhill and on down a steep muddy path to the canal at Elbow; the same path I took in the mornings when helping mum with the Post.

From the kitchen garden we walked through an arched wrought iron gateway in the wall into the front flower gardens. The house was over to the left of us with rose gardens between and a huge pond roughly eight feet by fifteen; even at ten years old I was awed by its stunning beauty.

We walked on down the path and then swung to the left to walk along the house frontage. All the time Hazel was pointing out this and that; the flowers, the shrubs, the trees. Where I could go and the areas that were out of bounds to me. As imposing as the side of the house was the front was even better. From the huge front door a flag path led to stone steps at least ten feet wide. From the top of these steps the lawns literally roll away below you to a ha-ha wall a hundred yards away. Over to the left is a small Copse with tall Beech trees growing from a grassy knoll. From the top of these steps you can look right across the valley to the village of Westwood three miles away on the other side.

Hazel walked with me across the lawn to the Copse. He pointed out an area tucked away out of sight, which was the compost area for the flower garden. He told me the Lavington's owned the fields both below the ha-ha wall and to the left of the house, the fields in which they kept their horses.

(Ha-ha walls typically formed a boundary between the estate's gardens and grounds. These walls were constructed so as to be invisible from the house, ensuring a clear view across the estate, a deep ditch on the hidden side of the wall made an effective barrier to livestock).

A year ahead I would enter this Copse with a wheelbarrow load of cuttings and drop them directly on top of a wasp nest. The wasps swarmed all round me stinging my bare face, legs, arms, and hands. I ran screaming through the gardens with the wasps swarming behind me, I never even bothered to grab my bike I just kept running and running through the village down Vinegar Path till I eventually got home. I could barely talk when I got home; my running had pumped the poison from the stings around my body and I was in shock. There were still wasps in my clothes so mum had no need of a verbal explanation. I was shaking with my teeth chattering. Mum sent Pete for Pat while she stripped me and treated the bites with vinegar; there was no antihistamine cream at that time, at least not in our house. Pat came running to see what was wrong then shot off to the phone. When Dr Thomas came and he came very quickly he gave me a sedative injection and also antihistamine tablets. I'd swollen up like a balloon. It took me a week to recover. Dad went to get my bike and told Mrs Lavington what had happened. The lovely lady came to see me in my bed in our little house on the estate. For me at eleven years old it was like being visited by the Queen. She sat on my bed and told me Hazel, who had driven her down to ours like royalty in her big car, had smoked out the wasps and nothing like that would happen again. Hurry up and come back she said. It cheered me no end. Anyway as yet that was some way ahead.

We walked on around the back of the house and up the side of the Copse to the ash tennis court; across the front of the court and up the small footpath to the parking area inside the main gates.

Attached to this side of the house was a small church or chapel. Although this was the main entrance to the house and front door it is in truth the most boring side of the house. You never really got to appreciate the majesty of the place in the way you would if you came in through the kitchen garden gate and walked through the massive garden. This is because a large Beech hedge prevents a view from the front parking area across the lawns and valley beyond. We'd now come full circle and walked back down the steps next to the boiler-house to the kitchen court yard.

Winnie brought me another lemonade and I began work.

Hazel furnished me with a hoe and put me to work hoeing and weeding in the veggie garden.

During the remainder of the holidays I worked a few hours two or three times a week, coming away most days with three shillings in my pocket; not bad money really for a ten year old in the mid-sixties.

Of course my friends got to hear of what I was up to and within a short space of time Jeffery was also employed to help in the garden. Then John Phelps, and so on and so on...

In truth we were only kids, we were ok when we were given a job on our own but as soon as more than two of us were in company we reverted to acting like ten and eleven year olds.

For some working at Mrs Lavington's, the days were numbered.

As bonfire night approached Mrs Lavington generously offered the cub scouts to use her field below the house to hold the bonfire and firework display.

With help from our parents and others we built the fire over the course of a couple of weeks and on the big day Jeff and I went to see Mrs Lavington to thank her and invite her to come down that evening and join in. We were greeted at the door by Winnie and told that Mrs Lavington was ill in bed, but she had asked to see us. Winnie led us through the grand old house to Mrs Lavington's bedroom where she was sitting up in bed with a light blue housecoat on. We were on our best and most polite behavior. I asked after her and said how sorry I was that she was, as I put it, 'poorly'. We chatted for a while and then she took a pound note from her bedside cabinet and gave it to us.

'Steven' she said 'I would like you and Jeffery to buy some fireworks with this. It's a small thank you for your help here during the summer.'

A pound was a great deal of money. You could buy a whole mixed box of fireworks with that!

'WOW, thanks Mrs Lavington,' we said as we were escorted by Winnie from the room. *I remember this as if we'd been invited in to meet the Queen. I felt like bowing as I left...*

Later with our dads, Jeff and I went to Little's and spent the money on a variety of fireworks.

That night we had a great display. All the cub-scout kids turned up; their parents plus many more people from both Winsley and Murhill.

Ross Daniels our scout leader had got hold of a big drum and converted it to a barbeque and using the burning embers of the fire he cooked sausages and baked potatoes.

Most people bought their fireworks from Stephen Little's dad in the general store and on the night small family groups huddled around their boxes and bags letting off their collection of catherine wheels, rockets, and bangers. Of course Jeff being Jeff he couldn't help acting the fool and he dropped a banger into Chris Strickland's firework box. The whole lot went up in a crazy explosion of colour. How no one was hurt heaven only knows.

Some of the older lads had come down from the village and stood around drinking beer and cider. They were there to disrupt what in essence was a get together for the Cubs and their families. My dad would have none of it and one lad found himself flat on his back after using bad language in front of my mum. A very disgruntled bunch of older boys drifted away and let us get on with it.

That was village justice; dad would never have got away with it today. He would have been up for assault. In fact the culprit went home and told his dad who came down ours banging on the door; dad told him to bugger off or he would get the same as his son.

We got into a great deal of mischief; going into places we weren't allowed; playing in barns or on the bales; running away shouting and laughing when we were caught.

These were the simple things that never really mattered. But I was also involved in some more serious petty crime that had PC Ford the village policeman knocking at our door.

One summer a group of us broke into the cricket pavilion just before the season started and stole all the lemonade. We hid it in the caves in Murhill woods. To begin with there must have been eight kids involved in that raid which took place one summer's afternoon around 4pm. But as we progressed the less brave (or sensible) went home.
I was the first to be caught.

The cricket field belonged to and bordered on the Manor house. Mrs Knatchbull the owner of the Manor and a friend of hers, a Mrs Vernon, were sitting drinking tea on the back lawn while we struggled across the cricket field with our crates of lemonade.

My tanned arms and legs clad in German lederhosen were a major giveaway on their own without the almost white blond hair and the fact that everyone in the village knew the Post lady's son. It could have only been two hours at the most before Fordy as he was affectionately known to the kids of the village was knocking at our door.

Of course trembling in my shoes I held out for only seconds before breaking down and splitting on my co-conspirators, Malcolm Holt, Trevor Pryor, and John Phelps. Jeff once again slipped through the net because he went home during our walk through the village to carry out the dastardly deed. Why did he go home? Don't know… will have to ask him one day but I suspect it was the sensible side to him that I never had.

Jeff rarely got caught doing anything wrong. Maybe he had that fear of getting a damn good hiding from his mum that kept him clear of serious trouble, or the knack of knowing when to leave the scene of the crime, the inbuilt voice that told him 'hang on this is a step too far'. Or of course the memory of the marble up his nose; 'don't do it just because Steven did it.'

Dad as so often in the past hit the roof with me. Put me over his knee and took the belt to my backside. Sent me to my room and banned me from going out for 'X' amount of weeks.

However I was not to be deterred, I would climb out through the landing window lower myself onto the annex, hop across the shed roof and down to the ground; within the blink of an eye I was again with my pals playing. Getting back in was a reverse procedure.

An amazing coincidence happened in 1987 while I was working in Turkey. We had a family hire one of our sailing boats, their name was Vernon. During the holiday Mrs Vernon said she liked my accent, was it from Wiltshire. I replied yes and told her I came from a little village called Winsley. She said she had an old friend who lived there, Mrs Knatchbull who lived in the manor and did I know her?

Of course I said I knew her very well through my mum being the Post lady and also the fact that back in the mid-sixties Miss Knatchbull had spotted me, the kid with the blond locks and half a dozen others raiding the cricket pavilion of lemonade and had reported me to Mr Ford the policeman. 'Well', said Mrs Vernon, 'I was there that very afternoon. I was sitting with Miss Knatchbull on the rear lawn having afternoon tea. In fact', she said, 'it was me that pointed out to Miss Knatchbull that you kids were up to no good and that we should call PC Ford.' That story caused quite a laugh over the course of the holiday.

However I got my own back after all those years. I had a holiday romance (wink, wink) with her daughter!

1967 was my last year at Winsley Juniors. As I had hoped I became games captain and also the captain of the school football team. Jeff was head boy, Janice Forsyth head girl and Angela games captain for the girls.

As mentioned previously the games shed was next to the boys' toilets in the playground and contained a pile of coconut mats, step benches, and other odds and ends; now and again Angela and I were released from class to tidy the shed.

We rarely did; what I do remember is us lying side by side on our backs on the matting holding hands and talking.

The final school year finished for me on a real low, I failed my 11 plus exams miserably; it wasn't just failure but total failure.

The exams were in two parts, if you got through the first part then you took a further section, passing this second section would see a child into Grammar school; I never even passed part one. Mum and dad were very disappointed in my results, but junior school had been a constant struggle for me and I don't think in all honesty my final report surprised them, they hoped against hope I would improve in secondary school.

Following the exams only a couple kids ended up passing both parts and going on to Fitzmaurice Grammar.

Taking after his mum, Jeff was very arty, gifted at drawing and painting. Pat had planned for some time to send him to Bath Art rather than Trinity. She had applied for Grant funding as Bath Art was in fact a private school. She succeeded and it was the beginning of what would be a long and very successful career for Jeff within the printing industry.

On the strength of my poor results my parents decided to send me to secondary school in Trowbridge, to Nelson Haden Boys; not to the catchment school of Trinity in Bradford on Avon.

Why did mum and dad want me to go to Nelson Haden Boys in Trowbridge? Well, Chris Strickland's parents had sent him there the summer before and they sang the praises of the school to my mum and dad.

Also at the time Trinity in Bradford on Avon had a very bad reputation (I would have thought I would fit in there nicely, after all I didn't have a very good one myself).

Nelson Haden also had an excellent record for sporting achievement, which in all fairness suited me down to the ground.

I think mum and dad wanted to see me into a better class of school; they wanted better for me than 'Trinity'.

Nelson Haden may not have been a grammar school but it was a specialist school where sport was concerned.

So I was a member of the September 1967 intake. In a smart new blue secondary uniform I left for my first morning at school with Sticky.

Sticky who was a year ahead at Nelson Haden took me to school that first morning and talked me through what would take place on that first day.

The motto of the school was 'Manners Maketh Man'. We had to wear grey trousers, plain collared shirt and blue blazer with the Nelson Haden badge on the pocket. We also had a school tie which would be swiftly removed into a pocket after assembly. How many times a day would a teacher shout at a pupil 'Where's your tie?'...hundreds of times I should think.

Nelson Haden Boys School front entrance. Cooky's office to the left of the door, staff room to the right.

We boarded the bus with our tuck shop and school dinner money. The bus meandered along the top road to town, down Masons Hill into Bradford-on-Avon town centre, over the town bridge and on to Trowbridge. Along the way we would pick up pupils from Trowbridge High and the Catholic School of St Augustine's. These catholic kids would keep themselves to themselves never mixing with the other school kids. I think their parents and teachers told them they would become polluted with protestant ungodliness if they did.

One girl and her brother got on the bus at Priory Close - Steve and Lynn Earl. Lynn was an attractive blonde and lots of the lads on the bus fancied her like mad but there was no chance of even trying to chat her up, her brother would keep her pinned in the seat. He did that for the four years we travelled on that bus.

I think one of the big issues with the St Augustine's kids was that whenever we played them at sport we won. Also every time we did play them a mass punch up would ensue on the route home. I remember one such punch up being stopped by two police cars.

The bus dropped us at Christchurch in Trowbridge and we along with hordes of other kids made our way up Gloucester Road then along the footpath beside the high school, left into Rock Road and on to the main Frome Road at the other end. On the other side lay my new school, Nelson Haden Boys.

Nelson Haden was a segregated school. Although the girls and boys shared the same grounds the schools were separated by the main drive, the administration building, the pond and a footpath that ran across the sports fields. The girl's side was a mirror image of the boys except for a group of old army huts on the far side of the playing fields used by the boys as spillover block.

Classes were segregated and the only mixing of boys and girls occurred at either break times when both girls and boys would sit on their respective side and talk across the middle of the path, or at lunch when the boys had to cross the girls playground to get to the school dinner canteen.

This I was to rapidly find out was an ordeal that subjected boys to taunts, name calling, wolf whistles and sometimes the indignity of finding a pack of girls surrounding you, kissing you and trying to get your trousers down.

But as the years passed and you progressed further up the school hierarchy and up the playground pecking order the girls were more friendly and flirty and you'd get 'Eh! Steve, Sylvia wants to go out with you' or 'Steve fancy meeting up at the canal?'

It wasn't all harmless fun though; girls seem to grow up far quicker than boys and when it came to a grope or a fumble behind the hedge it was the girls more often than not calling the shots.

The class allocations were based on your junior school results; A+, A, B+, B, then two other classes for those with a really low junior school performance called (and this sounds really awful), Lower and Upper remove! This highlighting of a child's lack of ability would no longer be permitted in today's politically correct world, but there you go, those were the times. Oddly the form room of lower and upper remove contained the school printing press and the kids in these two forms were taught how to print; they collectively produced the school newsletter plus any flyers for sports day, open evenings etc.

They had the foundation to a really good trade and lots of them found employment on leaving school within the printing industry which paid extremely well and was quite prolific in the area.

I ended up in form 1A, quite a surprise really when you take into account my disastrous junior school exam results and end of term reports. I don't think it would have surprised either me or my parents had I been in B+ or even B.

Lo and behold there was another lad in my class with the same name; not only the same name but spelt the same way with John as his middle name. This was going to cause confusion as the years went by, with mixed exam results and me being raised a class in English when it should have been him and him dropped a class in Math's when it should have been me.

Nelson Haden cup fine run

All in all we had a good bunch of kids in our class. But eventually Paul Stubbens, Clive Chisling and Rob Doel and I would become firm mates and most of the time we'd be found together. Clive and Robbie were local lads from Trowbridge and Paul had moved down from Cambridge when a parent had been relocated through work.

Paul was very good at all sport, he and I were in serious competition when it came to the field events, but I couldn't match him at football, he really was very good and played for the school team throughout his time at NHBS.

During the years 1967 to the early 1970s we had a formidable football team that topped the area schools league almost every season.

Our first day at our new school was to put it mildly a bit daunting. Our form master was a young teacher called Mr Sangster. He was reasonably friendly, but we found out over the course of time he was just as odd as some of the other teachers.

We were given our rosters for the term ahead and also had to pick a sport. This took place in the play-ground, all the teachers would stand along the front of the building, each responsible for a sport; then the sport would be called out and the name of the respective teacher. If you were interested in doing one of the wide variety of sports on offer you left the crowd and went and stood behind the teacher. Baseball, basketball, table-tennis, cricket, and many others. However because of the demand for football no first year boy was allowed to play the game during his first term. We had to pick an alternative sport.

After our first term if we wished to change our sport we could.

There was then the possibility of doing football but it wasn't guaranteed; by this time, thirteen weeks into secondary school if you were a good footballer you would have been spotted and noted. The best players were brought through first to the football club.

This football restriction came very hard on most kids whose only sport while at juniors, especially in the small rural schools, was football.

I ended up playing basketball, which I discovered I was very good at and enjoyed. I never really went back to serious football again while at Nelson Haden. I ended up running for the school cross-country team and playing basketball for the school. On a couple of occasions I played as a substitute for the football team but the full time craving I had at juniors for football was to diminish till I joined the army.

We slowly got into the routine of secondary school.

The catchment area for Nelson Haden covered many local village schools and all the junior schools within Trowbridge itself; there were over 500 boys.

A whole new pecking order was to emerge. Not only at classroom or form level, but year level and ultimately at school level. Who were the hardest and who was the weakest? Who were the oddities that were constantly bullied?

We had one lad in our year, a lad called Lewis, (that was his surname), who was constantly bullied in just the same way that poor old Johnny Gibbs was bullied in Winsley. He would be in the middle of any playground fracas. I think he was picked on because he had ginger hair and a vicious temper and he would be taunted until he could not control himself any more. When I look back on it now it was very mean; at the time it was looked on as very funny by all the kids.

Then you had the pack element; kids who went round in gangs, grabbing and abusing individuals. Individually these kids wouldn't say boo to a goose, but together there wasn't much you could do about it if you got picked on. We had a gang like this in our year. I won't name names, but if they ever read this I'm sure they'll know who they were. They would run round catching individual kids and giving them dead-legs, Chinese burns or debagging them, which means getting a lad on the ground, then pulling down their trousers and pants and finally standing over the person laughing; not pleasant if you're the victim.

You also had the individual; kids who never really belonged to a group, but drifted around in twos and threes and never really bothered anyone or got bothered by anyone.

Secondary school was a jungle where you had to be able to stick up for yourself or suffer the consequences and it was all sorted out quite early on.

I never arrived at Nelson Haden with any illusions of being a hard nut. I was just one of those kids in the middle ground, 'I don't bother you, you don't bother me.' But occasionally I had to defend my corner and I never lost a school fight. I don't suppose in any way I had a reputation as a scrapper, but I never got picked on and I never picked on others. It was generally recognised that when it came to the crunch I could more then look after myself so it was very rare over my four years at the school that serious confrontation cropped up; but when it did I never backed down.

When I left school in 1971 and went as a Junior Soldier to Dover the same sort of standards applied. Although I do remember getting held up against the wall by one giant of a lad at Dover, but we'll come to that in volume two.

My behaviour got worse. Maybe this was due in part to the disappointing end of my junior school education, maybe not; either way the barometer of bad behavior was moving upward from naughty to juvenile delinquency. I was beginning to really draw attention to myself with the Police.

Two further serious incidents had me in trouble with PC Ford.

The first was one autumn evening when we went cherry plumb picking. We would collect this wild fruit by the bucket load and take them home for jam or pies. Walking past the church I loaded my catapult with cherry stones and let fly at the stained glass windows. Mr Holbrook the Verger caught me red handed.

The whole routine with PC Ford and my dad was repeated. Dad took the belt to my backside again, a regular occurrence that never did any good. I would be sent to my room and confined to the house for a week but once in my room I'd again escape out of the landing window. I knew the repercussions of my jumping out the window when I was supposed to be nursing my wounds and repenting in my bedroom but I just didn't seem to care.

As I got older my parents just couldn't cope with my misbehavior. The only answer they had was the big stick, the slipper or the belt. Being the belligerent little bugger I was I took it all on the protective leather of my lederhosen; the sting was short lived and life went on.

The mischief that came closest to getting me sent to Borstal was the cutting of the plastic sheet.

I'm sure most villages had one and Winsley was no exception; how can I put it, the girl who's pretty liberal with her affections, the girl who, when you whistle, her knickers fall down.

Winsley had Miss X.

Although still at secondary school she had a very advanced business head on her young shoulders, she also knew she had a pot of gold tucked away under her knickers; and was quite willing to exploit it... if of course, you were willing to pay.

The sixpence my gran left under the bell often paid for a few of us to look at what she had... or should I say didn't have, while she lay sprawled on her back, skirt up, knickers down.

Sometime there would be three or four of us all gawping at once, eyes popping out of our heads wondering how it worked.

One day while her parents were out she lay in the recognised viewing position on her bed in her room, while we boys queued outside the bedroom door; we got about thirty seconds each to look and we all had to pay, the price had gone up by then and it was sixpence per head.

Gran would have had a blue fit if she'd known where her sixpence was going.

Sex education wasn't taught in school until the fourth year; by this time a pupil was fifteen years old.

Even when the time came round to learn about the birds and bees in the classroom it was only briefly skimmed over. Up till that point it was rumour and hearsay from older kids or found out by fumbling around with your girl or boyfriend; not the best way at all to prevent teenage pregnancy.

One evening we were all out playing and Miss X asked if a couple of us wanted a look. Oh yes of course we did.

'Let's go to the hay field then,' she brazenly said.

It was probably the summer of 1967 because Fordy was still the village copper.

The corn had been cut and the bales of corn had been stacked. Over the top of this was a huge plastic sheet measuring at least fifty by fifty feet. We would crawl under this sheet and make burrows and tunnels in the bales underneath.

The burrows and tunnels had already been made so all we had to do was slide ourselves under the sheet... but, when we got there we found the sheet laden with rainwater, which had filled the indentations of the tunnels below.

There was no way we could get under the sheet.

'Hasn't anyone got a knife? 'Said the very advanced Miss X seeing her income for the evening slipping away.

I had been given a really lovely pen-knife by gran for my tenth birthday.

Gran had asked mum and dad and it was no problem, most kids had sheath knife, a pocket knife or pen-knife by the time they were ten or eleven. Gran had taken me to 'Browns' general store in Bradford-on-Avon and I was allowed to choose one; I still have that knife to this day.

I had my knife with me and without thinking of the consequences I started to slash the sheet to allow the water to drain away.

Had I made nicks in the thick plastic cover they probably would have gone unnoticed or unbothered about. But the satisfaction of feeling my pocket knife slice through the thick plastic sheeting dispelled the thought that I was bound to be found out and within a very short space of time I was going to bring a whole heap of shit down on my own head; which I did.

When we eventually got rid of the water, the bales underneath were too wet to lie on so the whole exercise was in vain. The farmer, Mr Mumford, lived in Avoncliff and when he discovered his sheet ripped to shreds he went to PC Ford to report it. Of course Fordy knew which houses to start with but this time the normal ringleaders were not involved. He went to Malcolm Holts, Malcolm was innocent. So he went to the house where Miss X lived to question her older brother, he too was unaware of the incident.

But, during the course of the questioning Miss X, who was also in the room listening, broke down in tears. 'Do you know who did this? 'Said Fordy.

Of course she did and she broke down confessing all, well nearly all. I don't think the true purpose of us wanting to get under the sheet was ever disclosed. But that was irrelevant. I was nicked big time and was seriously in the shit. The farmer was adamant he wanted action taken by the police and charges were going to be brought against me. My dad was furious but at this point the hiding was put on hold while he tried to rescue me from a stint in a remand home.

PC Ford and my dad had known each other for many years. 'Is there anything at all I can do?' My dad asked.

'Well apart from paying for it I don't know, Mr Mumford is hopping mad and wants an example made of the culprit. It's a slim possibility that if you took Steven to see him and he apologised in person and with an

Avoncliff in winter. Mr Mumfords house just to the right of centre.

offer to pay for the sheet he may relent. But as it stands at the moment Steven is for the high jump. John you have got to get Steven into line. Keep him away from the older problem kids, you know who I mean, if not he will end up in Borstal; the next incident if not this one, will be one too far.'

My dad took PC Ford to the door and saw him out. He came back into the front room with a face as black as thunder.

'You silly young fool,' he said.

'It's not worth my while giving you a hiding. You heard what PC Ford said. If you don't mend your ways there will be nothing I can do to save you from going to Borstal; on your head be it. Now get your coat and let's go and have a word with the farmer.'

It was around 8pm when we arrived in Avoncliff and parked on the Winsley side of the aqueduct. Mr Mumford's house was plain to see on the side of the hill across the valley, a very imposing square stone building with five large sash windows and a big wooden front door. A steep straight garden path led up to the door from the narrow winding road leading steeply up the hillside to Westwood.

Dad and I walked over the aqueduct then across the dried up bed of the canal before arriving at the farmer's front door.

'Right,' said dad. 'When Mr Mumford comes to the door I'll do the talking and I'll tell you when I want you to say something.'

'Yes,' I said. I was trembling in my shoes.

Dad knocked the knocker and we could hear someone coming down the hall. A lady opened the door; Mrs Mumford.

Dad knew her but I'd never seen her before. She probably did all her shopping in Westwood not Winsley.

'Good evening Mrs Mumford,' dad said.

'Sorry to disturb you but I wondered if your husband was home that I may have a word with him?'

'Certainly... John Burt from Winsley isn't it? Just one moment and I'll get him.'

Mrs Mumford went back up the hall into the kitchen and I could hear her talking to her husband. The door reopened and Mr Mumford came toward us.

'John good evening and this is your son Steven is it?'

'Good evening,' I mumbled.

'Come into the front room and sit down,' he said.

We followed him in and both the adults sat down. Dad told me to remain standing.

'Now what can I do for you John?' Asked Mr Mumford.

'Well,' said dad, 'you've recently had your stack cover vandalised and you may have heard already from PC Ford that my son is the culprit. Mr Ford has told me that you want to press charges and I don't blame you. The thing is if this goes to juvenile court and Steven is found guilty, which he freely admits he is, in all probability he will end up in Borstal. You probably know from PC Ford that Steven has been in trouble on a couple of previous occasions in the village and feels that he should be made an example of. The thing is Steven going to Borstal is not going to help matters. I'm making no excuses for his behaviour, he's got to take whatever is coming to him; but I do believe Borstal would probably do more harm than good in the long term.'

Mr Mumford sat quietly and listened to what dad had to say. I quaked in my boots.

'Well John what do you suggest? What guarantee do I have, or for that matter the village in general, that he isn't going to get up to further mischief? Like you said this is not the first time.'

'He'll be paying for the sheet Mr Mumford out of his own earnings. He's got a job and works hard for Mrs Lavington at 'The Chase', she would tell you the same if you care to ring her. Also he's banned from hanging round with certain other kids on the estate. And he knows full well that all his chances have been used up.'

'What have you got to say for yourself Steven?' He said looking sharply up at me.

'I'm sorry Mr Mumford, nothing like this will happen again.' I said and quickly added 'and I will pay for it.'

'Well you're right on both counts my lad... Do you know how much a sheet like that costs?'

I shook my head, 'no,' I whispered.

'Thirty pounds. That's a great deal of money for a lad of your age to have to pay back. How much pocket money do you get a week?'

God that was a lot; If I gave up all my pocket money for 2 years I would only just pay for it.

'Whatever I earn at Mrs Lavington's mum and dad contribute the same again, I suppose around a pound a week during the holidays.' I woefully said.

'Oh, that's not so good then, you'll still be in my debt two years from now.' I could just detect a hint of a smile at the corner of Mr Mumford's mouth.

'I'll tell you what I'll do. I'll continue with my insurance claim for the sheet. That's a process I've already got underway.' *Mr Mumford was now looking at dad as he spoke.*

'If your mum and dad are agreeable, you help me on the farm for a couple of weeks during the rest of the summer holidays and we'll call it a debt repaid. That's my offer.'

There was no negotiation, I either accepted or faced a juvenile court.

'Any objections John?' Mr Mumford asked looking at my dad.

'No,' said dad' I think you're being more than fair.'

'Right tomorrow eight-o-clock sharp,' said Mr Mumford getting up to see us to the door.

We all shook hands and as we departed down the path; Mr Mumford's parting shot was -'and don't be late.'

And I wasn't late. I ended up working all the summer holidays on the farm and loving it. It kept me out of mischief and wore me out good and proper.

I would ride my bike down to Avoncliff in the mornings or turn up at a certain field where we were working. I took a packed lunch and a bottle of drink. Slowly Mr Mumford thawed toward me and by the end of the holidays we were on good terms.

At the end of my last day he called me over. I had worked three weeks for him apart from Saturdays when I had to go to Lavington's. I was worried I would lose my job there unless I turned up at least once a week.

We were in the farmhouse having a drink before I went home.

'I've got to go up the village, I'll give you a lift home.' He said.

My bike went in the back of the Land Rover and I jumped in the front; he asked me how I'd enjoyed working on the farm. How I felt about not being paid? Had I learnt my lesson?

He told me he believed he'd got his money's worth out of me and more. While he spoke he drove with one eye on me and the other on the road. He wasn't smiling now. He was seriously trying to make me see sense and not get into trouble again. I squirmed in my seat.

'You're welcome to come back and work on the farm again,' he said. 'Next time I'll pay you.'

I nodded and thanked him. I said I would see how it went at the Lavington's. Now the holidays were over I only had Saturdays anyway.

We got to Poston Way, stopped the Land Rover and removed my bike from the back; Mr Mumford walked with me to the front door.

I knocked, mum answered; I left my bike against the wall and I said goodbye, shook hands and went into the house.

Mum stood talking to Mr Mumford. After a while I heard the door close and mum came through.

'Mr Mumford was very pleased with the work you did for him. He likes you, you know? He doesn't want to see you go down the wrong road.'

I sat there saying nothing.

'Anyway he gave me this to give to you.'

I looked up and there was mum holding a five pound note. A five pound note! Wow! I had never had so much money in one lump.

'Why?' I asked mum.

'Well he paid you fairly by the hour. When your debt was paid, he said he thought you deserved to have the money that was owing to you. He's a fair man.'

He was, and once again I'd had a lucky escape. Would I ever learn?

At Nelson Haden the sporting ethic of the school was something I really enjoyed. We had the whole of Wednesday afternoon for sport as well as two other PE periods within the term's weekly curriculum.

We had an outdoor pool within the school grounds and swimming began as a once a week lesson from our return after Easter break. The pool was not heated and we would stand there shivering while Terry Baker hollered at us to get in. In the end he had to physically push us over the side. You'd never see the like of it today.

We also used the 'Lido' pool in the park in Trowbridge when it opened at Whitsun. This was also an outdoor pool and I believe it was heated. It was fabulous with diving boards and a spring board. The school swimming and

The open air Lido swimming pool in Trowbridge. Knocked down in the early 70s to make way for new housing and never replaced.

diving competitions would be held there prior to breaking up for the summer holidays.

I was pretty good at swimming getting thirds, fourths and the occasional second in our school pool and annual gala; I could go the distance but lacked the perfect stream lined technique needed when it came to speed swimming.

What I enjoyed most was high diving; I had no fear and would think nothing of hurling myself off the top board and did do well in the diving competitions.

Everything was pretty relaxed and on swimming days we were told to make our way to the pool, and off we went in dribs and drabs. We'd walk, or cycle if we had our bike with us, the mile down town. We'd turn up at the pool and wander into the changing rooms. We didn't realise it at the time but a great deal of trust was put in us by our teachers and I believe that ninety-nine percent of the time we never let them down.

The school like all other schools of the time provided dinners and many of the kids from the outlying villages stayed in school for lunch. This was carried out in two shifts; boy's first sitting followed by the girls.

We would wait on our side of the school driveway until given the ok; then we would follow the Beech hedge around the outside of the playground in a long line. Meanwhile the girls would be playing netball or standing around watching, pointing and giggling. There were a few awfully brazen girls who would make a point of flashing their knickers. Those who had boyfriends would meet the boy they knew at the entrance to the playground and walk across to the dining hall chatting along the way.

As a first year this whole exercise was daunting to say the least. When you'd negotiated the girls playground you had to find a seat in one of the two dining halls, as 'year one' you were expected to occupy a seat at the end of the table. This meant when the meal was over you scraped all the slops onto one plate, piled up the plates for collection and wiped down the table top with a disgusting rag from a bucket of lukewarm water; a creamy colour due to all the bits of food floating in it. Yuk!

Not having an older brother at Nelson Haden my school dinner experience started on the bottom rung of the ladder; the end of the table. But I was determined that I should not remain there long. The positions at table were regulated by the year you were in or your family status in the school, meaning... you avoided the bottom two seats if you had an elder brother in year four or five; or, how far you were prepared to go to secure your position.

Generally 4th or 5th years occupied the head seat. The lad who controlled the table dictated whom he had as his servers; they were the two lads sitting directly to his left and right at the top of the table. These were coveted positions and returning to school dinners after the summer holiday break there was a scrabble for these head server seats and they would on occasion be fought over.

I got into a scrap for my table, the one just inside the door on the right hand side in the second canteen. On another occasion it was taken over while I was away from school ill and when I got back a stranger had occupied my place. Again I had to front-up to the imposter to get it back; head seat reoccupied I threw my two servers off the table and moved two other lads in. It was their job to keep the table for my return.

However in year one with no older brothers in the school I was destined to start at the bottom, but I didn't stay there long. The boy to my right moved to another table and I moved up one place. I was determined not to go back to slopping. By the end of the second year I was a stand-in server and by year three I had obtained a permanent server place. I can't remember now who was opposite me on the table but you have to remember we were both vying for the top spot the following term. Of course my competitor may have decided to remain a server or may have decided to try going for the head place on another table rather than have a 'Barney' with me.

The scrabble and scraps for the top seat were part of school routine and that first day of school dinners was awaited with anticipation by those determined to get a head seat; the older boys pushing their way to the front of the dinner line prior to walking across the girls playground.

The strangest thing was the teachers occupied tables at the other end of the dining room facing the pupils. They saw everything that went on but hardly ever intervened. Strange how this kind of hierarchy went on but it was how school operated and I'm sure it was not just our school.

When my brother started in 1970 he sat on my table. He was my young brother and he had my protection. He was never hassled in school or out of school. This was how it was. Word got out long before Pete arrived that he had a brother in the 4th year. It was like this with most kids who had elder brothers. He didn't even have to slop the table; he had a year two seat. He really, to this day doesn't realise how lucky he was and all I ever hear is that I wouldn't give him seconds of roast spuds at the Christmas dinner meal. And I don't remember that!

School finished at 3.45 or 4.00pm and our bus left from Christchurch at 4.20. If we got out early we would walk slowly across town and pick up the bus at the Ushers brewery terminus. The bus would get us to Winsley by 4.50. Sabrina Hill who was at Trowbridge High, Sticky, and I would walk home up Dane Rise.

When I got home, gran would already be there waiting for me.

Pete was still at juniors and he would leave school at 3.30 and head for gran's house. Then she and Peter would walk down to our house in Poston Way.

One of my jobs was to light the fire. You can't credit it now in 2014 that a child of eleven, (because that's how old I was) would have the job of lighting the open fire but that was my job on getting home from school; not only lighting the fire, I cleaned out the ash-pan, chopped the kindling and taking pages of old newspaper from the shed, rolled the sheets into tight balls to go beneath the kindling.

First the paper in the bottom of the grate, then the kindling laid crisscross on top of the paper and the pieces of coal of a certain size laid on the kindling; with the front of the ash pan cover removed, I'd apply a match from underneath the grate to the rolled newsprint.

So, up to this point it sounds pretty safe, doesn't it? However two in five attempts would result in needing some extra draw to the fire and this is where the fun began. If the fire looked like dying, drastic action would be needed or the whole rigmarole would have to be gone through again...

which meant stripping the fire of the smouldering kindling and hot coals and laying them in the grate; although this would fill the room with smoke there was really no other option.

To prevent this misfire a double sheet of newspaper would be held across the front of the fireplace. A vacuum or suction would occur, so great that the middle of the news-sheet would be pulled into the fire like a boat's sail full of wind.

The fire would roar into life behind the paper and you'd feel the heat transfer through the paper onto face and chest as you hung on behind the now growing inferno.

Now the trick here is to remove the paper before it bursts into flames, if this should happen the only answer is to let go of the paper which will shoot burning up the chimney... definitely not good! As this could ignite soot in the flue and before you know it you've a chimney fire on your hands.

The idea is to closely watch the paper and as soon as it began to go brown in the centre of the sheet pull it quickly away. This was the knack of the good fire lighter, of which I'm proud to say I was one. Add a few more coals and when the fire was burning well replace the ash-can cover. Twenty minutes later the room would getting nice and warm. Oh, and stick your arm up the chimney to adjust the hot water cylinder damper! Another hazardous undertaking.

Dangerous maybe, but common place at the time and I'd had good instruction from dad who taught me how to do it.

Of course the open fire only heated the one room, the front room or sitting room whatever term you wish to give it; the rest of the house was freezing unless you had electric fires plugged in.

In winter to contain the heat from the front room fire the only doors left open would be those between the front room and dining room and the dining room and kitchen. Doors to the hall and upstairs were firmly closed. The bedroom window frames would be frozen shut from the inside with condensation icicles hanging from the old style single glazed metal frames.

Once again my progressive and forward thinking mum and dad took on the expense of having a 'Parkray' solid fuel fire installed with a couple of radiators, the council were still years away from providing such luxury in state owned housing.

The 'Parkray' would remain burning continually night and day through the winter so one of the worst chores, lighting the fire everyday disappeared until we got to North Bradley, then I started the whole thing over again.

Gran would turn up with Pete and make me a couple of rounds of pickled beetroot sandwiches to tide me over till tea time which I would sit and eat while watching Scooby Doo, Thunderbirds, or one of the other popular kids programs of the time. Pete would normally demolish a tin of Ambrosia rice pudding which he adored and later we would have a cooked meal with mum and dad.

Both mum and dad would get home from work, gran would leave us and return to nineteen, the dog would need to be walked, the table laid and normality would reign with Pete and I doing homework or the family sitting round after tea watching our favorite TV programs of the time, Coronation Street, On The Buses, Bonanza, or Till Death Us Do Part.

In the light evenings of summer we could grab a couple of hours outside playing football on the green before bed; this was the family evening routine.

1967, my first year at Nelson Haden was also a year of change for the family in general.

For my entire life dad had worked at the Avon rubber company in Bradford-on-Avon. With a second factory in Melksham it was probably the biggest employer in the west of the county; good money could be earned with Avon, especially if you worked 'piecework' which paid a set hourly rate and then further payments on what you produced.

But it was soul destroying work in a hot noisy factory. He worked a three shift rotation over three weeks, six to four, four to ten and ten to six.

Dad had worked this way all of his married life. One of the reasons he'd grin and bear it was because of mum and her being German. He had promised her on marriage that he would take her, or failing him being able to go with her, she would go on her own back to Germany every year.

A couple of times when money was really tight and when I was very young mum had gone back to Germany on her own or with me. But this was not the way my parents wanted things to be. Mum wanted

Bradford-on-Avon town bridge looking from the old swimming baths. Avon factory on the right hand side, dad worked behind the bottom window. We could talk to him from the bridge.

us all to go as a family for a family holiday. So dad worked hard at the 'Rubber Factory' as it was called locally, to make this happen and it did happen every year, sometimes twice a year.

But I knew both my parents wanted change, mum hated dad working at the factory and as the years went by dad got more irritable and it was all due to his job and place of employment.

The first change occurred in the summer of 1967. Mum had enough of the Post round. I was at secondary school and Pete was a very capable eight year old. Mum wanted to spread her wings and use some of her skills that had not been put into practice since she married dad.

She was highly educated and very intelligent and felt it was time to get a proper job. Also her best friend across the road, Pat, had started at

Bristol University, training to be a teacher and I think mum was slightly jealous.

She and dad discussed this and it was agreed; mum would look for another job and in the meantime they would also look for a second small car. A two car family in 1967 was unheard of.

And so arrived the Isetta bubble car; so named because that was just what it looked like. Made in Italy it sat two people side by side. It had a single cylinder engine generating no more the 10hp and a little gear stick on the side of the steering column. Three wheels... well at least it looked like it had three wheels, in fact it did have four, the two rear wheels were close together.

The original prototype had three wheels but they were prone to tipping over so a fourth wheel had been added at the back with a small gap between the two.

Dare I say it, a death trap on any amount of wheels.

To get in the thing you had to open the whole front of the car. The driver had to climb in first, squeezing behind the steering wheel which was also attached to the open front door and being careful not to get tangled up in the three pedals on the floor. It was not advisable to enter or exit with the engine running, if by chance you got caught in the gear stick you could find yourself half in and half out of the car while careering down the road. In the event of (God forbid) a head on collision and you lived and all your limbs functioned the escape route was through a sliding canvas trap in the roof... a so called, sunshine-roof. I came very close to having the indignity of exiting by this hole in the fuselage later in the year.

But mum was delighted, she had passed her test years before and often drove the family car but really it was dad's car and dad's choice of car. Now she had her own little car; which, during the short time in our possession would cause some heart stopping moments and for all its short-comings, I, over a short period of time persuaded my parents to let me drive the car every morning out of the drive. A procedure mum did not enjoy, having lost control one morning during the reversing manoeuvre and shooting across the road into Jim Burdon's front garden.

This was my first taste of being on the road in a motor vehicle.

The next item on the Burt's agenda of change was mum's job. The options for finding a new job in those days were pretty limited; the paper or word of mouth.

Word of mouth was fine if you lived in a bustling town where people had a finger on the pulse, but in Winsley where probably only one in fifty women worked outside the village the verbal grapevine did not exist; it was the Western Daily Press or the Wiltshire Times where you looked. There was no job shop or careers office.

However mum was offered a job surprisingly quickly. A receptionist at Volkswagen headquarters in Trowbridge.

Of course the big factor in obtaining the job was that she could speak, read, and write in German, her own birth language.

She and my dad were over the moon. It was a quality job and very well paid. The only down side was with me, I would have to travel daily to school in that awful little car.

How embarrassing. It wasn't as if mum worked over the other side of town; although within a couple of months that did happen. After only a short time of mum being with the company VW moved to the Canal Road industrial estate on the Hilperton Road but when she first started VW were based 100 yards from my school on the junction of Frome and Bradley Road. I would shuffle down in the seat as we drove through town and turned into the car park so I couldn't be seen. I would wait till we were round the back of the building before jumping out and walking the final few yards to the school front gate.

I still took the bus home in the evening as school finished at 3.45pm and mum didn't finish till 5pm.

School went on much the same the changes continued to be family orientated.

From the moment mum got her new job she encouraged dad to leave the Avon. Deep down this was what he wanted but he was earning good money; money that he wouldn't earn anywhere else.

The 'Marcos' team. Cyril five from the right in the white overalls.

Also there was the comfort element, a bit of fear of the unknown. But help and encouragement came from my uncle Cyril, dad's cousin, my granddads brother's son who lived in a lovely house in the old village.

Cyril was an engineer and a very good one; he was a few years older than my dad and had served in the Merchant Navy during the Second World War. His claim to fame was being torpedoed three times on the

Atlantic convoys and being rescued from a lifeboat on three occasions. He was a very lucky man.

Not only did he convoy the Atlantic but also served on the awful convoys to Russia through the Arctic Ocean.

Cyril was a great guy and I liked him immensely, I loved listening to his Naval war stories. His wife my aunt Betty took over the Post round when mum left to work for VW.

Cyril worked for a small sports car manufacturer in Bradford-on-Avon, Marcos Cars; a sleek looking machine made from fiberglass or GRP (glass reinforced plastic)with a marine plywood chassis. They produced their cars in an old mill, Greenland Mills at the end of Bridge Street. A multi-storey building, the cars would begin life on the top floor and get lowered through a hatch having more work carried out on every level till they reached the bottom and the engine was added. They were a hot competitor of Lotus at the time and the rivalry was fought out on the race track with both cars competing in production sports car racing, and at the Le Man 24 hour race where Marcos had a great deal of success.

Cyril worked on the engineering side but heard that a carpenter was needed and gave the word to dad. Dad grumbled that he wasn't a carpenter but with mum firmly pushing, dad took the bull by the horns and went for an interview with Jem Marsh the Owner/Director. Jem and dad hit it off from the word go and dad was offered the job; however the salary was a stumbling block. Dad was used to a fat weekly wage packet and Jem could offer nowhere near what dad was used to. Mum was having none of it. She was determined to get dad out of the factory and into a job in which he was happy. So the move was made. Mum's new income more than compensated for dad's loss. Dad settled in and was happy in his new job.

Dad at Marcos 1969

Marcos was a young company and the drive to improve the product was ongoing, dad was a very inventive person and within a short space of time had ideas for improving many aspects of the car; small things to improve the quality and longevity of components. He became foreman of the body shop and Jem's blue-eyed boy. He became involved in testing the cars at Castle Combe race track, meeting clients, many who were famous singers and musicians of the sixties; he even delivered a car to Paris for Nancy Sinatra; Frank Sinatra's daughter.

Dad at last was very happy.

I loved going to the Marcos factory. Some Saturday mornings I would go with dad and do some cleaning up around the workshop, if one of the young sales managers would be around I would ask if I could have a run out to the Wingfield Straight, a long stretch of road just outside Bradford where the car could be opened up to over 100mph; great fun.

Marcos worked closely with two brilliant car designers Dennis and Peter Adams, their workshop was in the oddest building, the old forge in bridge street across the road from the swimming pool.

Through dad I also got to know Peter and Dennis and when in town would often visit their small office and workshop where I would be fascinated with drawings and modelling of their next sleek four wheeled idea. They designed the Marcos Mantis which was years ahead of its time in appearance, I never really liked the finished car but the one car that I considered magnificent was the XP, the forerunner of the Probe 16. If my memory serves me correctly this car was built initially for the

Le Man 24 hour race, not for production, the Mantis evolved of the back of the XP. The photo shows the XP at its press launch which was held in a rented office next to the Canal Tavern on Frome road. I remember begging dad to let me have a day from school so I could go.

I loved Marcos and if the company hadn't got into difficulties in 1970/1 I would probably ended up working for them. But at that time the once a month or so Saturday morning would earn me a spin in a car and ten bob in my back pocket, earnings from my cleaning duties.

Pete and I enjoyed camping. Most of our summer holidays had been spent with mum and dad camping across Europe.

We started under canvas with our small tent from 'Tommy Best' army surplus and progressed to a lovely ridge tent with two sleeping compartments which we considered luxury; then came a caravan; a very small 14 footer, a 'Sprite'.

By the time dad's next venture came around in October 1967 we were serious caravaners. This next project was mega!

Our 12 foot Sprite at the Phillip's caravan site Church Knowle Dorset. Just look at those Lederhosen! What were our parents thinking.

It was the rebuilding of a burned out residential caravan.

In conversation one evening Ross Daniels told dad that he knew of a twenty eight foot caravan that had been gutted by fire.

Immediately dad saw the opportunity of a bargain. Get the caravan, strip all the aluminum and sell it to 'Drinkwater's' the scrap people in Trowbridge. He sold mum on the idea. No one could ever argue with dad once he had an idea in his head. So we resigned ourselves to the arrival of the van and sure enough it turned up on Ross's tractor and trailer one evening in August. The idea was to strip it and sell the scrap.

But no, within 24 hours dad had another brainstorm. We would cut five feet off each end, gut it and make it into a touring van. We would design the inside to suit our family needs.

And that's what happened; it took two years for our family to complete the project. I say family because it really was a family effort. Peter and I spent many an hour helping dad on that van. The new Tyning building site came in handy and quite a few materials found their way into the van helping to keep the costs down.

When it was finished it was a picture.

Painted in light blue with pretty curtains in the windows made by mum we were all very proud of the achievement. We had to have it weighed and inspected for road worthiness but in spring 1969 eighteen months after its burned out arrival at 2 Poston Way it passed all the road worthiness tests and we looked forward to many a happy holidays in that van.

Mums Isetta bubble car and the caravan project well underway in the drive at 2 Poston Way.

Meantime the bubble car chugged precariously on, an accident waiting to happen and the first incident happened on a wet windy afternoon in October.

Pete was off school for some reason and mum was also at home so she decided to take Pete to Trowbridge to an afternoon movie. They got as far as 'Bindings' shop in St Margret's Street in Bradford and the car stopped. Now at this point the road bends to the left while going up a slight rise, not the best place to breakdown.

It was chucking it down with rain, and this was the cause of the failure; simply water getting into the magneto, the mechanical part that sends a spark to the plugs. Try as mum might the car would not restart.

Across the road in the entrance to the railway station yard was E.W. Stones 'Station Garage' so mum decided to run across and ask them to push the car across the road and have a look at it. She told Peter to stay where he was while she quickly went for help. In her panic dash across the street her glasses fell off her nose and were crushed under a passing car. She now had a broken down car and no glasses.

Stones were great. They had the car in the garage, dried out the electrics and had it up and running in no time.

However mum's glasses were in smithereens so there was no point in going on. Also she was soaking wet. Slowly she drove home with nose pressed against the window and my brother saying 'left a bit, right a bit' and so on until they arrived back in Winsley.

Dad's comment on arriving home was, 'instead of coming home why didn't you leave the car walk into Bradford and sort out some new glasses?'

Mum's reply isn't printable.

Any kid going to school from Winsley to Trowbridge had to go on the public bus. School buses were only for kids in the catchment areas and Winsley didn't come under the Trowbridge area.

It was almost six miles by bus and the bus came from either the depot in Bath or Trowbridge. Whichever way the bus came and went it had to pass through the Avon valley before climbing steeply up the hill to Winsley. The valley ran round the great peninsular of land with Winsley perched on the high point above.

In winter and spring the weather would dictate when we could get to school. In times of even moderate snow there was no way the bus could get up Winsley Hill from Bath, or the hills leading out of Bradford. Even if the bus had managed to get from Trowbridge as far as Winsley which was highly unlikely. It would not get down Winsley Hill into the valley below.

Regardless of the weather, we kids would be driven out the house by our parents and told to get off to school; in bad weather Sticky, Sabrina and I would walk up to the main village bus shelter outside the pub and wait with Jeff our fingers crossed that the bus couldn't get through. We would wait a token ten minutes before going home and telling our parents (if they weren't at work) with glee, 'No buses today mum.' Then quickly get changed into our play clothes and wellies; out with our sledges we were off to Turleigh Downs.

The same happened in the springtime. Heavy rain would cause extensive flooding along the valley. The river would burst its banks in Limpley Stoke flooding a mile of road from the viaduct to the railway bridge at the bottom of Winsley Hill. In Bradford on Avon the water would flow either side of the town bridge and along Church Street up to six feet deep. Again this was a great excuse to stay home. The buses couldn't make it through and for days the army would shunt people backwards and forwards across the center of town.

Us kids would cycle or walk down to the town just to get a ride on the army amphibious vehicles. The only down side to this was in late 1968 Terry Baker our school sports instructor and my form teacher moved to the village and woe betide if he got to school and I didn't. At that time very few people owned a telephone, if we had one he would've been phoning me and Sticky to offer us a lift in.

During the summer I could avoid travelling in the bubble car by riding my bike to school. Roughly seven miles from Winsley to Nelson Haden the twice daily trip, either alone or with Sticky, was nothing to kids who lived constantly outdoors.

We would start at 8am and cycle down through Turleigh to Bradford and up the Trowbridge road. It was a hard slog. Neither one direction was easier than the other. Both had their fair share of downhill and up. Coming home we would generally take the top road. Leaving Trowbridge was hard work till we got to Trowle Common, then a long descent into town as far the footbridge where the library at the time, was housed in a large portable building. From here we pushed our bikes up a full mile to the top of Wine Street a hill so steep it is almost vertical. Then another grinding slog as far as Beale's farm before the road flattens out into the village.

In the summer we would do this ride twice a day during school term. Our legs like iron, it's no wonder both Sticky and I ran for the school cross country team. Even when it rained we had yellow cycle capes that covered our clothes; although the capes looked pretty naff they done a good job in keeping us dry.

Annual floods in Bradford-on-Avon. The car in the background is stranded on town bridge.

Our bicycles were our transport and once we all moved up from junior school to secondary we went everywhere on them. For my twelfth birthday gran bought me a lovely red racing bike with 10 gears alloy frame and drop handlebars. It wasn't new; it came from a second hand bike shop just up the road from my school, but I really loved that bike.

As summer moved into autumn the days of cycling to school were over and I was back in the bubble car. By this time VW had moved to Canal Road and mum would drop me at the bus stop at the end of Newtown by the church, our usual everyday bus stop.

Autumn moved into winter and along came the first flurries of snow. Now this car was not very stable at the best of times, and I dreaded the thought of having to ride in the thing on a road covered in snow; bear in mind the closely spaced drive wheels at the back would run in the centre of the road; the area where all the slush gets thrown from normal four wheeled vehicles.

Finally the morning came when it had snowed heavily in the night. I reluctantly got into the car and cautiously we started our journey to Trowbridge. By the time we got to Beale's farm mum was terrified. The back of the car was all over the road and I was hanging on for grim death. I pleaded with her to turn round and go back. We hadn't seen a bus which was a strong indicator the road leading out of Bradford toward Winsley was not passable. Mind you it didn't take much to stop the 264. We slipped and slithered our way through the town over Trowel Common and into the outskirts of Trowbridge. Just at the bottom of Cockhill where you now turn into the estate of Broadmead (which was still very much on the drawing board at the time), there is a small stone bridge which at one time had a narrow stream running beneath. Possibly by now mum was losing concentration, whatever the reason this is where she lost control of the car; a slight hump in the road and the merest hint of a twist to the left. Probably, right at this critical point mum either touched the brake or the accelerator, either way we were head on into the bridge. In all honesty we were lucky, our speed was minimal and fortunately no one was walking on the pavement. Now in 2014 the picket fence has gone and the brick work extended. But at that time had we not hit the bridge brickwork we would have been in the river, either side of the bridge was a very old wood-picket fence, a bramble infested embankment and cold water.

Mum sat there a brief moment in shock, while I, like a crew member of a burning bomber prepared to take to the escape hatch in the roof. However before I was able to move I felt the car being physically manhandled back on to the road by a helpful public one of which was my metal work teacher Mr Donnelly. Damn! I thought I would be able to pull a fast one, pretend I was suffering from shock and skip a day at school but no such luck I was bundled into Mr Donnelly's car and once the Isetta was running and mum was away I was taken to school by my teacher.

During the day the wind got up and the weather worsened. After lunch they closed the school and we kids were sent home. The coach companies were called to collect the kids from Hilperton and Westwood. There were no public buses running into Bradford so Sticky and I got a lift home with Terry Baker. It was snowing lightly but worse was the wind which was buffeting the car and driving the snow across the road horizontally. Terry drove past the entrance to the Tyning's estate turning in to Dane Rise and dropped me at my front door then Sticky at his house.

I had my key but instead of going in, I trudged with head bowed against the snow up to gran's for a cup of tea with her and my brother.

Mum normally got home around 5.30 with dad getting in around fifteen minutes later. At 5.45 I took my brother and walked the 100 yards home.

Dad got home at six but there was no sign of mum. I told him of our accident in the morning. Dad was worried and decided to drive back along the top road to see if she was stuck in the snow. He hadn't left the house before the door opened and there was mum in tears with Maurice White. We all went through to the kitchen wanting to know what on earth had happened. In fits and starts mum got her story out. It seems she had nursed the car back from Trowbridge. To avoid the steep hills in and out of Bradford she had decided to come home via Hilperton, Staverton, and Bradford Leigh; which in truth was a good plan. She had avoided the rise and fall and the bad bend at the top of Wine Street by going through Churches and what we called the Beazer estate (Downsview). She was just beginning to breathe a sigh of relief feeling she had made it as she passed Beale's farm when a gust of wind so powerful hit the car that it lifted it off the road, over the wall and into the field. It was a miracle mum was unharmed other than shock and a bit of bruising. The car didn't have seat belts, and I doubt mum would have worn one if it had. At the point where the car went over the wall the field is a good three feet below the road, quite a drop. Luckily during the course of the day the snow had built up against the bank and formed a big snow drift cushioning the fall.

Another driver had seen what happened, stopped and tried to help on his own. Unable to right the car he had flagged down the next person coming along, who just happened to be Jeff's dad; together they had got mum out the car, over the wall and into Maurice's works van.

Mum sat down and had a cup of tea; she was starting to regain her composure. The events of the day were recounted starting again with the bridge incident in the morning. Dad said he would get the car the following day and bring it home and check out the damage at the weekend. In the morning the wind had died down and the snow had stopped. Dad got up early and drove to Beale's to look at mum's car. He would go on to work from there. Mum stayed home from work. She walked up to the village to phone VW. I made my way to the bus stop with Sticky, we waited quite some time, then a lady in the bungalow across the road came over and told us she had rung the bus station in Trowbridge and the buses weren't running, they hoped to resume service by midday. Sticky and I went home. By the time I got back mum was also home from the phone box and we sat and had a cup of tea together and talked through the events all over again. Mum was adamant that the car would never again go out in the snow. If the snowy weather returned, she would catch the bus in with me; it was only a 20 minute walk from the bus station to the VW warehouse at Canal Road. I was horrified; it was bad enough going with mum in that bloody car but fancy having your mum on the school bus with you, Aaaaah!

Dad came home early and with Maurice went to collect the car. Small and basic it may have been but it was very robust. The front right hand bumper bar was bent; that was damage sustained when we hit the bridge abutment and the left hand headlight had been smashed and the mounting bracket bent when the car had flown over the wall. The headlights stuck out like Will Smith's ears on either side of the car. (Sorry Will Smith) giving it an even greater comical appearance than the car's odd shape in general. The car fired up in the farmyard and dad drove it home. It stayed in the drive until the weekend when dad made good the damage. By Monday morning the roads were again clear of snow and off we went in the car.

Christmas came and went, and winter moved into spring. The caravan project was going flat out and as the weather warmed up dad spent more time on the reconstruction. Mum had been promoted in her job at VW and with this promotion came a decent hike in salary. She took Pete and me into Trowbridge and bought us both a complete new wardrobe of clothes. This really was a rare extravagance.

So here we were ticking along nicely; mum as Personal Assistant to the Managing Director at VW in Trowbridge and dad settled in his new job with Marcos.

Then came the incident that for once and forever sealed the fate of the bubble car.

Someone had left the boards off the pit; the pit that dad had built into the drive for servicing the car.

We kids would use the pit to hold puppet shows, so it could have been us at fault, however for once the act of negligence was never proven and the blame was never placed. The pit was left open and anybody or anything could have fallen, walked or driven in and that's exactly what happened.

Whoever got home first parked at the end of the drive and today it happened to be mum. The pit was uncovered and mum drove straight in.

Not the two front wheels, no, they had miraculously passed either side of the void but the back wheels in the middle of the car dropped straight in.

Of course the car was triangular in shape, wide at the front and narrow at the back so what happened was the whole car fell backward with the front 45degrees in the air.

Mum was pushed back in the seat like a fighter pilot heading for the heavens. The door couldn't be opened either; she was stuck inside. Pete and I were in the house and so was gran, with its distinctive sound of a petrol driven lawn mower we'd recognised the car as it pulled into the drive. After five minutes Pete said 'where's mum?' We were watching kids TV so we were in no rush to leave the box. We thought gran being in the kitchen would go and look but in truth at the back of the house she wouldn't have even heard mum's entry to the drive. A few more minutes went by and I reluctantly went to look. 'Has mum come in?' I asked my gran. 'No,' said gran, 'I didn't know she was home.'

So I walked outside to look and there was the bubble car stuck in the pit with mum stuck inside. The only thing she had managed to do was switch off the engine.

She had opened the little sliding window next to the driver but was reluctant to shout for help because of the embarrassment of her situation.

Quick witted as we both were my brother and I grabbed a length of wood and pushed it under the back of the car and the edge of the pit. With hardly any effort, the fulcrum effect lifted the back of the car and mum was able to make a dignified hop to safety avoiding the couple of feet of unprotected pit that was still in front of the open car door. I asked mum to grab one of the boards and slip it under the back of the car, otherwise we would have to lower it back to its 45 degree angle with the back end hanging loosely in space. Job done we all retired indoors.

Pete and I thought this was hilarious, we were rolling with laughter. Mum too could see the funny side. But then the question came, who left the pit uncovered? That was a different story and of course Pete and I knew nothing about it.

But this was the final straw. When dad got home we shuffled the car to safety and put the boards back. Dad again looked at the damage caused to the sides of the car by it dropping onto the concrete edges of the pit. By the following morning our parents had decided to trade the bubble car in for a real four wheel machine. Pete and I were told the pit was out of bounds.

When it came to cars things never moved slowly with dad. By Saturday evening 5pm, it had to be by 5pm because that's when the football results came on the telly and dad needed to be sat down with his 'Littlewoods' pools coupon and a cup of tea, the bubble car had gone and mum was the proud owner of a Ford Anglia, a black ex-police car. It wasn't a case of keeping up with the Jones's. In Winsley when it came to cars you had to keep up with the Burt's. Mum now had a car that had four wheels and with a squeeze could sit five.

The summer school holidays would follow an annual pattern. As a family we would load the car and set of across the channel to do some touring, camping, and to visit Oma, and my uncles Ralf and Hans Dieter. This was our regular summer two week holiday trip abroad.

On our return the rest of the holidays would be spent playing around the village and being looked after, and fed by gran at nineteen.

When the summer holidays finished, and Pete and I went back at school, gran would go off to Torquay for a week with an auntie who lived in Wick just outside Bristol.

This had been a regular week away for gran and granddad before he passed away.

Daisy, my auntie, a Sartain before marriage, was married to Sammy and it was Sammy who drove the four of them to Torquay.

In 1964 while they were on their south coast holiday Sammy passed away. His sad demise happened during the night, in bed, in the hotel; it was an abrupt end to the holiday and a genuine 'Fawlty Towers' moment.

Daisy, who hadn't driven a car in years, managed to get the car plus remaining holiday makers back from Torquay safely. The car was then shut away in the garage till my grandfather died in1967.

Following the death of our granddad Daisy and gran decided to get the car back on the road and take their holidays once again in Torquay.

The car was a Morris 1000 and I hated going in that car; she wasn't in anyway a confident driver and drove everywhere at twenty miles an hour with traffic backed up behind her as far as the eye could see.

Not only was it a frightening experience travelling in that car, it was so bloody embarrassing, my friends used to laugh their heads off about it.

The Saturday before my gran returned dad asked me to go over and mow gran's lawn. We had an electric rotary lawn mower and it would take very little time and I didn't mind, gran did heaps for me and it was the least I could do. Pete wanted to come with me so off we went together.

Trixy my gran's dog, a vicious little Jack Russell that would have your hand off in an instant, was in the kennel, so with the key from dad we were able to let ourselves in the front door and plug in the mower.

Gran had a lot of lawn at nineteen. It was a corner plot and built at a time when growing your own veg was the thing; the back garden on its own was almost 50 yards in length.

Before granddad passed away most of the back garden was turned over for vegetables; but after he died dad had levelled over a big portion and put it down to grass.

Besides this large area leading up to the hedge bordering Bowels field there was another square of grass outside the back door; this area was fenced in for the dog. At the front and side of the house were another three lawns.

Pete and I were only one lawn away from finishing the job when Pete, who was holding the cable and walking along side of me, asked if he could have a go at driving the mower; he had asked a couple of times before but I'd said no. This time I said ok and let him get on with it while I held the cable. When we got to the end of the lawn he swung the mower to the left and went straight over the end of my toes. I wasn't quick enough to pull back out of the way and felt the blade slice through my baseball boot and then slice through the end of my big toe... the pain hit!

Pete of course stopped the mower and burst out crying. I was hopping around with a big lump of boot missing and blood flowing freely over the lawn. I done no more than head home as fast as I could; I think I was crying as well, more from shock than pain but also the fear that my footballing days were over. This was my primary concern as mum removed my boot and tended to my wound. Yes I'd lost a chunk off the top of my toe but it would heal over in a very short space of time and have no effect on the possibility of me playing for England. Pete remained at my gran's. Dad had to go and get him and the mower. He thought he was going to get a hiding for running over me, poor kid was found by dad sitting on the lawn howling his eyes out.

The toe, like all my injuries from the past to the present, healed very rapidly and after twelve months you couldn't really see where anything was missing.

I was a real schemer, into all sorts of money making ideas. I wanted and needed more money than I got from Mrs Lavington or mum and dad, who really didn't believe in dishing out pocket money for no return, it had to be earned by car washing, gardening, or some other household task.

I decided a way of making some extra pocket money was to keep rabbits, breed them and sell them. I bought one initially from Mrs Painter who lived opposite the junior school. It was a little brown and white Dutch rabbit and I called her Tess. Dad helped me build a hutch for her.

In the body shop at Marcos, one of dad's jobs was to fit the sunshine-roofs. In those days the sunshine-roof was a canvas affair that slid back by hand, the same type of mechanism that mum had in her bubble car.

The rectangular panels that were cut from the car roofs were very good for making up the sides, roof and floor for my rabbit hutches.

With a bit of help from dad in knocking-up the first hutch for my own rabbit I continued to make more and sell them to other people.

It didn't take long to dawn on me, that there was money to be made from selling rabbits as well as the hutches. So I bought another small black and white Dutch rabbit, a male, (a Buck) and put him in the hutch with Tess. Of course we've all heard the expression 'going at it like rabbits'; well they did, and the inevitable happened, and the results of this rabbit union, once they were weaned of their mother, I sold. I was quite an entrepreneur.

After seeing my rabbits Bernard asked Pat if he too could have one. 'Yes' said Pat; so Bernard went out and got himself a small black rabbit with rather long back legs. He called it Twink.

Twink was a breed of hare, a 'Belgian Hare'; the thing grew and grew till it was larger than a small dog! I remember one afternoon Bernard putting it on a lead and taking it out on the green for a walk, a pack of kids gathered round and thought this was great, Bernie taking his rabbit for a walk.

Twink done a bunk one winter; my brother went round Jeff & Bern's and there was the cage door open and hare prints disappearing into the snow. They followed the prints but to no avail, Twink would never be seen again...

We also used the fiberglass sun-roof sheets as sledges. We discovered one winter they really shifted over the snow; with two holes drilled in the corners of the narrow end and string tied through the holes, we would sit on the sheet and bend the front up in the air and away we went. With the smooth polished fiberglass in contact with the snow this really was like an Olympic sport, scary fast! The sheets were in great demand and selling them for a couple of shillings each contributed to both mine and Pete's holiday savings tin.

During the mid-sixties the structure of the village began to change. A new private housing estate was planned; it was to be built on the north east side of the village and would stretch from the back of Dane Rise through to the Bradford Road at Beale's farm. In all when completed there would be around 300 houses, a row of shops and a new school. The old Victorian school in the heart of the old village, the school our families had attended for over 150 years, would become the working men's social club.

It didn't happen quickly; test holes were dug while we were still at the junior school, no doubt to check on the soil type and ground composition. Because of this multitude of test holes this area was nicknamed by us kids the 'holefield'.

The first houses started going up around 1966.

Suddenly after a long time our big slide, swings and see-saw that had been taken from the old playing field reappeared.

They had been stored by the parish council and now a new playing field had been designated they were resurrected including a new roundabout.

This was our place of play; bombing around on our bikes, playing football, all in wrestling matches, scrapping, or just hanging out.

Bickering, fighting, and little flair-ups between us happened now and again. It may read as if they happened all the time, and I apologise if my story makes it seem that way, but actually it wasn't the case, we all got on pretty well, Chris Hill and Gibbo included. However, like the brick thrown at my brother's head, play did turn into war and when that happened no prisoners were taken. When a fight broke out it continued until the loser ran from the battlefield or collapsed on the floor; no one intervened.

An example of this was a fight between my brother and one of our peer group who shall remain nameless. We were in the 'holefield' when this lad stole my brother's bike and went riding off around the field.

Now this particular individual and I don't mind putting this in writing, was not a nice kid, read on...

Pete came moaning to me with -'so-and-so has nicked my bike.'

'Well,' I said, 'go and get it back.'

'He's bigger than me and won't listen,' said Pete.

'If he won't give it back, just pull him off the bike and take it.' I said.

You may think this is mean of me, but at some point Pete had to stand on his own two feet, he had a protector in his older brother and that would serve him well when he joined Nelson Haden with me already in the fourth year, but there does come a time when he needed to sort out problems for himself and this was it. Said child was a prize bully, overweight and aggressive, but only to kids younger than himself. He liked to throw his weight around and he had plenty of it to throw. Admittedly he was eighteen months older than Pete but that doesn't necessarily make a great deal of difference. I knew my brother could do for Lardy and he needed to make a stand for his own self esteem.

'Pete,' I said, 'he's is not a fighter and he's not quick on his feet you can get the better of him, now go and get your bike back.'

On this note I got on with whatever I was doing.

The next thing all hell had broken loose; a pack of kids had gathered round in a circle and there was Pete slogging it out with bully boy.

I ran across to see how things were going but at this point I dare not intervene, if I pulled Pete out of it he would be seen to have lost face and any future conflict would go against him, basically he'd be seen as weak.

As it happens every child was shouting for my brother and the support had kept him in there.

Pete's opponent was trying to grab him and had he succeeded it would have been game, set, and match, he was a half times bigger again than my brother.

'Don't let him grab you Pete!' I shouted. 'Keep out of his reach and hit him!'

They were exchanging blows of which most of Lardy's were missing but one fist caught Pete on the nose and blood shot everywhere. Pete had always been susceptible to nose bleeds and it didn't take much for him to have a gusher. Blood was everywhere and this startled the boy giving my brother a window to lay a couple of good punches. Pete was crying but his adrenalin was really pumping and unlike his Lardy opponent was not tiring and he just kept lashing out.

Suddenly it was over; vanquished, although still with fists up the boy was walking backwards toward the hole in the wall. Pete in a right mess of blood and tears was still walking aggressively towards him, fists up… suddenly in defeat the boy turned and walked off every now and again looking over his shoulder.

Pete was the hero, he was grinning and the other kids were patting him on the back. The lad concerned was not a popular kid among the younger element who tended to get the brunt of his bullying.

I was very proud of my brother and told him so. I went and picked up his bike for him.

'Come on mate let's get you home and cleaned up; God knows

what mum will say.'

As we walked down the road home Pete between tears and laughter told me he'd done exactly as I'd said; asked for his bike back and when he'd refused Pete just pulled him off. Then the fisticuffs began.

To be honest when I'd told him to get on with it I'd expected him to come back after a few minutes having failed. How wrong was I?

It was a huge boost to my brother's confidence and he never again was bullied or bothered by this individual.

However...mum was in the drive as we came round the corner by the flats and looked up and saw the mess Pete was in and came running over in a right old state. Not surprising as he looked like he'd been through a combine harvester.

I was chastised by mum for allowing my young brother, as mum called it, 'get beaten half to death' (slight exaggeration) but dad thought I was right to let Pete get on with it. It comes to us all at some point dad said.

To top it off his mum came down and had a go at mum saying that Pete had picked on her poor little boy. She got short shrift at our front door that's for sure.

Another scrap in the 'holefield' was a gang fight between us kids from the council estate and those from the new estate over the use of the football field.

We watched as the new houses were erected moving slowly toward our own council estate.

More families came to live in the new houses. Posh kids from private housing, kids who we didn't necessarily get on with. We would fight viciously with them for no reason at all and if we caught them playing on our football pitch there was all out bloody war. Of course quite a few of them ended up in Winsley School.

The Wallace twins from Scotland, Cameron Melrose from another Scottish family. I don't think they had it easy with us locals but the Wallace twins were pretty good at football and won a place in the junior school team. This didn't in any way change the situation when we were outside of school; they belonged on their own estate, whereas we went where we wanted to. After all it was our village and the new estate building site continued to be our play area.

We got to the field one day for a game of football and the new estate kids had already set up. We told them where to go and then it started, first as a slanging match, then a pushing in the chest competition, then the fists began to fly.

Everyone was hitting everyone and I ended up sitting astride one boy, pinning him down by his arms with the intention of giving him a sorting when I suddenly saw stars. One of the others had hit me across the back of the head with a lump of two-by-two timber (that's 50mm square for those on metric).

My hands went to my head and I protectively rolled to one side.

Our gang had seen this and jumped on the kiddie who did it, I'm pretty sure it was Cameron Melrose. The wood was grabbed from him and he ran for his life. I had a lump the size of an egg and was bleeding profusely from a long cut to the skull.

The use of weaponry was considered very unsporting conduct and our gang went for the jugular which saw the new estate kids running home as fast as their legs would carry them.

I was assisted back to 2 Poston Way suffering another open wound to be patched up by mum.

Incidents like this were not uncommon and these are only two of many battles that were fought either as a gang or as individuals, the council housing estate jungle... I suppose it still goes on today but the kids use knifes and even guns; at least we fought it out using our fists.

Back then a building site was not protected or wired off as it is today. No health and safety policy decreed that fencing had to surround the site or that measures of any form had to be put in place to keep the public out.

When the workmen clocked off at the end of the day the site was open to anyone wishing to take a stroll around it and for us kids it became our new, very large adventure playground.

We would go in the evening and play on the scaffolding. Sliding down poles and swinging from one level to another. We would play war games or hide and seek. Now and again a worker would leave a starter handle for a dump truck in the tool box and we would swing the machine into life and drive off around the site screaming and shouting. The older boys all knew how to do this. We would abandon the dumper when we got fed up and they would be found the following day somewhere other than where they left them and from that point the starting handles would be locked in the site office.

But after a few weeks things would be forgotten and again we would find a starting handle and have an hour of fun. One evening we started a diesel roller. With a control stick that either went forward or back we rammed it into gear and let it go... it demolished a porta-loo and yards of kerbing before becoming stuck nose down in some footings.

Some of the surrounding houses would occasionally phone the police to report us, but by then the village police house had closed and the 'Panda Car' as it was called, or the police mobile unit, had to come from Bradford-on-Avon. We would see them coming and scarper. None of the policemen knew the village kids so they wouldn't go knocking on doors like old Fordy did. They never caught us and miraculously no real life or death issues arose so I'm guessing they didn't really care. We of course ran off and kept away from the site for a few days afterwards.

Attending different schools Angela and I began slowly to see less of each other. They do say that adolescent girls grow up faster than boys and I think this was the case. She was turning into a stunning looking teenager and had made new friends in Bradford-on-Avon where she went to school. After all it was only two miles down the road so she could visit her school friends whenever she wanted.

We still played out together during the weekday evenings but she didn't seem to be around so much at weekends.

A new girl had turned up on the new estate. She caught my bus to school in the morning and went to St Augustine's catholic school. This didn't bother me, but when I showed my interest in her I was quickly rebuffed and she told me in no uncertain terms that I was not welcome and her mum and dad would not allow her out with a Church of England boy. However I persevered and eventually got to sit next to her on the bus; her name was Marianne Hannie, another Scot, (they must be shipping them down from North of the border by the busload). I liked her very much but she was never allowed out and was in fear of her mum and dad.

I remember one evening her parents went out somewhere and she let me in. While I was there they returned and the only escape was out the kitchen door, over the fence at the bottom of the garden and through the neighbours.

It was going nowhere this chasing of Miss Hannie and I still held a candle for Angela who was still in our gang be it not as much as in the past. I concentrated on trying to keep my old flame interested in me and let my short term fascination for Marianne die out. Little did I know then, that within a few months a German girl would enter my life who would capture my young heart good and proper.

In Germany my auntie Marlene was expecting her second child; the baby was due in August so mum and dad decided to delay going to Germany until after Marlene had given birth.

Following the birth of the child Marlene and Gerhard her husband would wait a week or so and take the train to Mulheim so my Oma could see her sixth grandchild.

My parents planned that we would go at the same time so our visit would coincide.

My little cousin Horst was born on August 14th 1968.

My parents discussed with my uncle when they would arrive at my Oma's house in Mulheim; they wanted a fortnight with my grandmother; but also they needed to leave it as late as possible for my auntie to get her strength back.

The other factor was that Pete and I had to get back to Winsley for the new term at our respective schools, so it was a fine balance of just when to go and how long we would have with my aunt and uncle. We eventually made plans for the last two weeks of the school holidays.

We were at Oma's for a week and a bit before Marlene, Gerhard, Elke and Horst (the new addition) arrived. It was cramped in my grandmother's little flat, a smaller flat she had moved to a year previously. My uncle and aunt with the kids moved into the second bedroom. The couch in the front room made down into a double bed for my mum and dad and Pete and I slept on the floor.

It did us just fine for the couple of nights prior to packing up and returning home.

It was our first time of meeting my uncle. He came across as being a really nice guy. My auntie I hadn't seen in a few years and Elke my little cousin was a lovely little thing, almost 18 months old, and of course the new addition Horst who was literally only three weeks.

So for a couple of days the house was chaos with baby's crying and people moving around in the night but it was nice for us all to be together and of course my other uncles, aunties and cousins all turned up to drink coffee and eat cake. A real 'Hopp' family get-together, which delighted my grandmother.

We left from Mulheim early on the Saturday and arrived back home in the evening.

We took it easy on the Sunday with Pete and me preparing our stuff for our return to school the next day.

Monday morning saw me returning to Nelson Haden in year two.

Summer holidays over and back to normality; mum had spare seats in the Ford Anglia and dropped Jim Burdon's daughters off at the grammar school on the way through Bradford. Sticky and I were on our bicycles and made the most of riding to school before summer turned into autumn; we both knew that as soon as the rain came we would have to share the car with the girls. It was the way of things, people helped each other out; my mum had spare seats in the car, others were going in the same direction; in the case of the Burdon's a big family with less money than us, you helped out where you could.

The next major incident in the village for once involved someone other than me; but it did involve a family member... my brother.

As kids we carried pockets full of junk, most of us had a pen-knife and it wasn't unusual for one or two kids to have a box of matches; when we went anywhere it was normal to ask if anyone had matches... just in case we needed to light a fire. Well the fact is we never had to light a fire but we lit one anyway.

In Murhill woods, down by the river when we were fishing, wherever; one of us would grab dry twigs and a fire would be lit. It was no big deal; having a box of matches in your pocket was really no different to carrying a pocket-knife or an air pistol. No one seemed to get stressed about it.

However it was a different kettle of fish when the fire got out of hand. This happened to Kev, my brother, and Ruth Godfrey.

What happened and who was to blame has never been resolved with each parent blaming the others. The fact is the three of them decided to light a fire next to the biggest hay stack in the village.

The three of them headed off up the lanes. Pete in possession of a box of matches which Kevin had persuaded him to pinch from our kitchen (so says Pete). When they got to the top of the lane at the cross roads by Freddie Burton's farm they turned right walking toward the Bradford Road and Beale's farm, a part of Winsley called Ashley.

Along this lane on the left was a huge hay stack belonging to none other than Ross Daniels. It was at this point they decided to light a fire...

Was one of them a secret arsonist?

Was there the thrill of watching the biggest fire the area had ever seen and thinking they could get away with it?

Sadly Kevin died of a heart attack in the mid-eighties so we can't get his story. I wish we could.

Here is my recollection of events as the story unfolded for me.

I was on my way home from school with Sticky on the bus and as we left Bradford we could see this giant pall of smoke in the distance over the fields toward Conkwell.

Everybody on the top deck of the bus had a clear view and as we got closer to Winsley we could see the smoke was not that far from the main road. As we swung around the corner at the top of Cottles Lane (Beale's farm) the smoke looked no more than a half mile away on Ashley Lane. It was an unbelievable sight.

Another half mile and Sticky and I were off the bus; dying to get home, get changed, and go to see what and where the problem was.

I dived into our gate telling Sticky I'd be round his in ten minutes and shot through the front door to get changed.

Gran met me in the hall totally distressed. 'What's up gran? What's mums car doing in the drive?' I questioned.

'It's Peter,' she said. 'He's burnt down a hay stack with Kevin and Ruth Godfrey.'

I couldn't believe what I was hearing. Gran had to repeat it for me.

'Where?' I asked.

'Somewhere up the lane,' she said, 'you can't miss it.'

'I know gran I've seen it from the bus.'

'Where are mum and Pete now?'

'They're up the fire with the police and fire brigade' she said.

So for once it wasn't me.

'I'm going up there gran.'

'Oh be careful, be careful,' my gran was crying.

I quickly shot up stairs and got changed grabbed my bike and shot round to Sticky's.

His mum had forbidden him to come with me (Mrs Stickland knew what was going on because they lived next door to the Godfrey's) so off I flew toward Ashley as fast as I could pedal.

It was no more than a few minutes on my bike, I passed people along the way who were also off to see what the heck was going on.

The sight that greeted me I'll never forget. There were three haystacks in a row; big ones, each the size of a small house and they were all ablaze.

Two fire engines stood by, the crews doing nothing and also a couple of policemen keeping back what was slowly becoming a large crowd.

My mum was there holding Pete, both were crying; no sign of Kevin or Ruth.

'What's going on mum?' I said, 'why aren't they putting out the fire?'

'There's no water supply,' she said 'and even if there was the two engines wouldn't be able to cope.'

The local rag had turned up taking photographs and was asking questions. I knew what would happen next, they'd be over questioning my mum and brother.

'Come on mum,' I said, 'let's go home. There is nothing you can do here. The police will come to ours if they need to speak to Pete.'

I went and told the police officer we were leaving and gave them our address. We walked slowly home both mum and Pete sobbing.

Slowly I dragged the story out of them. Mum had been called at work by gran after Pete had come running back from the blaze. She had acted swiftly and come home but there was nothing she could do; the fire was roaring and the different services had been called. To this day she doesn't know what prompted her to go with Pete back to the scene, she would have been better keeping out of the way at least she wouldn't have ended up on the front page of the local press.

The police came and interviewed my brother. Not Fordy, he had retired by then. The police came up from Bradford-on-Avon. They also interviewed Ruth and Kevin.

My brother was a good kid; hardly ever in minor trouble let alone anything of this size.

Pete had been gullibly led astray.

Fortune had it that the stacks were owned by Ross Daniels our family friend. Ross came round and spoke to my dad.

It transpired that that the stacks were covered under the farm insurance policy for fire and Ross would not lose financially. Ross told my mum and dad not to worry. He would tell the police that he wanted no further action and we could all rest easy.

Just before we left the county in 1971 mum and dad went to say goodbye to Ross. In the meantime he had lost his wife, I believe she was killed in a tractor accident on the farm and he was selling up. He took mum and dad into his confidence and told them the straw that had been burned that day was worthless. It had stood in the field for two seasons and was severely water damaged. He had been postponing dealing with it and had just left it standing there until he had time available to sort it out. He pocketed a good wedge that day.

Pete, Kev and Ruth of course were local celebs among us youngsters. Big write ups in the Western Daily Press and the Wiltshire Times, although the photo of mum and Pete that appeared in the paper was far from flattering. The two of them stood there howling. That photo must have been taken before my arrival as no reporter approached them while I was at the scene.

We had the usual lecture about matches, Pete was confined to the house for a period and life went on.

Another great universal pastime to which we applied ourselves fully was making and adapting 'Stuff.'

'Stuff' knew no limitations; in the same way we made trolleys from prams so we made skateboards from roller skates and adapted any old bit of junk we could get our hands on.

We made our own version of the now popular mountain bike and called them scramblers and I had my own version of a home-made BMX bike that I bought from Jimmy Francis during the third year at Nelson Haden. Jimmy's nick-name was Raggy because he looked like Shaggy in Scooby Doo. For anyone who's never watched the original animated series of the sixties, Scooby Doo is a dog who communicates with Shaggy his owner in his own weird language, when he calls Shaggy it comes out as Raggy... get it? Hence the nick-name.

The bike had odd sized wheels and tall 'Ape Hanger' handlebars. I used it for my paper round hanging the bag over the brake levers. I wasn't allowed to ride it to school because it wasn't considered roadworthy. I called this bike the Rag-mobile.

No such thing as a BMX or a mountain bike; we adapted our bikes to look like oddities from a Mad Max Movie.

In Conkwell we had the unofficial 'Tip'; the tip that Gibbo, and not to be outdone by Gibbo, also my brother as he has recently reminded me, fell down.

Gibbo remained in the pit for some time before being rescued. My brother was scavenging with dad when he went over the edge and badly cut the top of his thigh. He was brought home covered in blood and had to have stitches. He was most indignant to think I had forgotten this.

The Tip was an old sandstone quarry where stone had been removed in the late sixteen and early seventeen hundreds for the construction of the Dundas aqueduct down in the valley.

People unofficially chucked all sorts over the edge into the pit below and you could stand on the top and view all the new additions almost on a weekly basis.

The experimental conversion of push bikes was the big thing.

Using different diameter wheels; having a small wheel on the back and a big one on the front for some reason gave us a great buzz.

Also adapting the bicycle frame to take the wheel of a moped; this was top of the cool scale. Kevin had such a bike made for him by his elder brother Malcolm; it may have looked good but it was a pig to ride.

Bike parts, old prams and all manner of stuff like this appeared in the 'Tip' and was precariously retrieved without any mechanical aids such as a crane, a winch, or a hoist, then dragged home and put to use.

Another prize acquisition was a tandem. Getting hold of an old tandem frame was like winning the lotto for us kids.

We had a couple over the years. Jeff had got one from his cousin Stephen White who lived in Bradford on Avon.

Maybug scramble
Farleigh Hungerford.

To quote Jeff - *I couldn't get hold of the proper wheels for it; an ordinary wheel just buckles. I was getting through a different wheel about every 3 weeks – I sold it to Mark Edgell.*

So now I know where it went.

Sticky got his hands on one but it only had one set of pedals so the person on the back did nothing other than get chauffeured by the person up front.

Jeff can't remember Sticky having a tandem, he thinks it was a fixed wheel bike but fixed wheel were not uncommon. My Rag-mobile was fixed wheel. It's where the pedals act as the brake, the rear hub locks and only goes in the one direction causing the pedals to turn continually, bloody dangerous, and you can get quite a whack from them if you take your feet off the pedals while moving and then try to relocate them. Basically you've got to keep pedaling all the time, but with practice you could turn round sit on the handlebars and pedal backwards.

These weird aids to mobility where used in our adventures near and far and occasionally caused some form of argument along the way.

Kev had been known to abandon his moped come bicycle because it was so heavy to pedal and control; we would encourage him to ride it on the promise of swapping over at some point on route, but when the

137

time came none of us wanted to get on the thing, it was too much like hard work. He would demand one or other of us take a turn at riding it. If Angela was with us on her bike he'd go ballistic at his sister to take over; Angela would have no sympathy for her younger brother; ranting 'you promised, you promised,' he'd burst into tears, throw the bike in the hedge and stomp off calling us 'piggy buggers' as he went. (More on piggy buggers later).

One evening overhearing Pete and I laughing about Kev dumping the bike, my dad after reprimanding us for being so mean, went round to Mrs Holt's and took Kev in the car to get it from the ditch in which he had thrown it.

In the spring we would ride to the Farleigh Hungerford May-Bug Motocross Scramble, a great day out watching the bikes churning up the mud and flying through the air.

It took place at Whitsun; we left as a gang of ten but by the time we got there our numbers were down forty percent; the others having turned back due to rain, punctures, tantrums, or mechanical breakdowns. Sticky and Jeff on the Tandem, Simon Beale, Paul Orchard, Mick Gardner and me on our standard non-customized bikes.

That particular day it was chucking it down but the six of us, soaked to the skin stuck it out watching the thrilling racing.

Farleigh Hungerford was a fantastic hilly course, one of the best Motocross Grand Prix tracks in the UK and attracted world class riders. We would get plastered from head to toe in muddy spray that flew from the rear wheels of the bikes and get home wringing wet in a filthy state.

I have a memory of sitting on the top of the hill watching the riders flying over the ridge six or eight feet in the air. Sticky had just opened his flask of hot tea for a drink when a lump of mud the size of a golf ball flew into the air, curling over at the top of its flight path it dropped cleanly through the hole in the top of Sticky's flask. Scolding tea shot out like a geezer. Sticky dropped the flask and that was the end of his hot drink for the day. It must have been a ten million to one chance that this could happen, and while Sticky grumbled on about losing his drink we others rolled around laughing. It was a very funny incident that I'll never forget.

A river ran through the field where the motocross was held with an area below the ancient ruin of Farleigh Castle being designated as a swimming pool. There were high banks from which to jump and swings off the trees overhanging the river; loads of kids would go there to swim in the summer from Bradford, Trowbridge, Westwood, Southwick and the small villages between. We all knew each other from our different schools and being a neutral venue we all got on pretty well.

Other acts of madness that came under the heading of 'Playing'.

'The Splits' this was a game of dare using a sheath knife, or a good solid knife nicked from the kitchen cutlery draw. I had a lovely sheath knife that had been bought for me in Austria, around 7" long it had a beautifully engraved stag horn handle; again it was no big deal at the time to go out to play with a sheath knife hanging from your belt.

The idea of splits was to see who chickened out first; two of us would stand a yard apart and throw the knife into the ground as close as possible to your mate's foot. He'd slide his foot up to the blade and then it was his turn to throw the knife; as your legs became further apart it was harder to keep balance and to throw the knife. If the knife failed to embed itself into the ground you lost, or if you lost balance and fell over you lost, I suppose if you put the knife through your friends foot you probably lost as well, madness, but I don't remember any of us actually putting a knife through a friend's foot, probably more luck than anything else.

Then there were bows and arrows, but wait for it...not just normal bows and arrows, read on...

We made them, and spears from 'Hazel' branches we cut down in Murhill woods; we would sharpen the end of the arrows with our pocket knives and then shoot at each other. Even in this form the arrow could have done terrible damage had it hit someone in the face.

But we took this lunacy one stage further by fixing dart heads to the tip.

Yes, that's right, metal pointed dart heads over the ends of the arrows and shooting them at? No, thankfully we weren't so daft as to shoot directly at each other - although we may have considered shooting at the new estate kids.

However a live target seemed a great idea and Kev once again drew the short straw; but not to worry, we did protect him - by putting him in a pram, a metal sided, hooded, 1960s kiddies pram; so no problem there then...

In climbed Kev and from 25 yards away we lined up with our dart tipped arrows and let rip at the pram. How we perceived this to be any less dangerous heaven only knows.

He couldn't even get completely into the pram, he had to lay on his back with his legs bent. His knees stuck up above the rim, protected by a metal topped dustbin lid, referred to as 'The Shield'.

The caravan in the first stages of reconstruction, the forward end having been removed and reshaped.

He would shout ready and we would let fly with our metal tipped arrows. They would go straight through the side of the pram and the lining by a good inch (25mm). Then we'd go running over to have a look. Kevin came out of this madness completely unscathed, which is an utter miracle.

My father found out about this lunacy when I came very close to putting a dart tip through his head.

Dad was working on the engine of our Vauxhall in our drive, the car in this photo.

Out on the green I fired an arrow high in the air; up it went, up and up, turning over at the apex of its flight down it came into our garden and straight onto the wing of the car next to dad's head. Luckily it never landed directly on the top of the wing, or God forbid, on his head. But it did land on the beveled outside edge of the front wing.

Had it landed directly on the top of the wing, without doubt it would have punctured through the metal just as easily as it would have penetrated dad's skull from tip to barrel; *doesn't bear thinking about*. As it was, it bounced off leaving a dent and bare metal. This was another bloody good hiding from dad; fortunately I was wearing my lederhosen.

After three successful 5th November bonfire nights arranged by our Cub Scout leaders and parents, us kids gradually took over and managed the whole thing on our own.

The 'hole-field' became the new site for Guy Fawkes night. It became the field where we built the bonfire.

The new estate was still an ongoing project; houses had not yet started to be built on our field. Eventually this part of the field would become 'Poppyfield's' bungalows for the elderly, but in 1968 the new estate still ended at White Horse Road.

People in the village would save any old burnable items for us kids to collect and during October we would go round with our trolleys and wheelbarrows picking up newspaper, wood, old furniture, tires, anything burnable we could get hold of.

We would then go, in a big gang to Murhill woods to cut down a tree for the bonfire center-pole. It doesn't seem credible looking back that our parents let us loose in a gang in the village with axes, bill-hooks and ex-British army jungle machetes.

Fred & little grannies house next to the Wheatsheave. Photo taken 2013

It's even more surprising that we weren't reported for cutting the tree down. We would hack away at a thirty-foot young tree and then strip all the branches. We'd then tie ropes along its length and half a dozen kids would drag the pole up through the woods to the road. All the others, girls included, would carry or drag the branches stripped from the main trunk. It was a long haul back up the hill to the old village, here we would rest for a while outside the empty cottage that was previously the home of my great grandparents.

We would quench our thirst from the outside tap in the garden before starting the second easier half of our trek down through the council estate to the 'hole field'; in all a good mile and a half from the hamlet of Murhill.

Then if we had time, or perhaps the next day, we would dig a hole to take the end of the pole and with strength and ingenuity way beyond our years pull and push the pole upright, fill in round the base and stamp it down. The centre pole was up and from here we started piling the rubbish around the base. Over the next few weeks it would grow and grow.

If anyone stopped us and asked why we were chopping down a

young tree we told them as bold as brass 'its bonfire night and we need a centre pole.'

After all it was only a once a year thing for the village; a special night bonfire night; they would say 'oh yes of course,' and leave us to it. I can't ever remember anyone telling us off, or telling us not to do it.

We also made an effigy of Guy Fawkes. A pair of old trousers, a coat and an old woollen sock would be stuffed with straw. The sock would be the head, tied down inside the coat with a mask on the front and some old piece of headwear plonked on the top. We would then sit our Guy Fawkes in a wheel barrow and one evening after tea go out annoying the pants off people by singing a penny for the guy outside their front doors. Occasionally people would shout at us to bugger-off or I'll phone the police, but in the main people would put their hands in their pockets and give us a bob or two toward our fireworks. One year we didn't even bother with a real guy we dressed-up Kev in all the old clobber and stuck a paper mask on his head with an old cap. The only person who noticed was my auntie Dot who opened the door with a cheery, 'hello boys' and 'you've been talked into something else then Kevin?'

At the end of the evening we would go back to one of our houses and split up the spoils, a few shillings each would be a good bounty and buy quite a few bangers rockets and jumping jacks.

This was long before the introduction from America of the boring 'Trick or Treat'.

Halloween at that time wasn't really celebrated; bonfire night was the special night where a large percentage of the village families got together, chatted, watched their kids have fun; ate baked potatoes and sausages and let off fireworks. Now, sadly it's all but forgotten; people still go to arranged firework displays; but the days of the effigy on top of the fire and the centre pole have faded away; again another sad loss of tradition.

A few days before the event Pete and I would go with dad to buy a couple of quid's worth of rockets, roman candles, Catherine wheels and bangers from Stephen Little's dad at the Wheatsheaf. Long before the fifth we had done our best to get hold of fireworks, bought for us by the older lads like Kevin's brother Malcolm and Andrew Rendell. We would nick a box of matches from home and in the dark November evenings run round the village creating havoc putting bangers under dustbin lids, in dog poo, or leaving them on the door step of people we didn't like; light the banger, drop it on the step, ring the bell and run away, what a hoot!

Only once in all the years us kids built the village bonfire was it

Mr & Mrs Little's shop, The Wheatsheaf. Fred and Annie Sartain's house next door. Old Colonel Walkers stately home behind the wall on the left.

Deliberately burned down prior to the day. It was November 1969, about a week before the big night.

I was at home and a knock came at the door. It was Bernard.

'Quick get your coat and shoes on, someone's burned our bonfire down!'

Sure enough from our front door I could see the sparks flying high in the sky behind Sticky's house. Even mum and dad came running to see what was happening. The blaze was so big the fire engine was on the way from Bradford-on-Avon. However by the time they arrived, connected up the hose and got the water flowing the fire had lost its intensity, so the firemen stood with us and watched it burn.

We were dumbstruck. Who did this? The kids from the new estate? A bunch of kids from another village? That wouldn't be unusual, there was inter-village rivalry and burning down another village bonfire was not unheard of; but 7.00pm was quite early in the evening and no one had heard or seen any gangs of kids.

Rumour went round later that it was a boy from Murhill, but it was never proved.

We had five days to rebuild. And we did it. Everyone in the village chipped in; we didn't bother with another centre pole we just piled the rubbish as high as we could get it. Dad even brought home three old Marcos Car fiberglass mouldings, which really bumped up the volume.

The bonfire night celebration was held on the 5th November.

It didn't matter if it was a work or school day, or whether it was raining, the bonfire went ahead. This year it was a Wednesday and we rushed home from school full of anticipation; got changed into our scruffy old clothes, crammed a sandwich in our mouth and headed up to the 'holefield'.

The fire was due to start around 6.30pm.Maurice and dad would come along with a can of petrol to get the fire going. We kids had sticks with paper wrapped round the end and after dripping petrol round the base of the fire the paper would be lit and the sticks hurled onto the fire.

When we arrived at the field it was dark, we walked up Dane Rise with our fireworks under our arms and arriving at the field we saw what must have been a hundred people standing around in groups waiting for us the village kids, the stars of the show to ignite the fire and get the festivities started. It was a great night.

I remember it being dry but very cold, but once the fire got going people would soon warm up and gather in groups and let off their fireworks. Many people were from the new estate, people we didn't even know. Once the fire got going the heat was so intense that we would be pushed further back into the long dried winter grass. This went on for a few hours and people would slowly drift home. The fire would burn itself out overnight with just a few of the older boys and girls hanging out chatting and smoking.

In all the years we kids built the village bonfire and I suppose there were six in all, three arranged by the Cubs and three arranged by the village kids themselves; no one ever got hurt.

They were great fun and showed just how we kids had great tenacity and initiative in planning and working together to get the show on the road.

Our parents never really interfered. We weren't mollycoddled we were left to get on with it. Either our parents were completely naive or they just trusted that we needed to be allowed to form our own awareness and personalities by being allowed (by today's standards) this unprecedented freedom. Whatever it was, it was great, none of us would have wanted it any other way. It didn't really vary from one house to the next. Only Gary Hancock's parents restricted him to the estate but in truth he was a few years younger and Wendy his mum being younger than most of our mums was more switched on to what we got up to.

Following the birth of my cousin Horst in August 1968 and our brief meeting with my auntie and uncle in Mulheim, plans were made to visit them at their house in Bavaria.

Mum especially looked forward to seeing her younger sister at home, and the house in which she lived.

Their flat was in the small village of Geltendorf in Bavaria, south Germany, thirty miles to the west of Munich,

Mum and dad decided we would visit over the coming Christmas and New Year.

Of course, as usual the trip would take place by car. The trip would start with our normal 180 mile trek to Dover, a trip we were so used to doing we could almost do it blindfold.

Then from the ferry a 550 mile drive south almost to the border with Austria. Not only was this trip across Europe three times longer than our usual trip to Mulheim, but we were doing it in the middle of winter.

We'd done a long trip down into Austria and Switzerland in 1964, but that had been a summer holiday four years earlier, and it had been done in little stages, stopping for a few days in different locations with no deadlines to meet.

Dad meticulously prepared the car, changing the drive belts fitting new wipers and any engine hoses that looked in the smallest way to be perished. A new thermostat was fitted, and a collection of tools and spares boxed in the boot. The one thing we never even considered were tires, of course we only had summer tires and cross-ply's at that. The last thing you'd want to be driving on with snow and ice under the car.

It was a long, long, journey. We left just before midnight on Friday 20th December booked on the 6am Saturday morning ferry from Dover to Calais. We took the A4 as far as Slough joining the recently completed M4 section into London; then coming off the Chiswick flyover to join the A205 South Circular road till it hit the A2, then the last leg to Dover. We did this route so many times that by the time I was thirteen I could direct dad through the suburbs of South London like a local.

The crossing was short and by 8am we were heading directly across France to Luxembourg then Saarbrucken, Karlsruhe, and Stuttgart. This was a grave mistake. No real motorways made for a slow journey and it took us 10 hours before we hit the Autobahn at Karlsruhe. We were tired and so was dad. As well as the long distance the weather was getting colder with freezing fog and snow flurries. However we were now on Autobahn, except for the last 40 miles, for the remainder of the journey. Our stops for coffee, toilet, and leg stretches became more frequent.

Snow lay deep on the high ground to the west of Stuttgart but fortunately the Autobahn was clear. It was bitterly cold and well below freezing. We eventually arrived in Geltendorf at midnight, twenty four hours after leaving home.

Over the last hundred miles the snow on the ground had increased and in Geltendorf it was a thick carpet half a meter deep.

Entering the village we stopped at a phone box for mum to get the final directions from my aunt; as she got out the car she fell flat on her back, the roads were like glass with ice. Dad had been flying along without a care in the world. It's a wonder we hadn't ended up in a ditch!

My aunt and uncle's second floor flat was warm and welcoming. With three bedrooms we weren't that crowded. Pete and I had a good sized room with bunk beds and after a quick wash and a cup of hot chocolate we were soon asleep.

We awoke to a wonderland of white.

During the early hours of the morning the temperature had risen and it'd started to snow, huge flakes falling like 'down' from a pillow. Pete and I had never seen anything like it. This was real snow!

Mum and dad were already up and organised. Some of the cases were out of the car and our wash things were in the bathroom. I looked forward to a lovely hot shower, a luxury we didn't have in 2 Poston Way.

As I got dressed after my shower I could hear the village church bells ringing; a lovely sound you hear all over Germany on a Sunday morning.

It was a Sunday morning; Sunday 22st December 1968, three days away from Christmas.

This would be a very different Christmas for Pete and I; we didn't even know if mum and dad had brought us any presents. If they had then they had been smuggled into the car when we weren't around. But I knew that we would be doing some great stuff over this holiday; presents this year were not important.

My auntie's flat had a big balcony and my brother and I were longing to open the patio door and stand looking out over the village in the snow; as we entered the kitchen we asked if we could go outside but we were told to sit down we were about to have breakfast with the family.

But my uncle had other ideas, he was tuned in to mine and Pete's excitement and with a wink he disappeared returning a few minutes later with a scooped shaped snow shovel from the cellar. He promptly opened the patio door and cleared the standing area by shoveling the deep snow into the garden below. Then with a laugh and a few words to mum which I interpreted as telling her not to be so stuffy, he pushed Pete and I out onto the balcony.

When I first met my uncle in the summer I liked him instantly, he was good fun; he knew Pete and I had never seen snow like this before, he also knew that the snow could ease-off or even stop before we had finished breakfast. We wanted to stand and watch a blizzard of snow unlike anything we had ever seen in Wiltshire, even taking into account the snow of 1963 and he was quite prepared to indulge us.

On our auntie and uncles balcony our first morning in Geltendorf, Bavaria, Dec 1968.

Reprimanded, mum sat with my auntie, little Elke and Horst in his high chair at the table; but after a few minutes everyone wanted to come outside.

It was amazing, as odd as it sounds you could actually hear the snow falling it was like a murmur coming in waves. The bells had stopped, there was no one to be seen and no sound of traffic; a scene from a fairy tale; then we went back inside for 'brekkie'.

Breakfast was a long drawn out affair with lots of chatter, questions and catching up. I looked at my lovely little cousin Elke. She was approaching her second birthday and she was adorable. Horst as well, like any baby of four months not yet a person in my juvenile eyes, whereas his elder sister was a walking talking little doll of a thing. But they were both lovely and we, especially Horst, Elke and I were to become firm friends for life.

After breakfast Pete and I got dressed up in our warm winter clothes to help dad unload the car, which after a night in the drive looked like a big white bubble. We went down with the snow shovel and under my uncle's direction started clearing the snow, neatly in good German tradition I might add, to the side of the drive.

The neighbours from the flat below came out to help and we were introduced. I was amazed how strong the Bavarian dialect was; it sounded very different to the German spoken in the Rhineland and I would come to learn that different words were used for certain things and that in Bayern they were a very independent people.

The baggage was taken upstairs and the snow removed from the car and the drive. Pete and I were free to get on with building a snowman. The plan discussed over breakfast was that the morning would be spent indoors generally relaxing, talking and

Dad clearing the snow from the car our first morning in Geltendorf Christmas 1968

drinking coffee. After lunch we would all go together with the toboggan to a field on the other side of the village for some sledging fun.

The first thing Pete and I discovered was Bavarian snow is not like English snow; it's dry, soft and crunchy and very difficult to bind together. To make a snow-ball we really had to push our two hands together hard to form the ball, otherwise it would just crumble back into individual flakes; even then we had to do it with bare hands, in our mother's knitted woollen mittens there was no chance, the snow stuck to the wool.

Pete and I spent the morning building our snowman; we didn't see a soul, it was like an uninhabited village.

Snowman unfinished but suffering from the cold in our inappropriate English style winter-wear, Pete and I went in the house for a hot drink. Already our clothes and gloves were wet; our only footwear apart from our best shoes were our wellies, which may have kept our feet dry but they done nothing to keep our feet warm. We could see my aunt casting a disapproving eye over what our parents considered acceptable winter attire. I was certain that before Christmas Pete and I would own a lovely pair of chunky German snow boots and possibly some new winter clothing as well.

We had brought games and books to keep us occupied, so until lunch was prepared that's what Pete and I amused ourselves with.

Following lunch we all dressed in our winter clothes for a trip to a favourite hill in the village for some sledging. The neighbours downstairs lent us a second toboggan and all together we made our way along footpaths and bridleways across the village.

When we arrived we were amazed at the number of people; it seemed the whole village young and old had turned out for a Sunday afternoon of fun. It was a pretty decent hill... not perhaps as long and steep as our own 'Turleigh Downs' but not bad all the same. The snow had been compacted from the morning's fall and we had a great afternoon, all of us taking turns to fly down the hill and trudge wearily back to the top. By 3.30pm it was getting dusk and we were all whacked and so made our way home. We knew the hill and the snow would be going nowhere, Pete and I could return more or less when we wanted during our stay.

Everyone was early to bed that night. We were still very tired from our trip the day before, especially dad. Also my uncle still had two days of work before he finished for his Christmas break.

The town square Landsberg. Pete in wellies, me in my aunties mountain boots.

We had our evening meal and by 8.30pm Pete and I were in our bunks asleep.

At home in England both Pete and I had full blown feather quilts, the real McCoy; bought by our German grandmother when I was six years old; they were in no way similar to a British style eiderdown or the modern day duvet. They were thicker fluffier and far better, and I had slept under one of these quilts for so long I could no longer sleep comfortably under the old style top sheet blanket and eiderdown. These feather quilts were massive, one big cotton pouch filled with feathers under which you just snuggled and no matter how cold the bedroom, (remember in England this was still a pre-central heating era for most houses), I would be as warm as toast.

My auntie had given us quilts like these to sleep under and I slept the sleep of the dead.

I woke to the sound of my aunt and uncle moving around the flat; she was looking after the little ones, while at the same time seeing my uncle off to work.

A constant banging radiated from the kitchen which sounded very much like Elke smacking her spoon on the table top.

It was 7.15 and I was wide awake. I heard my uncle say goodbye to my aunt and the door open and close. I climbed out of bed and went through to the kitchen. My parents weren't around, Marlene had probably asked them to keep out of the way until Gerhard had left the house and the children had been fed; but I wandered into the kitchen said 'Gutten Morgen' and squeezed in at the window end of the corner seat where my cousin was sitting in his high chair. He just looked at me with his big blue eyes.

'Gutten Morgen Horst,' I said; then I looked at Elke and said the same.

Early days... Horst started crying and Elke slipped off the seat and hid under the table. Not the greatest start with my young cousins. Marlene laughing brought me a glass of fresh orange juice, a luxury we didn't get at 2 Poston Way and lifted my cousin from the high chair bouncing him in her arms. He stopped crying instantly and the next thing I knew I had him and my aunt had gone off to do something else. When I meet with my cousin now 46 years later a strapping lad taller than me, I remember back to that first morning we got to know each other. This time he didn't cry he just lay there gurgling and looking up at me, then mum came in and laughed saying perhaps I should stay behind when they go home and work as the nanny... maybe I should've.

The weir in Landsberg with the old town in the background.

Today was Monday; the plan was to go into town, the closest town being Landsberg am Lech roughly 10 miles away and do some shopping.

It was crispy cold but the sun was shining when we all piled into our car and headed out onto the main road for Landsberg.

Landsberg is a beautiful medieval town whose history goes back a thousand years. It was on the Crusader routes to the Holy Land nine hundred years ago and is now part of the historic romantic road which runs from Wurzburg in Northern Bayern, 220miles south to Fussen on the

Austrian border; a route that meanders through a hundred medieval towns and villages along the way.

This holiday, when I was twelve years old was going to be the start of a lifelong love affair with Landsberg, Fussen, and the mountains in Bavaria. I would also in later life come very close to moving to, living and working in Landsberg, but sadly to date have not fulfilled the ambition.

The old town of Landsberg sits in a valley on the river Lech. The buildings are old and the streets narrow and cobbled. A protective fortress wall surrounds the old town and like other fortress walls surrounding medieval towns in Germany you are still able to walk around a great deal of the town on top of them. Each street into the town leads through a large towered gate; similar to the type of gate you would expect to go through when entering a castle.

In the middle of the town is a large open area with a fountain and surrounding shops. This was also a car parking area but on that particular day was being cleared of snow by large bucket loaders and tipper trucks. 'Where are they taking all that snow?' we asked mum. Mum in turn asked Marlene who told us that the snow would be tipped over the railings and into the river over the other side in the park. Of course Pete and I wanted to see this, I suppose dad was just as interested as us, so as a group Marlene led us in that direction. We actually approached the river from the town side where a footpath followed the embankment the length of the town. Over the other side of the river we could see the latest tipper truck of snow pull up and guided by a workman standing to one side, reverse to a gap where the railings had been removed. Then the snow was tipped into the river below.

At this point a weir crosses the river, it curves across just below the road bridge and I suppose in length it would be nearly two hundred yards across. The large pool of still water above the weir was frozen solid with hundreds of ducks and other birds eating bread and other food being thrown by people onto the ice from the bridge. During the winter months the river level drops and the current runs quite slowly, it's not till the thaw in spring time that the river becomes a ragging torrent of melt from the mountains up stream.

At the end of the weir I could just make out a statue which appeared to be facing away from us. I asked my auntie what, or who it was. She said it was the statue of the 'Old Man of the Lech' the mythical old man who watches over the river.

On another day we would return to the town and explore the footpaths and visit the deer park which followed the river on the other side of the bridge. Pete and I really looked forward to this. Little did I know then that when we did return in a week's time we would be accompanied by a young teenage girl slightly younger than me who would become another lifelong friend; Monika Michenfelder.

We turned round and headed back into town. Marlene needed to do some food shopping and dad took Pete and I to find some decent winter boots. My wonderful aunt had already given her sister earache over my brother's and my footwear.

Boots adequate for the snow had not been written into my parents' holiday budget but all the same we were going to get something more appropriate then wellies. Well done Marlene!

Old man of the 'Lech' statue on Landsberg bridge

By the end of the day Pete and I did end up with a lovely pair of boots each; proper winter style boots, high over the ankle with tags rather than holes for the laces. Lace holes of course let in the water and snow. By the time I went in the army in 1971 I had outgrown my boots but they were still going strong and they were passed on to my brother. In the long term mum ended up wearing Peter's. I'm sure my aunt and uncle paid for these boots.

I have a great selection of photos from this holiday and when I look at them I recognise none of the clothing; I'm sure the majority of it was borrowed from my aunt, uncle, and perhaps dare I say it even friends of theirs.

We came to minus fifteen degree Bavaria totally unprepared in the dress sense but at least dad put anti-freeze in the radiator of the car.

All finished in town and with the food stocks replenished we headed home. Pete and I were looking forward to trying our new boots that afternoon and taking the sledges back to the hillside.

After lunch off we went again with mum and dad and had a great afternoon.

The following day was Christmas Eve. Pete and I were allowed to explore the village and play out until lunch time, but then we were expected to clean up for the afternoon, as after all it was a religious holiday and these are taken very seriously in predominantly catholic

Bavaria.

The local kids were skating on the village pond which Marlene said was common in all the villages. The ice was almost two feet thick and there was no fear of going through. My aunt had a pair of skates which fitted me, although not perfectly, as they were slightly tight but I was keen to have a go. I'd never been on skates before and didn't know that men's skates differed in appearance to women's. I had been on roller skates which I was reliably informed would make ice skating come as second nature. However I had no intention of making a fool of myself in front of the village kids and my plan was to wait until no other kids were around.

The sledging hill in Geltendorf.
Pete, mum with Elke, me, Gerhart on the sledge.

It doesn't always go to plan. Sure Pete and I turned up at the pond when only a couple of kids were there, but after all, schools had broken up and children were at home all day so it was inevitable that one or two would be around. I sat down removed my boots and put on the skates, lovely white figure-skating skates... for a woman!

By the time I had staggered drunk like to the middle of the pond, falling a few times on the way the word had gone round that the English boys were trying to skate on the pond; a reasonable crowd had gathered. I was not going to get off lightly.

My audience saw this as a mighty comedy act and my attempts on the ice were met with hoots of laughter; I made my way as calmly and dignified as my skates and inexperience would allow back to the side of the pond, removed the skates, donned my boots and made my way home.

In all the years Pete and I had been coming to Germany and other parts of Europe we had never had a problem making friends; on camp sites around my uncle Dieter's in Duisburg, and at my Oma's in Mulheim.

But here the kids didn't seem so friendly; I resented the laughter and didn't realise that some of it was due to me wearing my auntie's boots. I swore it would be a good few years before I tried ice skating again.

After lunch we would shower and dress in our best clothes. My uncle had finished work early and he, dad, Pete, and I would go for a walk through the forest while my mum and aunt stayed at home dressing the tree and finalising the cooking and baking for the next three days.

My uncle brought Elke with us, leaving Horst with Marlene while we went and had a long walk through the forest tracks in the snow. My German was better than dad's and I talked and interpreted between dad and my uncle. We came back into the village and as we walked up one of the footpaths two boys appeared laughing, pointing, and poking fun at Pete and me.

My uncle shouted at them and with a parting shot they ran off.

I asked my uncle what the problem was but he just said 'gar nichts,' really nothing... But I was annoyed; I knew they were mocking Pete and I and I wanted to know what it was all about. When we got home I asked mum to get an explanation from my uncle, I wasn't going to accept no as an answer.

My uncle said they were just taking the Mickey. They had seen me on the ice and were just poking fun; I should forget about it.

I was not amused; from now on I would be on my guard.

The house looked and smelled lovely, we had brought a Turkey with us that had been cooking all morning and the smell wafted through the house, making us feel really hungry.

After a light lunch mum sent Pete and I to our room. Have a lie down, snooze or read your books she said, it will be a long evening and you'll both want to see Christmas in at midnight.

The next thing I knew dad was shaking me by the shoulder. 'Come on,' he said, 'time to start Christmas.'

This year was going to be a real German Christmas a big meal of cold meats and cheeses on the eve, with Christmas music playing and the presents dished out before bed. No one would go to sleep before midnight.

The following day mum, with my aunt's help, would prepare a proper English roast dinner with all the trimmings, crackers and pud to follow. My parents had brought it all from home.

Pete and I showered and got dressed in our best. We went through into the open plan living room, kitchen. The table was laid, the lights dimmed down and carols playing on the record player. The tree all decorated and the lights twinkling had stacks of presents underneath. Some I could tell had been wrapped in England before we left.

It was now 5.30 and dark outside, I could make out the snow falling in the streetlights beneath the kitchen window; magical... a Christmas like we had never had before.

One by one we all gathered in the front room and my uncle opened a bottle of sparkling wine and we all had a glass including Pete and I; the beginning of a lovely evening.

We chatted and laughed, I had to recite my escapade with the skates and my uncle said I should never have been let loose with women's skates. He blamed my mum and aunt for my embarrassment and promised he would take us both skating proper in Landsberg before the end of the holiday. Slowly I too had to see the funny side and join in the laughter.

Around 7pm we moved to the table for our buffet meal of breads, hams, cheeses, and pickles; followed by fruit flan with cream, and a selection of wonderful sliced cake that my aunt bought in the Stadt cafe in Landsberg. It was gone nine before the table was cleared and we all sat with a drink. The little ones were asleep and my aunt would look in on them regularly. Horst of course needed far more regular feeding then Elke. Then it was time to dish out presents. I can't remember now all the gifts that were passed round. I do remember getting a pair of short ski type shoes from my aunt and uncle. I was very impressed until I came to use them but found they didn't really work unless I was on tightly compressed snow and that I also needed a steep hill for them to be in any way effective. A kind thought but a bit of a white elephant in Winsley. I also got a bottle green cardigan with black buttons knitted by mum. I don't like green now and I never liked green then, but wear it I had to and did so most of that holiday.

Years later when I was in the army mum was still sending me knitted items to my unit in Germany. I remember the Christmas parcel turning up in December 1974 with a salmon coloured jumper... God Bless her, it never got worn.

I was amazed to see my little cousin Elke at twenty two months getting her first pair of skis. This I was told was quite normal; kids are on skis as soon as they start to walk.

We went to bed just after midnight happy and contented, full of lovely food and with a pile of presents at the end of the bed.

Christmas day was a lazy day. We all slept late, except of course for my aunt looking after Horst and Elke; we had breakfast of lovely German rolls and boiled eggs.

Our big roast was planned for the evening so again it was time for some fresh air, and this time Marlene came with us and the children. We drove to a small village on the Ammersee, a big lake full of yachts in the summer but frozen solid in winter. It was only a short distance of five miles or so and when we got there I was amazed how many people were out on the ice. Hundreds; skating, curling, and in the distance I could see sails like dinghy sails. My uncle told me these were people ice yachting, sailing boats on long skis propelled by the wind.

We walked for miles along the footpath between the village and the lake then returned across the ice. We got home around 3pm and the vegetables already prepared were put in the roasting tin. Most of the food preparation had been done; the main item needing a long boil in water was the Christmas pudding. There was no microwave in my aunt's house in 1968.

The meal was wonderful and around 9pm Pete and I without any argument were ready for bed. Thanking our parents, our uncle and aunt for a lovely time we both cleaned our teeth and hit the sack.

Thursday was Boxing Day and another slow day. We had planned to go into Munich but decided to leave it till the Saturday. Nothing would be open in the city for the next couple of days, even the buildings for tourists would be closed.

But my uncle had a great idea. We would drive to the Olympic Park already underway for the 1972 games and have a look at the construction. Also beside the stadium BMW were building their new headquarters, a building that would become an iconic landmark; not only in the city but internationally. Four cylindrical towers with the flying saucer shaped museum below.

We drove into the city, the roads reasonably clear of snow, a pretty straightforward route. We left the car in the Luipold Park a half mile away from the Olympic park and walked back to view the construction. Much of the site had been sealed off, but we could walk the purpose laid pavements that ran though the site. It was a huge project. The base for the Olympic tower was already under construction; also the concrete pad areas that were to take the suspended metal frames for the glass roofs of the swimming pool, gymnasium, and the football pitch were nearly all underway. A huge plan mounted on a hoarding helped my uncle explain the site and layout and how the finished park would look with acres of grassed areas a boating lake and outside concert areas.

The BMW factory on the other side of the inner ring road was raising from the ground; the cylindrical towers symbolic of the cylinders of a car engine. Across the road my uncle pointed out the rows of flats being built to house the Olympic athletes.

This accommodation site in a few years would become forever synonymous with 1970s European terrorism when a Palestine terrorist group held the Israel Olympic team hostage.

On September 5th a group of eight Palestinian terrorists belonging to the Black September organisation broke into the Olympic Village and took nine Israeli athletes, coaches and officials hostage in their apartments. Two of the hostages who resisted were killed in the first moments of the break-in; the subsequent standoff in the Olympic Village lasted for almost 18 hours.

Late in the evening of September 5th, the terrorists and their hostages were transferred by helicopter to the military airport of Fürstenfeldbruck ostensibly to board a plane bound for an undetermined Arab country. The German authorities planned to ambush them there, but underestimated the number of terrorists and were thus undermanned. During a botched rescue attempt, all of the Israeli hostages were killed. Four of them were shot, then incinerated when a Palestinian detonated a grenade inside the helicopter in which the hostages were sitting. The five remaining hostages were then machine-gunned by another terrorist. All but three of the Palestinians were killed as well. Although arrested and imprisoned pending trial, the three PLO survivors were released by the West German government on October 29, 1972 in exchange for a hijacked Lufthansa jet.

This would be the start of a decade of extreme European terrorism.

The construction project was really interesting and we walked in a big circle around the area using the footpaths that had been specially constructed for the public to view. My uncle told us the whole venue would be covered with glass roofs and pointed out the tower under construction that would be almost three hundred meters high with a restaurant and rotating observation gallery at the top. I looked in wonder and hoped that one day I'd get to the top, the view would be fantastic.

It was gone lunch time before we got back to the car.

A great deal of people were out walking or sitting in the winter sunshine on benches watching the world go by, it was lovely; a little hut selling quick food was giving out a lovely smell of cooking and reminded us how hungry we were. These 'Imbis' huts as they are called were very popular with German people before the invasion of McDonalds and Burger King.

They cooked bratwurst, Bavarian weisswurst and schaschlick, meat squares on skewers with onion and pepper slow cooked in a curried tomato and onion sauce. This was going to be today's lunch and very yummy it was.

We were warm now after our walk but the temperature was only one degree so we grabbed seats in the sun and ordered our feast with beers to wash it down. I was also allowed a small glass of beer, but Pete had applesaft, German apple juice.

Dad, Pete, me and mum with Elke. Geltendorf 1968.

I had always loved this type of German fast food and tucked into my selection. The only sausage I really didn't like was the wiesswurst (white sausage) it just looked too insipid and unappetising to me. We returned home and by the time we got there it was dusk.

The following day Pete and I again took the sledge to the hill; dad and mum joined us and we had a great afternoon.

Saturday morning dawned bright and cold and wrapping up warm we walked to Geltendorf station to catch the train directly into the city centre.

On the way to the station the two boys appeared again watching us from a distance. I was beginning to find them very annoying.

The day was spent looking around the city centre visiting tourist sites and shops. At lunch we had cake and hot chocolate in a lovely café in Mairenplatz slap-bang in the middle of the city. After a couple more churches and Kauf-house's (big stores) we caught the train home. We had gone to the famous Hofbrauhaus for a beer but it was so packed with people dad and mum decided not to go in. 'To touristy,' dad said. I was really disappointed because my uncle had been going on about the massive beer hall and its history. Apparently everyone who visited Munich had this place on the list of places to visit for a stein of Hofbrau from their own brewery and we'd stuck our heads in the door and left. I don't think dad was comfortable with taking Pete and me into such a rowdy atmosphere. But unknown to Pete and me at the time, we would return...

Sunday was a slow start and after breakfast we went again to the Ammersee. This time however we drove down the east side to Monastery Andechs. The Monastery has its own restaurant and the monks brew their own beer. It was another beer tasting session for dad and my uncle. We took a walk along the lake and returned for a full blown Sunday evening meal.

Monday we had visitors coming from Munich, friends of my aunt and uncle; Mr & Mrs Michenfelder and their children Monika and Peter.

In the morning Pete and I amused ourselves in the village; we took the sledge to the hill and spent a couple of hours going up and down. I tried my new skate ski shoes (for the want of a better name). They weren't that successful but I wasn't going to let on and disappoint my aunt and uncle by telling them the shoes didn't work.

On the way home as Pete and I walked and talked pulling the sledge, snowballs rained down from behind us. Looking round I saw again it was the two kids who were becoming a prize pain in the ass. This time they were in for a shock. I'd bang there bloody heads together. I turned and ran back down the road toward them; a look of horror came over their faces. As they turned and bolted for it; I was only yards from catching the slower of the two when they turned into a driveway and ran round the back of the house.

I didn't go in; I stopped at the gate while they looked around the corner of the house shouting abuse at me. I was twelve and they were no younger than me, they should've known better and they bloody well would if I got hold of them. I pretended to walk away stopping a few yards and standing against the hedge hoping they would reappear and I could jump on them. They did look round the corner of the drive but seeing my young brother waiting a couple of hundred yards away quickly guessed my game and disappeared. Still I now knew where they lived and I would get my revenge.

I told Pete not to say anything to mum and dad, I thought they would forbid me to get involved and I didn't want to be told not to give the pair of them a hiding; I was determined their time would come.

Our guests turned up around 2.30pm and we were introduced.

Monika was a year or so younger than me and her brother Peter was two years younger than my brother. Monika was a really lovely looking girl, a tanned open face with big blue eyes and chestnut hair and I didn't do a very good job of hiding my interest; the adults were soon laughing at me. The sitting room table was laid for coffee and cake for the adults, while we four kids were placed together at the kitchen table. We tucked in. I was astounded at how well Monika could speak English; her grasp of the language was almost perfect with no shyness of using it. Listening to her talking to Pete and me at the table her mother and father were obviously very proud of her. She asked us what we had been doing and where we had been and as well as talking to Pete and me she translated our English into German for her brother. I was very impressed. We played board games at the table while our parents sat and chatted; then around 7pm Marlene dug out a strange looking pot with skewers that I'd never seen before; a 'Fondue set'. The container holds boiling fat with a flame burning underneath and you sit with piles of cubed raw chicken, pork, and beef and with your skewer fry the meat in the fat, apparently all the rage for dinner parties on the continent,(the expression used for any country on the other side of the channel).

Of course my mum wanted a set and that was the next, 'impress the neighbours', item on the shopping list.

Actually it was quite enjoyable sitting there drinking and cooking food over a stove like gypsies. Bloody dangerous though!

Lots of happy chatter going on around the table and I could understand a great deal of the conversation.

Monika's mum and dad were saying how good it was for Monika to be able to use her English and vice-versa; my Mum was saying how Steven and Peter must talk in German to her; a sentence she had rolled out continually over the years.

I didn't want the evening to end and Monika to leave. To me she was the best thing to have happened on the holiday.

Through the heavily accented Bavarian dialect I could grasp snippets of the conversation, such as, Monika bleiben, meaning to stay and schlafen to sleep... I began to realize that my mum, auntie, and Monika's parents were discussing Monika staying over. I pretended not to notice but my fingers were tightly crossed. Marlene was grinning and rattled a few sentences off at Monika; she laughed and replied in German I could understand as yes, why not. Then my aunt looked at me grinning and asked me in broken English -'you understand Steven yes?' I, in embarrassment just shrugged my shoulders and nodded, probably going red at the same time.

Monika said to me in her near perfect English, 'Steve is it ok if I stay till Wednesday?' With all the adults staring at me around the table I didn't know where to look; I just stammered my consent and said it would be fine.

So Monika was to stay over tonight, tomorrow which was New Year's Eve, and be here all day Wednesday. She would sleep on the top bunk, with Pete and me sharing the bottom bunk; then her dad would pick her up Wednesday in the afternoon.

So she would be staying with us on New Year's Eve, wow how lucky was I.

With the wink I got from my aunt, I knew she had been the one to set this up.

Monika's parents and Peter left very late and we tumbled into our bunks; Monika peering over the edge at Pete and I sleeping head to toe on the bottom bunk she said goodnight. I went to sleep a contented teenager. This was the beginning of a lifelong friendship.

The following day New Year's Eve, we all went to Landsberg for a walk around the town walls and through the deer park. Our trek complete, off we went to enjoy more coffee and cake in the Stadt Café; this pastime was becoming a very indulgent habit; but with only three days of our holiday left who cares; cake like this you don't get in Trowbridge.

We arrived back at my aunt's in the early afternoon.

We skipped lunch knowing that as it was New Year's Eve we would be having a special meal in the evening and nibbles on the table up till midnight. The three of us had already been told we could stay up and see in the New Year.

For a while we decided to go into the garden to do some repair work to the snowman and throw snowballs at each other.

We weren't in the garden long before they turned up; the two brats who had taunted me like an itch you can't scratch during the time at my aunt's. But oh boy, this time they had chosen the wrong day. Today I had a girl in my company and there was no way in the world they were going to show me up in front of her.

They believed they were secure on the road above my aunt's garden. The five foot wooden boundary fence and a steep embankment a couple of yards in height from the garden to the road made them feel safe. They were sorely mistaken... They stood on the road shouting and making faces. Monika stopped in her tracks looking at them in amusement and then at me. Then she shouted at them to go away. (I know this as I asked her afterwards what she had said.) Her shout had the two kids rolling round with laughter, but they weren't concentrating.

New Years Eve Dec 68.
Me, Pete, Monika & Elke.
Dad, mum & Marlene.

I was at the fence and over before they realised. They started to run but their house was a good half mile ahead of them and I was only yards behind. I rugby tackled the first to the ground pushing his face into the snow on the road then taking my fist to the back of his head. He was screaming. By now his mate or brother, or whoever he was, had come back and was stood near me shouting at me to stop. In a flash I was off the first boy and lashed out at the second. I hit him hard and he stumbled back onto the ground. I stood over the pair of them telling them to get up. Cowering they both climbed to their feet and I shoved both of them in the chest telling them in no uncertain terms, with raised fists making my point perfectly clear, that if there was a next time they wouldn't get off so lightly. They were both openly crying by this time and I just turned and walked away. When I turned back they had arms round each other obviously sobbing while shuffling their way down the road. They had it coming...

As I walked back I could see my mum, dad, well the whole family actually waiting for me at the junction across from my aunt's garden. Heated debate was going on. I didn't care in the eyes of my brother and my new found friend I was a hero. The kids got what was coming to them. I would hear no more piss-take from them.

I was escorted into the house by my stern looking parents, but it was only a sham telling off... The, 'you should have turned the other cheek,' type of lecture for the benefit of my aunt and uncle. Both Pete and Monika had risen in my defence telling the adults what had happened and in all honesty the adults all agreed the boys had it coming. It wasn't as if they were younger than me, they were roughly the same age and it was two against one. I went in for my shower pretty chuffed with myself.

Us kids sat down to play a board game, Mensch aerger dich nicht (Don't get angry);a game similar to Ludo where you have to get your four buttons home while trying to blast each other off the board; a great fun family game which we still have at mum's house to this very day.

The phone rang and my uncle picked it and spoke to the person on the other end. I could tell it was one of Monika's parents as she was listening in and grinning and nodding at me. I understood some of the one sided conversation but I was still having extreme difficulty with my uncle's strong accent. I knew the following day Monika's parents were coming to pick her up; I didn't know what time I only hoped it would be as late as possible. I really didn't want to say goodbye to her. My uncle was looking across at us and grinning and Monika was nodding saying yes, yes, yes... my uncle then handed the phone over to Monika and went to talk to my mum.

Monika came back and sat down. 'My father would like to take us to Munich tomorrow to the circus,' she said, 'just us children... would you like to go?' Would we like to go!? 'Yes of course,' Pete and I said in union. 'Your uncle will talk to your mum and dad and if it is ok they will tell my father when he rings later to wish us all a Good New Year. He will then pick us up in the car later tomorrow morning.'

Wow, that sounded fantastic to me. I ran through to my parents to ask if it was ok. They said if it wasn't too much trouble for the Michenfelder's then yes we could go. Fantastic!

That would give us two more days in Geltendorf as we were set to leave in the very early hours of Saturday morning to catch the afternoon ferry back to Dover from Calais.

We had a lovely evening and around midnight telephone calls were made to my uncles and my grandmother in the north of the country. Monika phoned her mum and dad and they were told it was ok for Pete and me to go with them the following day. Once again we kids were allowed some fizzy wine and laughing and joking off we went to bed.

The next morning dawned bright but cold. Mr & Mrs Michenfelder and Peter turned up around eleven. We were going to drive into the city and have something to eat at an Imbiz before going to the circus. The tickets had already been purchased. How Monika's dad did this thirty years before the internet was born heaven only knows, but not only had he got tickets, they were front row seats!

The circus was in the middle of the city and our tickets were for the afternoon. We never went to an Imbiz. Monika's dad took us through the centre directly to the Hofbrau house. That was so cool. It was the one place I had wanted to go and peering into that massive beer hall a week before I had been really disappointed that my dad had decided not to go in.

But here we were, in what was without question the world's most famous pub.

It was and still is the biggest pub I've ever been in.

Rows of scrubbed wooded tables, with benches that seat up to twenty; waitresses rushing in between in their traditional white and black Bavarian serving dresses, there must have been fifty of them waltzing round the tables with huge steins of beer in each hand and black leather money pouches at their waist; they dropped the beer on the mats and then marked your beer mat with a pencil line. No money exchanged hands until you were finished. A system of honesty and trust; I'm sure anyone could have walked out without paying had they wished to do so.

In the far corner they had an area set aside for food; sausages of course, bratwurst, brockwurst or the Bavarian weisswurst with bread and mustard; that was the simple choice of the food.

We grabbed seats at a table and you really had to be quick, the place was heaving with people. Once seated it was only seconds before a waitress came up to ask us what we wanted. She took the food order and the drinks order and disappeared. Monika and I had kid's beer, a kind of non-alcoholic black beer similar to American root beer; the two Peters had apfelsaft. With these drinks a plate of mixed sausage had been ordered. Monika's dad was rubbing his hands with glee; he was just as happy as us kids.

It all came and we tucked in. When we had drunk the top from our black beer Monika's dad poured some real beer in from his litre jug. We had a great time. An hour later we left for the circus.

I remember we had seats right at the front and it was an old fashioned circus with animals, horses, tigers and camels. At the intermission I bought everyone an ice cream from my own money... I felt very grown up doing that.

When we came out it was dark and we were tired. I knew this would be the last hour I spent with Monika and I was very sad. We had become firm friends in the few days we had spent together. I wondered if I would ever see her again.

When we arrived at my aunt's it was a quick hello and goodbye. This was the third trip Mr Michenfelder had made that day from Munich to Geltendorf and they still had to go home.

Goodbyes were said and promises to keep in touch were made. I gave Monika a hug and a kiss on the cheek. We could hear the conversation which had already begun whether it was possible for Miss Michenfelder to visit England... my fingers were well and truly crossed. We waved them off, me with a heavy heart.

Friday morning while dad checked the car over Pete and I once again took the sledge to the hill for a final hour of fun. I wasn't concerned about the two boys. They wouldn't bother us again. In the afternoon we packed and by 7pm we were in bed. We had to be up at 2am and on the road by three. I went to bed thinking of my new found friend. Maybe, just maybe she would get to visit us in Winsley.

We woke up in the dark, splashed some water over our faces and cleaned our teeth. This kind of midnight travel was not unusual to Pete and me and neither of us got disgruntled about it. We had 'brekkie' and said goodbye to my aunt and uncle.

My dad, mum and uncle had poured over the map to find a better route home. My uncle had travelled extensively over Germany and was well placed to advise.

It was decided that we would go as far as Karlsruhe then head north following the Rhine as far as Köln, then head west to Aachen. On the map this looked a great deal further than the direct route we had taken across France on the way down. But the return journey was Autobahn almost all the way and my uncle assured us would knock literally hours off of the journey.

He was right; with our very comfortable Ford Zephyr 2.5 able to cruise easily up to 85mph dad ate up the miles. It was the early hours of Saturday morning with hardly any traffic on the road.

We stopped every two hours to stretch our legs. We had food and drink in the car and munched on the goodies my mum and aunt had packed as we drove. Pete and I were hardened travelers, we'd travelled thousands of miles crisscrossing Europe since the day we were born and looking at the world go by out of the window was an education for us.

At Liege the Autobahn ran out and we were on single carriageway into Brussels. This was the only difficult part of the journey as there was no ring route around Brussels at that time. Normally when we visited Oma we would cross to Oostende then go on a more northerly route to Antwerp and Monchengladbach.

But once we had found our way through the city we had motorway to the coast at Oostende. Then it was just a case of following the coast road south to Calais. Mum booked us in and phoned Marlene while we waited in the car. Dad slept until boarding and then promptly fell asleep for the crossing.

Once in Dover we were on familiar territory. The trip up to London and round the south circular road to the Chiswick flyover, the familiar route, then the completed section of M4 as far as Slough.

Calne, Melksham, Bradford-on-Avon and home; car in the drive we were all sound asleep by 3am, almost twenty four hours after leaving my aunt and uncle's house.

It had been a lovely holiday.

Back to school Monday we would have to see what 1969 and a new year would bring for the Burt family and in particular yours truly.

We didn't surface until lunch time, had a snack and then unloaded the car. Clean clothes were put away dirty clothes piled ready to go through the twin-tub. There was a knock on the door, Jeff and Bernard asking if they could come in and talk to us. Mum was not happy with that, there was too much going on but she let us go over to Pat's for an hour. I think she was glad to have us out of the way. Pat and Maurice had a telephone and she said she would be over soon to ask Pat if she could phone my aunt. Pete and I went across to Jeff's to tell them the story of our holiday. In the evening my gran walked down and spent an hour, then after some food Pete and I got our school things ready and went to bed.

A new term began at Nelson Haden on Monday 6th January 1969.

As we headed into spring the final touches were being put to the caravan. It was truly a work of a craftsman and dad was justifiably proud of himself.

The caravan was finished on the inside with a teak effect panelling and curtains at the windows hand stitched by mum.

Following the standard layout of the time it had a table and seats at the forward end. The table served as the centre section of a double bed.

Inside the van on the left hand side were the kitchen units and worktop incorporating a sink with manual foot pump and a gas hob. Above the sink and hob were cupboards and below the hob was a small oven. Little wall lights surrounded the van and everything ran off bottled gas.

A second wide sofa ran across the width of the van at the back, this also served as a lower sleeping bunk for Pete, me, or both of us should a friend come along. A rolled up canvas hammock style bed could be suspended on cups screwed to strengthen points in the sides above.

Opposite the kitchen there was a full length hanging locker and a small WC room with sink and chemical toilet.

Nothing in the van looked home-made. It was, as I said, a very professional job.

Dad did everything; plumbed up the water pump to run from a water container that stood outside the van; next to this would be an empty container to catch the kitchen sink waste. He plumbed in the gas system and wired in all the 12v electrics.

We backed the car up to the van, plugged in and switched on everything to give it a try. Every service worked faultlessly. Then it was the turn of the neighbours to come round sit inside and inspect dad's handiwork. Most everyone in the street was interested, they had all watched for two years as the van changed from a burned out thirty foot square box into a lovely eighteen foot tourer.

Before we could use it in earnest we had to get it weighed and inspected for road worthiness; this happened in Trowbridge.

We arrived at the D.O.T (Department of Transport) depot in Trowbridge and the inspector came out to view the van... Everything seemed ok except there was a very mild smell of burning wood. We couldn't make out where this came from; nothing was switched on in the van. Everything including the kerb weight was in order so the van was signed off and we went home. Dad drove cautiously and had the driver's window wound fully down.

The following three page article is the build of our caravan taken from the Practical Caravan magazine January 1970.

NEW 'VAN FOR OLD

D. J. BURT TELLS HOW HE FASHIONED A NEW TOURER FROM A BURNT OUT WRECK

Early in the winter of 1967 my wife and I were offered a very delapidated caravan, 17 feet long, square and old fashioned, with small windows and big wheels. Furthermore, it had been completely burned out.

It was suggested that we might like to dismantle the van in order to sell the aluminium for scrap, and knowing the high price of aluminium we were only too pleased to accept the offer.

A local farmer put his tractor at our disposal, and one damp and foggy night in November we fetched the van from a field where it had been standing for many months and managed to manoeuvre it into our garden.

Unsightly

One look at it was enough; it was just too unsightly to stand in our drive very long and we decided that the quicker it was dismantled, the better.

During that first evening it suddenly occured that we could convert this 'van, cut it down, re-shape it and so turn it into a four berth tourer. I was certain it

could be done and after all, what had we to lose?

My wife of course thought the proposal quite impossible but once the idea started to take shape, there was no holding back.

I think enthusiasm started to run riot that evening and it did not take very long for it to affect the whole family. Well into the night we sat and discussed our plan, and before retiring our mind was made up. We decided to start the very next evening.

The first major task was to get into the van and rip out all the old charred wood and insulation.

This was a job for all, our two children included. A huge bonfire helped to get rid of everything that could be burned and quite soon only the empty aluminium shell was left.

A few wooden supports could still be used, others, too badly burned, had to be replaced later.

We had to decide what new shape we wanted our van to be and to what size we had to cut it to make it com-

fortable to accommodate a family of four.

As the van was so long, it was also somewhat wider than the average. But at 7ft 3ins it was permissible to be towed and we thought that width would give us the extra room to move about freely.

For want of anything else an old roll of wallpaper had to serve to draw and cut out a pattern. This we held against the side of the van, and with a sharp instrument marked out the new size and shape.

Cutting the sides

We next loosened the roof under the front guttering and then started cutting with an ordinary electric drill and saw attachment. First one side, then the other, until the front of the van came away quite easily.

Of course the chassis was much too long, so we cut that off as well after which we proceeded to do the same with the rear.

Where we had cut, the chassis had

● No one would believe, looking at this photograph, that this smart looking tourer was once the burnt out wreck of a seventeen foot long holiday caravan

● The 'new from old' tourer was beginning to take shape at this stage

52

55

● *This end view of the caravan in it's new form shows the advantageous width*

to be strengthened with new cross members and wooden battens before we could fix the two end pieces back into position.

Next the roof. What difficulty we had lifting it off the body, but with perseverance we managed and one evening, using a wanderlight we re-cut it completely in order to remove all parts which had been burned.

The roof was next put back into position and temporarily secured with pop rivets but not without first waterproofing the edges with rubberised sealing compound.

Our van was beginning to take shape. Still looking far from nice we could however, visualise the outcome and each step forward made us feel more eager to go on. Friends and neighbours were following each step with great interest and curiosity but quite often doubted our ability to finish the task. It had become a challenge which we were determined to see through to the end.

Having only weekends and evenings at our disposal we worked by wander-

light, each evening throughout the winter.

In order to complete the roof we obtained a pair of trestles and plank. That way it was easier to screw down the roof very firmly and fibre glass the joints to make them completely waterproof. We did not seem to feel the cold and often we had to brush away the snow before starting our evenings' work.

During this time we had ordered new windows for front and rear of the 'van and a toilet window and new roof light. These were quickly fitted.

The door could be reclaimed but we moved it to the rear, near the toilet compartment which had been included in our design.

The original windows were fitted on either side making our van beautifully light and airy.

Laying on the services

Before we could work on the interior the caravan had to be wired for lights and piped for gas. This was completely new to me and a task I expected to be most difficult. But by trial and error and after feeling slightly despondent at times, I completed the job to my satisfaction.

Now, at last, we had reached the stage where we could start working inside. What a pleasure it was after having worked out of doors for so long. An oil burner helped to keep us warm, and we were beginning to feel that we were making progress. We had bought two rolls of glass fibre insulation wadding and this we stapled in position between the wooden structure of the sides and the roof.

The next purchase was of three sheets of ½ inch marine ply eight feet by four feet for the roof, some ½ inch round beading and chromium screws and washers to fix along each joint. The beading was glued and panel

● *Work on designing and rebuilding the 'van was shared by the whole family*

pinned into position. The screws could not be used until painting was completed.

We were able to obtain offcuts of marine ply to line the sides of the van. Although it made our work slightly more difficult the outcome was most satisfactory and, after all, economy was of great importance.

What a great moment it was when at last we could get down to the task of designing and measuring the interior layout.

We knew what we wanted. Centre kitchen unit with plenty of cupboard space underneath, dinette at the front, converting at night into a double bed.

Major use of offcuts

At the rear, next to the toilet compartment we left enough space to fit a gas fire for which I had provided an extra point.

Marine ply was also used for the furniture, offcuts being bought whenever we could make use of them. The wood was rubbed down again and again after

● *The interior of the caravan was clad with light coloured wallpaper*

● *The side panels were marked and cut after the end panel had been removed. At this stage, the new ends are awaited before the roof is shaped and cut to size*

which it was varnished. The rubbing down had brought out the grain to perfection and the result was very nice indeed.

Every now and then we would review our financial outlay and as time went on we found that we were spending less than we had anticipated.

My wife and I went bargain hunting and we were able to obtain many useful things quite cheaply. The foam cushions were second hand, but washed they came up like new. Curtains and seat-covers had been a Christmas present and even friends responded and offered small gifts.

How well I remember one day, when Peter, our youngest, arrived home, his

pockets bulging with nails which he had we could take our van for its first test run.

Our next task was to remove the two big wheels and replace them with two similar to those on our car. These we obtained from a local scrap merchant who also supplied us two very good tyres.

The corners of the body had to be sealed with a compound after which we used 1inch x 1inch cope section and aluinium strips which I found would easily bend over a piece of wood.

We also fitted the window valances. These I was able to make myself by moulding glass fibre over a piece of cardboard tubing.

Financial outlay for materials used			
	£	s	d
Jockey Wheel, Hitch, Ball, Four Steadies, Brake Lever, Two Gas Lights, Four Gas Mantles and Bottle Carrier	18	0	0
Two Secondhand Wheels and Tyres	4	0	0
Brake Cable	1	5	0
Windows, Roof Light, Door Lock, Aluminium Coping, Guttering	12	0	0
Fibre Glass Insulation	2	0	0
New Rubber Beading for four Windows	2	0	0
Nails, Screws, Pop Rivets and Sealing Compound	6	0	0
Linoleum	10	0	0
Sponge Cushions (second hand)	3	10	0
Marine Plywood and Sprucing	14	0	0
Gas Fittings including Piping and T-Joints	1	10	0
Hotplate (second hand)	2	10	0
Paint (Sale bargain)	2	10	0
Grab Handles		12	0
Handles for Cupboards and Doors		10	0
Varnish for Furniture		16	0
Rearlights and Sidelights (second hand)	1	0	0
	£83	13	0

The prices quoted are only approximate, but £100 all told should be sufficient to re-build a touring caravan.

● This was the side of the 'van before the windows had been repositioned. The new arrangement allows much light and add to the overall living comfort

picked up from a nearby building site. No matter that they were rusty and quite useless, he had made his contribution.

As we had used marine ply offcuts for the sides of the van we decided that wallpaper would give a good finish. We used cream coloured plastic coated paper, two rolls were sufficient and well worth the extra outlay.

The table, which has a hinged centre leg, and forms part of the bed was made of ½ inch marine ply covered with plastic material. This same material was used for covering the top of the kitchen unit.

Attractive pelmets

No windows are complete without pelmets and ours look most attractive. They were made of plywood rubbed down and varnished to a high gloss.

The original floor boards were found to be in good condition and they hardly needed attention but to add to the pleasant appearnce of the van we covered them with a good brand of linoleum, again a worthwhile extra outlay.

Two gas lamps, well positioned to give a pleasing light in the evening, finished off the interior. Now we had but to finish the exterior and already we were talking of nothing else but that day, not now too far away, when

New corner steadies

One day was spent fitting the four corner steadies, and how much better our van looked after having been supported for so long by breeze blocks and wooden boards.

The original brake cable was useless and had to be replaced, as did the tow hitch, handbrake lever and jockey wheel.

Just before Easter the van was ready for painting. Sections of the aluminium cladding had been damaged by fire. These had to be filled in and carefully rubbed down to give a pefectly smooth finish. The job of painti~ was handed over to my wife. She h been looking forward to it, and one day, just after dawn, we were up and about ready to start the final stage of our enterprise.

Three days were taken to complete the painting (one undercoat and two top coats) and by the third evening we had truly finished our caravan.

Now followed the ultimate goal we had worked towards for 18 months. The van had to be taken out onto the road and thoroughly tested before we could tell whether our venture had been a success.

Towing stability

When the moment arrived, the following weekend, we were anxious

indeed. A thousand questions went through our minds. Had we remembered to do everything? Lights and brakes were working and the van was balanced perfectly. We hitched on, pulled up the jockey wheel, released the brakes and off we went.

It was a moment of triumph. The van was towing very well. No pitching, no rolling; it was marvellous.

Since that first test run our van has been on the road many times. We spent our holiday touring Devon, Dorset and Cornwall and had a wonderful time. It is now part of us and will always be our special pride. Next summer, it will accompany us on a long hodiiday abroad.

Time is our own now, the many hours of working are over. But not for very long. Plans are lying before us to build another caravan. This one will be built from scratch, from glass fibre; light enough to be towed by a small car, yet big enough to accommodate a family.

We weren't very far into our return journey; around Staverton I think, when dad stopped. We all asked why and he said he could hear a rattling, tinny type noise coming from the back of the van.

We got out and looked but could see nothing untoward. But the smell of burning was again obvious.

Dad stuck his head up close to the wheel arch; that was it, that was where the smell was coming from!

Dad got hold of the wheel and shook it; the wheel moved excessively without having much noticeable effect on the van itself. Dad guessed the problem. Removing the wheel trim we were horrified to see of the five wheel nuts on the hub, three nuts had come completely free of their bolt stubs. The other two were almost at the end of the thread.

Dad quickly realised the problem. There was not enough clearance between the wheel and the wooden arch. Every time we went over a bump the wheel hit the top of the arch, acting as a brake, causing the wood to scorch, hence the smell and slowly causing the nuts to work loose. The fact that they were contained within the wheel hub cover had prevented us from noticing while at the DOT depot. Also the chrome cover had prevented us from losing the nuts.

We got the wheel brace out and retightened the nuts on both sides of the van. We were very lucky; had the wheel come off completely the van would have crashed to the ground possibly doing irreparable damage, or even worse causing a serious accident.

However it was not a difficult problem to rectify, just a case of raising the arch by an inch or two. One of the arches was within the under kitchen sink cupboard, the other in the wardrobe, as they were not on display they were both bare wood, no veneer, just painted ply board.

We got home safely and over the following couple of weeks dad made the van ready for a Whitsun trip to Studland Bay in Dorset.

Studland in the sixties was a wonderful place to go and we went often. The route took us directly south through Trowbridge, Westbury, Warminster, Blanford, Wareham, and eventually to Corfe Castle.

Then the B3551 toward the Poole ferry; we would go through Studland village for another two miles and turn down a dusty track to the beach car park. Miles of sandy beaches, dunes and one solitary cafe; it was idyllic and at that time very few people ended up at our spot.

Below Corfe Castle where the A351 met the B3551 there was a great café with a big garden, small animal zoo, and kids play ground. This was always our stop-over place for tea, lemonade and ice cream.

The road also carries on through Corfe village to Swanage or goes off in the other direction, meandering through the little villages of Church Knowle, Steeple, and Lulworth; little by-roads following the coast through the Bovington military training area until it brings you back onto the A352 heading west to Weymouth.

Pete and me waiting to be blown sky-high on Tyenham beach 1969

This training area was, and still is thousands of acres in size. All the little villages that were within its borders had been taken from the local people during World War Two.

The reason being, that this area of coastline was crucial to preparing the soldiers for beach and cliff landings in Normandy.

The people must have been devastated by this government directive, but knowing they were helping the war effort and being promised they could return after hostilities ended, they left with heads held high.

The sad fact is that many of the houses, schools, and even churches were shelled, blown up, and smashed by tracked vehicles in the training leading up to D-Day. And even now sixty five years and more since the end of the war they still have not had their villages or land returned to them; a travesty of justice.

In 1969 a World in Action special was filmed on the beach at Tyneham, one of the derelict villages. A great many people including 'The Burt' family came to support the villagers and protest at the army's continued presence while the filming went ahead. During the filming a young boy had to be rescued by the emergency services from the cliff face above the beach. This rescue became the back drop to the ITV television interviews at the time. The boy in question was one Steven J Burt of Winsley, Wiltshire. This would not be my last appearance on TV in 1969, and not the last time I'd be rescued from a cliff face.

It was Church Knowle where we found a very small camp site. In the grounds of a farm belonging to Mr & Mrs Phillips; this became our chosen site; at first to put up our big ridge tent and later to park our caravan.

It was a lovely weekend. The fully laden van towed very well and dad soon relaxed into the journey. When we arrived dad arranged our van against the hedge, we had our lunch and headed for the beach.

Many a lovely weekend had been spent at our spot on the south coast and we'd drive the eighty miles to Church Knowle whenever the opportunity arose; nearly every trip one or two of our friends came along to share the day.

Although Pete and I were off school for the week dad and mum only had the Bank Holiday Monday, so for the rest of the week with our friends from the estate we followed the usual routine, down the canal, fishing, or riding our bikes around the area.

Another of our favourite places to cycle was the small hamlet of Iford.

Iford bridge with the statue of Britannia standing on top

Iford is so small it only just qualifies for hamlet status. There is only the Manor plus one or maybe two other houses, no more than a dot on the map but a place where we had a great deal of fun. Iford was on our circular route covering around 10 miles; we'd head down Winsley Hill under the railway bridge and then left through Limpley Stoke and on to Freshford.

In Freshford there has always been a lovely pub 'The Inn', we would stop, prop our bikes against the wall and buy a lemonade and crisps from the off-licence.

After our break off we'd go again, over the river bridge taking the right hand fork following the river for another mile to Iford Bridge.

The River Frome is very shallow at this point and flows gracefully through lush gently sloping meadows toward its final destination.

Here we would stop, leave our bikes and splash around in the crystal clear and very shallow water for ages our play watched over by the mighty stone statue of Britannia sitting majestically on a plinth half way across the bridge. When we finally had enough, tired and wet we'd collect our bikes and slowly make our way up the hill past the Manor to Westwood.

Up, down, up, down it was hills all the way, long slog up to Westwood then a steep descent into Avoncliff.

Over the aqueduct; a brief rest before the final killer of a trek up across the field and the footpath coming out at Winsley cricket field. At last on reasonably flat ground an easy mile back through the village and home.

As we moved into our early teens our parents would also allow us to camp further afield and we came up with the idea of night-time badger watching in the field below Ross Daniels' farm.

The water from Turleigh Trows flows as a stream underground though the old Turleigh Mill and from the Mill Pond across the bottom of the valley into the river Avon above Avoncliff.

On the 'Downs' side of this valley below the Belcombe road there is a steep

The Copse and the valley below where we camped to watch the badgers.
Through the gate and down the hill to the stream.

hill and a Copse of trees, home to a large badger set.

I have recently looked on 'Google Earth' at this area, and from above the route of the stream is still visible, however the stream itself seems to have dried up, this may be due to the numerous giant Willow trees that have grown up along the edge of the water course; these trees suck many gallons of water from the ground.

The field belonged to Ross who had no problem with us camping on his land, but laughingly told us to be careful with fires.

We loaded our trolleys with all we needed and tucked into a big meal before we left; with a good supply of crisps, nuts, other snacks, and drinks off we went. Down Turleigh Hill and right at the bottom into Green Lane, the same route we took to go fishing.

At the end of Green Lane where the track goes off to the right down to Elbow bridge and left to our fishing spot, there were a group of farm buildings and from here a farm gate led into the field sloping away to the stream in the valley below.

Now a new house stands on the corner where the gate used to be.

We dragged our trolleys stacked with gear down the field to our chosen position by the stream, unloaded and put up our tents.

It was still light so together we walked up the hill to look at the badger set and to collect wood for a fire, which we laid inside a circle of stones collected from the stream. We were in this regard very sensible and practical. Our camp site chores carried out we had to wait till dusk.

That was the time the mucking about started.

Wading about in the stream; making a mud dam and splashing water on each other getting uncomfortably wet until it became dusk.

Then it began to rain.

We had pitched our tents facing the stream looking up the hill toward the badger set. The idea being that we would lay facing out of the tent entrance and watch quietly for the badgers to come out.

When the rain came we all piled into our tents. Our flimsy 'Tommy Best' tent long since discarded, Pete and I now had a small ridge tent which had been given to us by our uncle Ralf. It was sturdy and had a fly sheet over the top and it was water proof... Jeff, Sticky and Kevin on the other hand had a flimsy affair with no fly sheet or sewn in ground sheet.

The fire went out and with it that secure feeling of warmth. We watched, waited and dozed until we became bored. The rain got harder.

Jeff decided he wanted to get into our tent as it was drier, but there wasn't room it was full with just Pete and me. So Jeff started letting down the guy ropes.

I'd had enough.

'I'm going home,' I said and told my brother to start clearing up our stuff. By 9.30pm soaked to the skin we were dragging our trolleys up the field back onto Green Lane and down to the bottom of Turleigh Hill. Everything was chucked in a pile on the trolley, we were all wringing wet. Jeff and I were arguing; I accused him of always mucking about and not taking anything seriously.

It was close to 11pm when we got home; everything was drenched including us kids. We left the trolley fully laden in the annex between the house and the shed, (the area dad had enclosed when we first moved into Poston Way) and went inside; our parents said they were just on the point of coming to get us.

The other kids went off to their respective houses.

Pete and I changed and sat in our dressing gowns with hot cocoa. A bit of an anticlimax to that particular adventure.

The next big family outing planned for the caravan was early in the school summer holiday, a week at Wells-next-the-Sea in Norfolk. We would then return home and dad would help Marcos move to the new factory in Westbury.

Changes were afoot with Marcos. New models had been introduced including a 2 litre V4 model and a 3 litre metal chassis model to replace the original design which had been fabricated from marine ply; put bluntly a wooden floored vehicle. This change of material was a necessity for the company to enter the American market.

Orders were growing rapidly and the company had outgrown Greenland Mills.

During the early part of the year a new factory had been sought and eventually found at Westbury, four miles to the east of Trowbridge, a total of seven extra miles from Bradford-on-Avon. Dad would be based there instead of Greenland Mills from August.

So the summer holiday plan for the family was a week at the beginning of our school holidays away in the caravan then two weeks in Germany at the end of the holidays before we went back to school.

As a family we had never been north of Swindon. It was Weston-Super-Mare, Woolacombe on the Somerset and North Devon coast or Studland Bay; Dover if we were going over to the continent.

Our coming venture heading north-east into the unknown was prompted by the Strickland family who went every year to Wells-next-Sea in Norfolk for their summer holidays and sung the resorts praises to my mum and dad.

It was a bloody long way; an eight or nine hour trip in those days. This compared to an hour and half getting to Studland.

Pete and I were not keen. We liked Studland, we liked Corfe and the army training area were we could pick up live ammo to take home and swap for 'stuff' with other kids; or fire the bullets in a vice with a hammer and nail. All good character building stuff!

I'm grinning here while I imagine a parent of today reading this with a look of horror on their face. Yep, dangerously true antics.

School broke up and the caravan was made ready for our trip to Wells.

We would leave at six in the morning. Our route would take us to Newbury along the A4 then up to Oxford across to Bedford, Cambridge,

Norwich, and then the North Norfolk coast.

What a nightmare journey. I didn't think it would ever end. We arrived at 3.30 in the afternoon after a nine and a half hour trip.

We were all grumpy and exhausted. To make matters worse when we got there we couldn't see the sea. The tide was out when we arrived and when I say out, it was really out, like half way to Holland.

We dejectedly got in the car and found our caravan site. We jacked down the legs of the van had a cup of tea and some bickies and decided to explore.

By the time we returned to the van for our evening meal our spirits had not lifted. We were not impressed. This place was not a patch on our usual spot on the south coast and the people spoke a different language... well so it seemed.

We played some games around the table, went to the washrooms and then went to bed.

Dad woke us at 4am. 'Come on move yourselves,' he said. 'We're heading down to Studland.'

He and mum had talked this over quietly while we were sleeping and realised we were all disappointed. The news cheered Pete and me. We bounded out of bed, over to the washrooms to splash some water on our faces and clean our teeth, a quick cup of tea and we were on the road.

It was much the same route till we hit Newbury but then we just carried straight on to Winchester, round Southampton to Poole and across the ferry.

Back in the county we knew and loved; I didn't care if I never heard or saw Norfolk again... little did I know!

We were lucky, the Phillips had a spot for us and we settled in for the last five days of our seven day caravan holiday.

There had been no other people around when we arrived, a couple of small two man tents and one other caravan slightly larger than ours with an awning zipped shut and no car. The owners must be out and about.

It was now gone 5pm and too late to do anything.

Mum made our evening meal while Pete and I kicked a ball around. Just as mum called us into the van for our meal four people turned up on push bikes, they belonged to the two small tents. They waved and wished us good evening.

We were eating when the other family returned. They pulled their car in by the other van and climbed out.

Mum, dad and two daughters my age. The parents went through

the awning into the van while the girls hung towels and swimming costumes on a line suspended between the van and the boundary fence.

'It looks like they have two daughters your age Steven,' commented my parents. 'You'll have to introduce yourselves tomorrow.'

We left mum to do the washing up and helped dad get the picnic table and recliner chairs from the boot of the car and set them up in front of the van. Our neighbours by this time had unzipped the side of the awning on their van and I could tell dad was impressed with the open but covered space it provided.

Our neighbour (I'll call him Jack and his wife Jill as I can't remember their real names) had settled down with what looked like a glass of beer while his wife and the girls were getting things ready for their evening meal.

Dad got up and wandered over to introduce himself. I couldn't hear what they were saying but watching the pointing and hand expressions it looked as though the discussion revolved around awnings and caravans in general.

Dad came back having invited the family over for a drink after they had eaten. It was after 7.30pm when Jack, Jill and the two girls came over bringing their camping chairs with them. The girls' names (and these I do remember) were Sally who was a year older than me and Sarah who was a year younger. They were very pretty and well spoken. Their father was an officer in the RAF and they were well travelled having lived in Cyprus and also in Germany. They were now based in Lyneham not too far from where we lived.

A very pleasant family; although a few years younger than my parents they weren't stuck for conversation; they had a lot in common with my mum and dad. Our dad had also been in the RAF based in Gutersloh in Germany for his national service. Jack had also joined as national service but had gone on to become a career officer.

Pete and I plus the girls sat and listened. In those days your parents did the talking unless you were told otherwise and this evening was purely an evening of polite introduction.

They were new to the area, this being their first visit to the south coast and had come down on Saturday, the day before while we were heading North East to Norfolk. Yesterday they had settled in and gone into the village of Church Knowle; today they had been to Swanage.
Mum and dad spent an hour talking about the area and things to do.

I could tell Jack was quite horrified that we went as a family through the ranges down to the closed beaches at Tyneham. He mentioned that there would very likely be unexploded ordinance laying around and possibly even mines on the beach. Dad didn't respond giving Pete and me a look that said 'please keep quiet' and Jack never pushed the issue further. But he probably spoke about it later with his wife wondering how long our family would last before we individually or collectively blew ourselves sky high.

We were all tired and the family left us around 8.30pm.

Pete and I said goodnight to the girls and we both secretly hoped they would follow us to Studland the following morning; that was the proposed plan.

However in the morning Jack had problems with his car and called the AA. We explained again how to get to the beach and left them to it. Alas we never bumped into them on the beach that day.

Pete and I were kicking the ball about when the family returned and after the hellos how did it go today etc, us four kids were left to it. The girls came over and asked if they could join us, so we stood in a circle kicking the ball back and forth. Mum could see that the girls quickly tired of this and came over saying why didn't we do something which was fun for all four of us. An obvious code that means sacrifice the football and keep the girls happy. So we played leap-frog.

It started out nice and innocently but then us boys began to show-off; or as mum says to this day Steven started to show-off. Jumping over Peter I got him to stand higher and higher.

Then my little brother wanted a go. Now instead of making it easy for him I stood so high he couldn't get over my back. Mum saw this from the caravan and shouted at me not to be so mean. Embarrassed at this public telling off I waited till my brother came up for the next jump; when he was half way over I stood up flicking my brother high into the air.

He came down with an almighty thump and a crack from the shoulder blade that could be heard the other side of the county. Screaming he ran clutching his arm to the caravan. I ran behind telling him not to be such a wimp, and it would be alright it was only a bruise... It wasn't a bruise it was a broken collar-bone.

Sarah and Sally were standing round cooing at my poor little brother and looking daggers at me. In fact everyone was looking daggers at me. That was the end of the holiday. We took Pete to Wareham hospital. An X-ray confirmed the broken bone.

Our neighbours were in bed when we got back to the site. Well at least the girls were. Jill came over to ask after Pete.

I was in disgrace.

The following morning we hitched up the van and went back to Winsley.

I remained in disgrace, my parents accusing me of showing-off in front of the girls at my brother's expense.

I got the 'how could you be so stupid?' lecture. The, 'you could have broken his neck, back, etc,' lecture and the, 'you've spoiled it for the family,' lecture.

My robust and outspoken response to this was, that we may as well have stayed down there; after all a broken collar bone is a broken collar bone whether you're in Dorset or Wiltshire. That fell on deaf ears.

(I might add that almost fifty years later this incident is still brought up at family get-togethers and I still need to robustly defend my corner).

So it was back to Winsley, football, fishing, and Murhill woods until we left three weeks later for Germany.

I was thirteen now, my group of friends roughly the same age and all football mad.

Going to football on a Saturday had been a part of my life since I was five or six years old; going to Bristol Rovers with dad was quite a common event although I might add, not every Saturday.

As we kids got older we all picked first division teams to support. (This was prior to the forming of the Premier League).

My team of choice was Manchester City, Jeff's Everton, Kev's Manchester United and Sticky's Chelsea, etc.

But we also followed the local teams of Rovers and City in Bristol and Swindon Town in division three. Town had a great team at that time and were progressing really well in the League. Earlier in this year in March they had beaten Arsenal at the old Wembley stadium 3-1 in extra time in the League Cup Final. A massive upset to pundits' predictions, Arsenal had lost the year before in the final against Leeds United, they were back with a second chance and thought Swindon two leagues below them were easy meat. How wrong they were.

This cup win had prompted stronger support from us local kids and our parents allowed us to go to the 'Town' home games on the train without supervision.

So when we had the money we caught the Saturday lunch time bus to Bath; walked a hundred yards across the road into the railway station and then on the train two stops and we were in Swindon.

The 'County Ground' as it was named was a stone's throw directly up the road from the railway station. I had cousins, aunties and uncles in

Swindon and if my parents were planning a Sunday trip to visit the Swindon arm of the family I could watch the football then go and stay the night at my aunt Ada's with my cousins Robbie and Christine. My elderly aunt Amy, Ada's mother lived in Manchester Road one of the terraces between the ground and the station, this was my stopping off point.

Football in the late sixties had started to become marred with violence with rival gang fights both inside and outside the ground.

The Police didn't stand a chance.

Crowd control was unheard of even in the big cities, let alone country towns like Swindon. There was really no coherent plan to deal with mob violence. At this time football trouble was in its infancy but would continue marring the national and international game for almost three decades to come.

We youngsters thought this was exciting and I suppose wanted to be part of the noisy chanting crowds walking up the middle of the road from the railway station.

However, as normal, Steve Burt had to take this one step further and on 22nd November

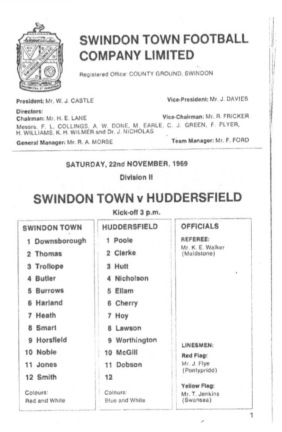

SWINDON TOWN FOOTBALL COMPANY LIMITED

Registered Office: COUNTY GROUND, SWINDON

President: Mr. W. J. CASTLE   Vice-President: Mr. J. DAVIES

Directors:
Chairman: Mr. H. E. LANE   Vice-Chairman: Mr. R. FRICKER
Messrs. F. L. COLLINGS, A. W. DONE, M. EARLE, C. J. GREEN, F. PLYER, H. WILLIAMS, K. H. WILMER and Dr. J. NICHOLAS
General Manager: Mr. R. A. MORSE   Team Manager: Mr. F. FORD

SATURDAY, 22nd NOVEMBER, 1969

Division II

SWINDON TOWN v HUDDERSFIELD

Kick-off 3 p.m.

SWINDON TOWN	HUDDERSFIELD	OFFICIALS
1 Downsborough	1 Poole	REFEREE: Mr. K. E. Walker (Maidstone)
2 Thomas	2 Clarke	
3 Trollope	3 Hutt	
4 Butler	4 Nicholson	
5 Burrows	5 Ellam	
6 Harland	6 Cherry	
7 Heath	7 Hoy	
8 Smart	8 Lawson	
9 Horsfield	9 Worthington	
10 Noble	10 McGill	LINESMEN:
11 Jones	11 Dobson	Red Flag: Mr. J. Flye (Pontypridd)
12 Smith	12	
Colours: Red and White	Colours: Blue and White	Yellow Flag: Mr. T. Jenkins (Swansea)

1

1969 when we went to see Swindon's home game against Huddersfield, I stole a loo roll from the toilet of the 1.30pm British Rail train from Bristol Temple Meads to London Paddington, stopping at Bath Spa, Chippenham, Swindon and Reading (change for Didcot) and Paddington. This toilet roll in true British Rail tradition had the logo and initials 'BR' stamped on every leaf.

I had seen toilet rolls being thrown at football matches and it looked harmless fun to me. I never thought in my wildest dreams I would get caught throwing it, or be interrogated like Ronald Biggs when caught.

However that is exactly what happened that very day and seen live at 10pm on BBC 'Match of the Day'.

I had the loo roll and I was determined that at some point during the match it would fly majestically from my hand unravelling as it went.

I got back from the toilet compartment of the train and whispered what I had done, taken, or I suppose stolen, to my mates. They didn't look that sure.

The encouragement was there, but I also got the feeling that they didn't actually want to be near me when I threw it. However I also sensed a feeling of awe from my mates that throwing the roll would lift my street-cred sky high. (*Street Credibility* as it is called today).

Off the train and along the road to the ground we went. We paid at the turnstiles, five bob or so... (Five old shillings, 25p of today's money)

then we moved round to the 'Town End' behind the goal.

Once again I was unmistakable. Just like my capture after the cricket pavilion incident I stood out like a sore thumb; I was wearing a black leather jacket with my almost white blond hair, I could have been picked out in any crowd.

It was my misfortune (and you would think that by now I would have learnt that I never got away with any wrongdoing, I always got caught) that to monitor and quickly clamp down on trouble, the crowd had been planted with random plain clothed police officers; one who just happened to be standing right next to us.

We had made no secret of the fact that I was going to chuck the bog roll; laughing and joking and taking it out of my inside pocket two or three times with the intention of a spectacular launch.

182

During the first half Swindon had a penalty awarded. Poole the Huddersfield goal keeper saved the shot by Butler, but the ref had the kick retaken because he moved before the whistle. A second chance for Swindon and again Poole stops the ball and the follow-up rebound. We stood there crestfallen. The half time break came with no score. One minute into the second half and Huddersfield are one up. This is my moment. As our keeper Peter Downsbourgh retrieves the ball from the 'Town End' net I let fly. Yeeeeha! Loo roll away.

Straight and true toward the penalty spot it flew; unravelling on the way it did not.

The policeman was ready and waiting to pounce.

I was unable to witness the aftermath of my action as I was grabbed by both arms from behind and marched down through the terraces by the plain clothes copper.

At the fence behind the goal which was only three foot high I was bundled over into the arms of two of Swindon's uniformed finest.

Was I escorted to the gate?

No, they marched me out onto the field to the spot where my toilet roll lay, as tightly rolled as when it left my hand and they made me pick it up. The players were stood round holding the ball and looking on at this young offender. Not the appropriate moment to request autographs...

The crowd were cheering and clapping and I was shitting myself. (Another of my life's episodes indelibly stamped on my memory).

With a burly copper on either arm I was frog-marched across the field and down the tunnel into a small interrogation room.

This is not an overstatement. It really was a cell. No windows and one bulb swinging from the ceiling; concrete walls and a desk with a hard looking uniformed police officer behind it.

The Gestapo officer behind the desk was handed the toilet roll.

'So what's he been up to?' He asked my escorts.

They explained the circumstances of my capture.

The officer I could see, regardless of my good looks and angelic face viewed me as a future hardened criminal; a boy who was on the road to ruin and a life of violence and crime. Given the chance he would have sent me to Dartmoor, instantly locked me up, thrown away the key and had me doing hard labour for life.

I was terrified and on the point of falling to my knees and begging for mercy. In fact I didn't need to fall to my knees, they were about to give out anyway.

'Suppose you think this big do you?' He said glowering at me.

Before I could answer he said, 'have you done this before?'

I couldn't get any words out so I just shook my head.

'Lost your tongue have you sonny? I'm expecting an answer.'

'No sir,' I stuttered.

Where do you come from?'

'Winsley sir.'

'Winsley?...Where the f--k is Winsley?'

'Between Trowbridge and Bath sir.'

Brought this with you?' He said holding out the toilet roll out in front of him and unravelling a couple of feet.

'Yes sir.'

'Dad work for British Rail does he son? Don't lie to me, this roll has 'BR' stamped on every leaf. You nicked if off the train didn't you?'

At this point some inner resolve and self-protection mechanism took over. If I said yes I would be openly admitting to theft...

'No I didn't, I found it on the pavement on the way up from the station and picked it up. I didn't know it was belonging to British Rail.'

'So you're saying someone else nicked it, you found it and thought it would be fun to chuck it in the ground...? I think you're lying.'

It wasn't just my knees that were trembling, my voice was also on the point of giving out but I battled on.

'No, that's the truth,' I said.

There was a big book with names age and addresses open in front of him on the desk.

'Name?' He said.

'Steve,' was my reply.

'Not your f--king first name your surname.'

'Burt... Steven Burt,' I quickly offered.

'Age?'

'Thirteen,' I said.

'Thirteen? - Thirteen years old and you're dragged down here by two police officers and now your name is going to be recorded in this book. What do you think of that? Proud are you?'

Before I could answer he said, 'ever been in trouble with the police before?'

'No sir,' (what a liar) I said. 'It was just a dare that went wrong.'

At this point another bloke was dragged in from the terraces.

But this guy never came quietly he was kicking, shouting, swearing and struggling.

Only one of my escorts had remained and he was now needed. The copper behind the desk turned to him and said, 'chuck him out.'

He had someone else to amuse himself with.

His parting shot was, 'don't you ever find your way in here again.'

The police officer grabbed me by the scruff of the neck, took me to a wood bolted wicket gate and pushed me out of the ground. His parting shot was that I had been a lucky boy.

Jesus... I was feeling sick and trembling.

That really was a close call. I'd even got away with not giving him my address. I needed a drink. I found a stall selling cold drinks and sandwiches and bought myself one of each. I went over near the turnstile sat down with my back against the wall, ate, drunk and composed myself. Oh well... not so bad. I live to fight another day.

After all that the thing that irked me the most was the fact that the toilet roll hadn't unraveled itself on the way to the spot.

I finished my tea walked over to the waste bin and chucked in my rubbish. Although I was a little horror I always did the small things right like putting stuff in the bin, helping old ladies across the road and putting things back where I got them from.

I looked at my watch, there was only twenty minutes to go. Jeff, Chris and the others would be out. I may as well wait for them at the station.

I got up to walk away from the ground and just as I did a young copper walked past.

'Alright?' He asked.

'Yeah I'm ok,' I replied.

'How come you're not in the game?' He asked

'I got no money,' I lied.

'Here, come with me, I'll get you in for the last ten minutes,' he said.

I couldn't resist it. Instead of doing the sensible thing and declining his offer I allowed him to lead me to the gate and ask the bloke at the turnstile to let me in.

'Let him in,' said the bloke. 'We only threw him out ten minutes ago.'

'Is that right?' Asked the copper.

I had to admit it was and with a -'you wanna get yourself home son,' from an annoyed copper I sheepishly headed off toward the station.

Oh well, win some, lose some.

I waited at the top of the steps leading to the Bath bound platform for my mates to come. If I didn't find them on the platform I'd find them on the train.

As it happened we did meet on the platform and my experience had to be recounted while my mates looked on in awe at my almost unbelievable story.

We all knew I was lucky not to have my photo taken or receive a ban from the club.

I was feeling happier and more relaxed now. I'd had a lucky escape. I was a hero and my parents weren't likely to find out...were they?

We left Bath station, crossed the road for the bus and got back to Winsley at 7pm.

I said goodnight to my mates and asked them to keep quiet about my ejection from the ground. But I knew that it was only a matter of time before this got back to my parents. It would however give me breathing space to concoct a simplified and less damaging (to my backside) story. How wrong was I?

My parents greeted me with a cheery hello how was the game. I said it was good but didn't go into too much detail. We had a late meal and then sat down to watch the telly.

At 10pm came 'Match of the Day' and on a Saturday night I could stay up late to watch it; it was my one late night of the week.

It hadn't occurred to me this may happen, but - yes you guessed it. Match of the day Saturday November 22nd 1969 the regional game being highlighted; Swindon v Huddersfield.

I couldn't believe it, my blood ran cold. I was undecided whether to own up on the spot... this may dilute my punishment; quickly run upstairs, pack a suitcase and take the first ship to Australia, or deliberately smash the telly.

I took none of these avoidance actions; what I did do was sit there with my fingers crossed and pray.

Dad was jovial; 'oh, your match,' he said, 'how great, we may see you in the crowd.'

My god! How right he was going to be. He even got mum and Pete in to watch it.

Sure enough the moment came. I was squirming in my seat with what was to come.

While Downsbrough pulled the ball from the back of the net a toilet roll came flying over the cross bar.

'Someone in the crowd has thrown a toilet roll!' shouted the commentator. 'Play has stopped; the police have the offender!'

My dad is disgusted at the behaviour.

186

'They should be thrown out the ground,' he shouts at the telly. 'They should be banned!'

By now I wish I'd taken option 2 or 3... I just wanted the floor to open up and swallow me.

Then from the crowd comes this little boy in a black leather jacket and blond hair escorted by two of Swindon's finest. At this point you can't make out it's me but I can sense dad sitting up in his chair and glancing in my direction.

There's still hope, if only the camera doesn't zoom in.

But alas it's no good, as I stand up from retrieving the toilet roll the camera zooms in directly on my angelic face; my moment of TV glory for the whole of the UK football following fraternity to see.

My dad is rigid and speechless; staring across at me on the couch mouth open and nothing coming out.

I take the opportunity to get in first...

'It wasn't me dad,' I say, (quite convincingly I might add).

'They grabbed the wrong person, honest. It was none of us... another guy threw it and when they grabbed him he and his mates blamed me, they were older than us, I couldn't do anything about it.'

A spontaneous lie of genius; for the moment I was saved. I could see the indecision in my dad's eyes and quickly took advantage of this.

I went through the story explaining in detail; perhaps with hindsight too much detail what had happened.

I was given the benefit of the doubt. Dad was semi-satisfied. I think he could visualise the scenario on the terrace and understood that it was possible for me to be blamed.

But I could also sense the distrust... why always Steven? Was this just too much of a coincidence?

Mum's concern was more to do with what the neighbours would think. Nobody missed Match of the Day, especially when it was a local team playing.

While debate was going on between mum and dad I sneaked off to bed, hoping against hope that it would all blow over very soon.

Of course I was world famous in Winsley and Trowbridge, which is very heartening considering the drumming I got from dad two days later when the truth got out. I was hailed as the local hero on the bus to school, by the kids at school and even one or two of my younger teachers had a laugh about it.

It was impossible for this episode to be covered up. It was round the village in no time, all the kids I went to the match with told their brothers and sisters who eventually told their parents and it got back to mine.

My dad took the belt to my backside again, this time without me wearing my lederhosen; it hurt.

The punishment was mainly for lying. If I'd owned up to the wrongdoing when I first got home I think I'd have been reprimanded in some form but not as harshly as what actually happened.

I was confined to the house for a week (grounded I believe the kids today call it). But worse still I was banned from going to any further live games until my parents saw fit to change their minds.

This restriction would mean that I would not see a live football match in the UK again until the mid-eighties when returning from Turkey during the winter months I would go and watch Norwich play with my mate Nigel.

I need to thank Jeff for providing the match program which he kept for forty five years(he must have guessed I'd want it) and also the cartoon that he drew showing my expulsion from the ground. Thankfully however, I don't recall it ever making the front page of the 'Wiltshire Times & News'.

We entered the decade of the seventies with mum once again voicing her dissatisfaction with living in Winsley.

She now made the point, and it was a valid one, that with dad working in Westbury and her working in Trowbridge it was a waste of money both of them driving in the same direction everyday to reach their respective places of work and having to use two separate cars to do so.

It would be far better to look for a council house swap in a village the other side of Trowbridge, or even better, buy their own house.

Dad was unenthusiastic at the second idea. He had never grown up with ambitions of owning his own house; in truth it frightened him to death. As for mum, in Germany most people rented their house so to her owning a property was not a driving ambition either, it just wasn't in the culture of either of them.

However rather than another council house, renting privately might be an option.

Pete was in his last two terms at Winsley juniors and after the summer holidays would be starting secondary school. The plan already discussed and agreed was for him to join me at Nelson Haden. All these factors together pointed to a sensible conclusion; a house move out of Winsley somewhere toward Westbury. The plan would be worked on. Steve Burt was not happy.

Over the past twelve months I had corresponded with Monika regularly by Post, there was no email, Facebook, or mobile phones in 1969. Once every three or four weeks I would sit down at the dining table and laboriously relate life in Winsley and Nelson Haden schooling in long hand to my pen-pal in Munich and in return she would write to me.

The sad thing was and I only realise this today as an adult, that her writings to me were always in English and my return letters were also in English. This of course did nothing to help improve my second language.

Mum and dad encouraged my writing to Monika, especially mum who deep down wanted my bond with Germany to be stronger. She was willing to overlook the fact that I wasn't prepared to work at corresponding in German; something was better than nothing as far as she was concerned.

After both of us nagging our parents and a bit of tooing and froing it was agreed Monika would visit us for the Whitsun school half term, the week of 25th May.

The holidays didn't fall the same time in Germany as in England but her school and her parents viewed a trip to England as very educational and allowed her the time off. Her parents would put her on the plane at Munich airport and we would pick her up at Heathrow. She would have the full school holidays with us in Winsley; I was delighted.

When our family had returned from the Geltendorf holiday I had told all my mates, both in the village and at school of this smashing girl I had met. In fact I had a photo of Monika sitting at Marlene's dining table that I'd shown to all my mates. The general agreement was that she was a very attractive girl and I was a lucky sod. I must put my hand on my heart and admit at this point that I did somewhat embellish our association, possibly referring to her as my girlfriend, and possibly even being the future Mrs Steven Burt... a *decade up the road I was to be bitterly disappointed*.

Mum and dad promised that if the weather was fine we would have a few days in the caravan in Dorset.

School was plodding along and I continued to remain in the middle ground academically, still in group 'A', however realistically, based on results, I should have dropped a grade to 'B+' in Mathematics or probably even one grade lower to 'B.'

My overall results according to my reports were really appalling and they shouldn't have been as I was fundamentally a very bright kid.

I just hated school.

We had a strange selection of school teachers. Some were ok, a couple of them were pretty nasty.

Our head master Mr Cook was quite a nice bloke and was famous for his passion in all things to do with the school.

He would really get worked up and have his own motivational expression which he would bellow from the stage in assembly - 'Guts and Determination boys! Guts and Determination!'

(*My memory here has been prompted by Robbie Doel; thanks Rob*).

Ranting across the stage during assembly one morning while shouting at us 'SING BOYS SING!' He fell over the edge into the arms of the first years sitting below. We couldn't control our laughter; music and singing went to pieces as he tried to pull himself back up onto the stage.

His favorite hymn was 'Jerusalem' which we had to sing at the top of our voices. He would knock on the doors of the houses at the end of the playground and ask the people living there if they could hear us. If they could, all was well; it was his indicator of our performance. It was a case of quantity not quality with Cooky when it came to singing.

We had to give one hundred and ten percent in everything.

Our school football team as I have already mentioned were brilliant and cleaned up the opposition year after year. Pete Bristow, Paul Stubbens and Greg Suggett and one great little short arse hard nut Clive Bond so impressed Cooky that he ranted back and forth across the stage one Monday morning after hearing the result of his, (our), team victory against another school on the Saturday.

'That boy Bond!' He shouted at us. 'Guts and Determination! Guts and Determination! An example to us all, an example to us all... well done Bond, well done!'

Three hours later he gave him the cane for smoking.

That was another thing about Cooky; he could never give the cane without crying.

The cane was dished out in a corridor leading to one of the classrooms. Boys would line up outside and take turns going in.

Cooky would be inside crying his eyes out. His words to every boy were – 'this will hurt me more then it hurts you,'... yeah right!

Then he would put a book under his arm and with the cane in hand lift his arm.

When the book fell to the floor that was the point he brought the cane swishing down on your open palm. The pain was horrendous!

You would leave the corridor with tears in your eyes. The kids waiting their turn outside would look terrified as you came out. But it was always the same bunch of kids lining up... we never learnt and soon forgot the pain.

The idea was to keep your thumb out of the way. If the cane caught the edge of your thumb, that really was pain in the extreme. Also another knack was to drop your hand just as the cane hit. This took practice and guts because if you didn't get the timing right the manoeuvre would be noticed and the lash repeated. Smoking and skiving got you a single whack on each hand, but insubordination to a teacher would get you two or even three... so it hardly ever happened. There was a lot of laughter behind teacher's backs but to their faces there was only respect.

But that was the way things were. If you screwed up and got caught you got the cane. No good running home and crying to mummy. You got what you deserved and most parents had no sympathy.

Apart from Cooky there was only one other teacher allowed to dish-out corporal punishment and that was the deputy head Mr Rees.

He was a really nice teacher; polite to his pupils and fair. He gave respect and treated the older boys as adults.

He taught mathematics and mainly dealt with the fifth year non-leavers. Detention classes were held in his classroom, which were overseen by a different teacher every night of the week.

Detention was a lesser grade of punishment than the cane, but could last for weeks.

Mr Rees would assess what you'd done when you came into the corridor. He would downgrade your punishment to detention or give you the choice. Some kids didn't want to stay behind an hour after school for a week and so chose the cane.

But if Rees gave you the cane you knew it. He was not like Cooky crying and whimpering he really would dish out a stinger.

Mr Hewitt was the woodwork teacher. He was ok but his one hang up was smoking.

You learnt very quickly not to smoke before going into woodwork class. He would stand in his little corridor where all the work pieces were stacked on shelves and sniff you as you walked passed. (How bizarre is that!) If he smelt cigarette smoke on your clothing he'd smell your breath, you couldn't make this up could you. If he then came to the conclusion you'd been smoking you were sent to Cooky's office. The fact you hadn't been caught with a fag (cigarette) did not absolve you of guilt; you were, in the eyes of Hewitt, guilty.

Mr Gould was our chemistry teacher. He had a habit of standing behind you and heavy breathing down your neck.

Old Spitfire Watley our music teacher...he couldn't talk to you without spitting all over you; you needed an umbrella and for this we took the piss out of him something awful.

Rob found out years later that his dribble, spit thing, was caused by being hit by a Jap rifle butt in a POW camp during the war. Hearing something like that makes you regret your childish behaviour of the time. He was a genuine hero who had done his bit.

Mr Dutton the French teacher had strange yawn thing he did...very odd. We all thought he was gay; why we should think this heaven only knows, there was no proof, or at least I don't think there was. It was just a school rumour that had been handed down from older brother to younger brother for years.

He ran the Trowbridge Air Cadet Force and I found out during a school reunion in 2007 that he was a decorated airman from the Second World War and we had the audacity to call him all sorts of mean 'nick-names' behind his back.

Mr Sangster's punishment of choice was making you pick up rice or putting a chalk stick in your mouth... errrr what the hell was that all about, where did they get these ideas? Some of them were mighty odd, that's for sure, the teachers as well as the ideas they had. Mr Lowe was a prize Bastard with a capital 'B' he would lift you up by your sideburns, for those mature enough to grow sideburns, or the hair that grew down the side of your ear for the less mature. He would lift you up till you were on tiptoe. The Bastard; it hurt like hell. Another teacher I wouldn't piss on if he was on fire.

But then we had the really nice teachers like Mr Bruce who taught Maths, Mr Gregory Geography, Mr Boffin Physics (very apt name) and Biology, Mr Donnelly Metalwork, and I thought Terry Baker our PT instructor was a decent kind of guy until I read my final report in more detail... now I'm not so sure.

Terry was hard with us, but we all liked him and could have a laugh.

He would grab me and Sticky during the day and say 'do you fancy running tonight?' This was Cross Country running for the school. If I said I could do it he'd phone my mum at VW and get her permission. Then after the event he'd drive me or both of us back home.

We did all sorts of sports at the school and Wednesday the whole afternoon was donated to team games like football, rugby, cricket in the season and we even had a baseball team; this as well as the two other PT sessions per week when we would practice for school sports day; running, throwing and jumping events, we done them all.

Robbie says to this day high jump was the only sporting activity he was good at; hurling himself over the bar to land in a sodden rock hard sand pit...I couldn't remember this feat of sporting prowess from my friend so I questioned him on it; he was adamant, high jump and art, his two best subjects at school... He still has his school reports to prove it. We must be the only two NHBS pupils who still have, after all these years our awful school reports... I discovered that sadly they don't get any better with the passing of time.

The teachers were enthusiastic for the school and didn't seem to mind putting themselves out to do Saturday or after school activities. Although I didn't enjoy school that much we had some good times and I made some great mates. The school report is my final report before leaving. It makes grim reading and a total embarrassment.

These reports hardly varied during my years at Nelson Haden except in this my final year I missed school 38 days (although it states sessions on the report they were actual days) which must have been an all-time school record; most of them were days I spend playing truant; I was forever skiving-off.

However, regardless of my absenteeism I'm baffled when I read this report and others as to how ridiculous the marking system was. The comments don't make much sense either. Every year they said exactly the same thing.

I have all my reports from my Nelson Haden years and while hunting out this final report, laid the previous three years reports all together on the table and compared them. They are all bollocks!

NELSON HADEN
COUNTY SECONDARY SCHOOL FOR BOYS
TROWBRIDGE, WILTSHIRE

REPORT FOR YEAR ENDING 19 71

NAME _Stephen J. Burt_   FORM _4A+_

SUBJECT	GRADE	SET	MARKS	REMARKS	TEACHER'S INITIALS
ENGLISH	C+	II	C	Satisfactory progress this year.	Pml.
MATHEMATICS	C+	III	E	Very weak. Shows no interest at all.	LBI.
GENERAL SCIENCE PHYSICS/BIOLOGY RURAL SCIENCE	C+	III	D+	Has shown interest especially on project work	dS
RELIGIOUS INSTRUCTION	C+		C	Shows an intelligent interest	PW
HISTORY	D+		DH	Poor, shows some interest but little effort.	RJB
GEOGRAPHY	D+		D+	Tries hard but finds work difficult	DS
WOODWORK	C+		D	Has been on the slide for some time, despite my advice to avoid making the most of these opportunities	
METALWORK					
TECHNICAL DRAWING					
PHYSICAL EDUCATION & ORG. GAMES	C+		D	Little effort made.	JeB
ART & CRAFT					
MUSIC					
EFFORT/APTITUDE CO-OPERATION				Has not made as much effort as needed	JeB

CONDUCT _Quite Good_   NO. SESSIONS ABSENT _38_

GENERAL REPORT _This is a very poor report, reflecting upon the general attitude of Stephen's to work this year. If he wishes to make a success of his potential career in the army, he must make great efforts to improve_

J. C. Baker FORM MASTER/MISTRESS   _Denis Cooke_ HEADMASTER

A = Very Good ; B = Good ; C = Average ; D = Poor ; E = Very Poor
Gradings refer to the standard in the Set in which the boy is placed.

To be signed by Parent or Guardian and returned to the school please.

I have examined this Report.   Signed ....

194

It makes no sense; I was good at English and in fact I went on to get English 'O' level grade 1 at Dover (Dover comes later), I was in the top five of the class in Metalwork and Woodwork, yet look at the marking; physical training - I worked my guts out and represented my school in many sports for crying out loud. Biology no problem, I liked the subject and still do... I loved History and Geography and do to this day, but again look at the marks. Then to top it off the report says I show an intelligent interest in Religious Studies... bonkers!

The system stinks. These remarks which are totally random and not even dwelt on by the teacher who wrote them and had to write probably another three hundred beside could have very easily destroyed my future plans and ambitions... had I had any. It was not what I was good at or even the effort I put in, it was because of my attitude and behavior; this is what governed what went in the report.

Well who cares, my life turned out pretty darn good, far better than any of those teachers would have predicted that's for sure and probably more fulfilling than the lives they had led or were likely to lead.

But as a parting shot it strikes me as strange that after four years at the school and a form master who knew me very well they still couldn't spell my name correctly...Stephen with a 'ph' for Christ sake! Oh, and I wasn't in 'A+' I was in 'A'. Bloody hopeless the lot of em.

We had one a young trendy teacher called Bill Jennings. He was friendly and would talk to us as equals. We considered him a pretty decent bloke for a teacher.

He had a flat somewhere along Claverton Street in Bath, over the foot bridge behind the train station, or at least a friend of his did.

He held a party there one night during our fourth year and invited a bunch of us along.

A bit weird when I think back on it; fourth year pupils going to a party at their teacher's house and all boys at that.

Everyone was boozing and smoking and when at 10.30pm we left to walk back over the footbridge to the bus station quite the worse for drink; Martin Edmunds balanced along the top of the footbridge handrail clutching a beer bottle in his hand.

I lived in North Bradley by this time and so I spent the night at a friend's house in Trowbridge. It was a good job I did, because if I'd turned up at home drunk my dad would have gone ape-shit and probably torn Jennings' head off. He hadn't wanted me to go to the party in the first place.

Early in the summer of 1971 Jennings took us to Jersey for a camping holiday... I'll come to that later.

Another decent teacher was Mr Hill our English teacher (nothing odd about Hilly). He had a classroom in the spider block; the old World War Two Nissen huts that were our overspill classrooms. These classrooms had solid fuel 'Pot-belly stoves' to keep us warm. We had to fill them with coal which we collected ourselves! To quote Nora Batty, Last of the Summer Wine, 'They really don't know they're born today!'

Mr Hill was the only teacher that thought I would get anywhere in the world and at the last teacher parent meeting held before I left Nelson Haden my mum went to talk to him. Mr Hill told her 'don't worry Mrs Burt your son will be ok. He may not have been that good at school but he'll turn out alright.'

I was able to talk to Mr Hill at our reunion in 2007, tell him what I had been up to in my life and thank him for having faith in me all those years ago. He remembered me and the conversation with my mum. *It might seem odd he did, but it was the German thing again, people always seemed to remember us.*

School sports day was a major event where we would all compete against each other; class against class; year against year. In a school where sport was a major part of the curriculum winning counted for a great deal.

After the school events came the zone events. If a pupil had won at form or year level you were picked to represent the school in the zone sports; a similar system as we had at juniors; Secondary against Secondary, Grammar or High school.

It was a major day in the school calendar and lessons would cease.

For those in years three, four and five not picked to participate, two choices would be given. You could either come to school and watch and support the events taking place or join the cycle rally. The cycle rally was for the older boys and great fun. In groups of roughly eight boys and with packed lunches we were given a cycle route of roughly twenty miles to follow. I seem to remember it was a type of treasure hunt where clues had to be found to take you on to the next place. Years one and two weren't included as being too young; they were rounded up to support those participating in the sport.

For the cycle rally, bikes had to be roadworthy and they would be checked over before we set off. On the day we had a 'no uniform' policy and you could wear what you liked.

The route went from Trowbridge out through Southwick,

Beckington, lullington, Laverton, Woolverton, Tellisford, Farliegh Hungerford, Westwood and then back to Trowbridge. A pretty decent cycle ride and not for the faint hearted. The thing is, in those days there was nowhere near the amount of cars on the road that there are today, so you didn't have that ever present danger of being knocked off your bike.

The route would vary slightly year by year but in the main remain in the same area. The groups would leave from the school playground in five minute time slots; having your bikes inspected before leaving. We inevitably caught up with the group in front or stragglers would be left behind and join up with a group coming up behind. We would muck about, but if word got back to the school that we had been seen misbehaving we were in the muck cart big time and the following year you'd be confined to watching the sports competitions.

Me heading into school sports day 1968

There were of course kids who were representing the school every year at sports day, and others who represented the school only one or two years in the time we were there. I only joined the cycle tour once in the four years I was at Nelson Haden; that was in year four; all other years I participated in sports day events.

On the last day of term the whole school would go into the assembly hall in the afternoon to watch a film. It was always a war film; Rob remembers 'The Cruel Sea' or 'Above us the Waves', great British war time propaganda movies with John Mills.

I remember the 'Halls of Montezuma' a 1951 war film with Richard Widmark and Jack Palance. The US Marines fighting the Japs on some island in the Pacific. This film was in colour and showed real footage from World War Two. We all thought it was awesome.

Then the last night of term a disco would be held in the assembly hall. This of course would include the girls' side of the school as well.

Prior to 'Disco's' we had only two means of evening entertainment, Scouts or Youth-club.

The advent of the disco was something new and exciting; music, girls and dancing. I went to my first school disco wearing dark brown elephant cord trousers. Yes, you read that correctly, dark brown elephant cord trousers!...

A smart turnout from Nelson Haden Girls.

The choice of course made not by me but by my mum.

They were too tight and kept creeping up the cheeks of my backside which prompted one girl to shout across the floor at me (across the floor because girls sat one side and boys the other) 'been riding a horse have you!?'

I had the whole bloody hall looking at me.

I didn't get it... couldn't understand what she meant or the fact that a crowd of them had been sat watching me wriggling round in my trousers and pulling the trouser seam out of my ass-cheeks throughout the evening.

I looked innocently at them, and in red face embarrassment replied. 'No, what do mean?'

This had them rolling in hoots of laughter.

I looked on po-faced; I just didn't get it...Nelson Haden Girls took no prisoners. They were Trowbridge's answer to St Trinian's. You couldn't go wrong marrying one... you had a minder for life.

The school was very progressive and a great deal of trust was put in the pupils.

When very good educational type films were released and appeared in the Trowbridge Odeon, the school would pay for us to go to the cinema in the town and watch them. I remember going to see 'The Ten Commandments'; a film about Moses with Charlton Heston, Yul Bryner and Anne Baxter.

Also we went and saw a lovely film called 'Kes' about a poor boy in a Northern steel town who finds an injured Kestrel, he nurses it back to life and trains it to fly from his arm. His brother kills the bird in the end and puts it in the rubbish bin. A very sad ending but educational in the sense it gave us a perspective on life in other communities in other less fortunate parts of the country. Even now forty five years on I would recommend this film, a brilliant film to equal 'Billy Elliot' a film to pull on the heart strings.

The move from Winsley still featured prominently in the family plans and it was Easter 1970 when dad found us a house to rent.

It was a farm house belonging to dairy farm in the Village of North Bradley two miles from Trowbridge and four miles from Westbury, it was a lovely little village.

Martin Edmunds from my class lived there, also Alan Cooper he lived in Park Close a little road at the entrance of the village; he was in A+ the form above mine as was Martin Giles who lived at the bottom of Churchlands. Paul Stubbens lived in a new private housing development on Silver Street Lane just off the North Bradley Road.

These lads I knew from school, others from the village I was soon to make friends with.

Dad had heard of the house from a friend of a friend; the usual way.

The farm was a working dairy farm owned by Vic Turner who had this farm and one other where he lived in Southwick.

Vic's farm manager in charge of our farm was a guy called Nobby Bent who lived in the village in a council house.

During our first winter in The Rank farm house we realised why the manager had chosen not to live in it; it was bloody freezing! No cavity wall installation, just single 8 inch brick walls with open fire places and sash windows in every room.

The house hadn't been lived in for some time and needed some work to make it habitable, however Vic Turner assured us by the summer he would've had the work done and we could move in. We went as a family to look the place over; although it was in a bit of disrepair dad

The Rank farm house six years after our departure; looking very uncared for. The tree by my bedroom window gone; the porch gone. A drive in the veggie garden and a crappy lean-to over the back door. I was very sad to see this.

assured us it would be tip-top by the time we were due to move.

I loved farms; I had spent many hours helping out on Ross Daniels' farm in Turleigh and Simon Beale's farm on the top road. I loved the outdoors, animals, the countryside, and all things about nature. I loved the fact that the kitchen door opened more or less directly into the farm yard. I was no longer so unhappy about the move.

The stage was now set for our departure from Winsley.

From the time my parents signed up to The Rank farm house dad spent time over there sorting things out, chucking stuff out, and moving things over. This would go a long way to making our move easier when the time came.

During this time both he and mum began to make the caravan ready for Whitsun.

Easter had been lousy weather but Whitsun was expected to be dry and unusually warm, especially in the south.

Pete moved into my bedroom with me, and the small bedroom on the corner became Monika's room.

The day came for us to go to Heathrow and pick her up. I was very excited.

Heathrow in 1970 was easy to get to, just under two hours up the newly opened M4.

On arrival at the airport we parked and walked round the shops and out onto the roof to watch the aircraft coming into land. The whole experience far more relaxed than today. I had never been to Heathrow before or come to that any airport. It was a new experience. Dad had returned to Heathrow from Paris after delivering Nancy Sinatra's Marcos sports car but he never rated the experience and complained that his ears had hurt him the whole fifty minute flight. He would repeat this story of his flying related ear agony in conversation for years to come, or whenever mum suggested they fly somewhere for a holiday. That return trip from Paris was to be my dad's first and only flight.

I looked forward to the day I could take a flight. Little did I know that my first flight would be from Luton to RAF Gutersloh in Germany with the army in October 1973.I would be flying to join my unit in Osnabruck for the first time and the flight would be delayed through snow and end up landing in Hannover. *We'll come back to that story in the next volume...*

Monika came through customs into arrivals, bag slung over her shoulder and a big smile on her tanned open face. I'll be honest; my 14 year old heart gave a flutter. It was really lovely to see her again and looking as lovely as she did all those months earlier in Geltendorf.

Her English was faultless and we chatted our way back to the car. Dad's question was did she have pressure build up in her ears? She laughed and told dad how to counteract the effect by yawning or holding your nose and popping your ears. Information dad would never use.

We got back to Winsley and showed Monika her room, then we ate some lunch, it had been an early arrival so we had the afternoon to play outside. The following day we were taking the caravan to Dorset. This short two day stay would be just outside Wareham at a caravan park near the Blue Pool.

After lunch Pete and I took Monika over to Jeff's and introduced her to Pat, Maurice and the family. We then spent the afternoon wandering around the village, down through Murhill and along the Elbow track back to Turleigh. We got home around 5pm for our evening meal and gran came down to say hello. After eating us kids prepared our stuff for the trip to the coast the following day.

We left around 9am and by midday we had arrived at the site and set up the caravan. Mum made up a picnic and we headed to the beach.

This was all a very new experience for Monika. She came from the city, and lived a long way from the coast; the nearest coastal beach for her family to visit would be Genoa on the Italian Riviera or Trieste on the other side of northern Italy; both a good four hundred miles from her house. There are bathing lakes within Munich and bathing is permitted in other lakes throughout Bayern but it's not like going to the seaside.

We loaded the car with blankets, beach balls, and a small rubber dinghy that Mrs Lavington had given me; a one man survival dinghy from a world war two aircraft.

It was a very robust dinghy and very small measuring only six feet by three feet when inflated and those were the overall outside measurements. The inside space was just big enough to hold one person lying down. Enough space to keep you afloat if your plane came down in the sea.

Over the long weekend we had a great time. The Sunday morning and Monday were spent on the beach but Sunday afternoon we drove down to Church Knowle to the Whitsun Fete and dad played skittles for a pig in the grounds of the 'The New Inn' pub.

God only knows what we would have done with a pig should he have won. It probably would have ended up in our back garden like the Geese. In the evenings we went to Corfe village for fish and chips and to play around the castle walls and also to the Blue Pool where we played in the woods around the lake. It was completely non-commercial back then. We got back home late on the Monday night. It had been a lovely three days only marred by a small disagreement between Monika and me over the use of the dinghy. It had ended with a wrestling match between the two of us and Monika throwing my sandals into the brambles, I was astounded how strong she was and made a mental note not to go down that road again. My dad pulled us apart and we shook hands and all was forgiven and forgotten. My parents of course said I should be ashamed of myself for getting into a situation where I was fighting with a girl... I looked on it as self defence!

Following our return from the south coast we kids spent the rest of the week mucking about in Murhill woods, down the canal and wandering around the lanes.

Mrs Allen's Victorian glass conservatory. The twist bell is on the top right of the frame; we kids had to stand with one foot on the wall and one on the window ledge to reach it!

We had a house in the village belonging to a Mrs Allen. A lovely Victorian style glass conservatory covered her front door out to the pavement.

Her front door was effectively the conservatory door and in the top right hand corner of the frame was a bell.

We were fascinated by this bell which resembled a clock key. To ring the bell you had to twist the key and the quicker you twisted the key the shriller the noise became. When passing we could never resist mischief making by ringing the bell and running away. Monika watched us do this and really got caught up in the moment; she also wanted a go. I believe it was the sheer excitement of doing something she knew was wrong. She, like the rest of us, would stand on the small wall, reach up and twist the bell as hard as she could; we'd then run like hell laughing and shouting.

I can never remember anyone coming to the door when we rang

the bell, which remains on the door to this very day.

We were also allowed to swim in a local private swimming pool. This pool belonged to a family in Turleigh; the 'Fitzjohns'.

They had a big house at the bottom of the village with a pool in a field below the house. It was really lovely. I fail to remember how we first managed to wangle a swim in the pool, probably Ross Daniels or mum asked the 'Fitzjohns' on behalf of the Cub Scouts.

We would go and timidly knock at the big door on the street clutching our towels.

The door was set back in the wall up a couple of steep steps so when it was opened you were looking up at the person above you in the doorway. For children this was a bit intimidating and we would argue over who should knock and do the talking; it was inevitably me.

They were very generous to let a right rabble of council estate kids from the village use the pool.

Things were fine if we behaved and were quiet; however over the course of time word got out that a pool was at our disposal and more and more kids would turn up wanting to swim; there would be screaming shouting and a right old carry on. In the end one extra rowdy day we all got kicked out. Three children had knocked at the door while another half a dozen hid round the corner. Mr or Mrs Fitzjohn would always ask how many are you? If it was two three or possibly four they were ok with the numbers. But any more and the answer was no. On this particular day they said three when of course it was more like seven or eight. Mrs Fitzjohn said yes and shut the door. The path to the pool through the rear driveway avoided the house so it was easy to sneak down in numbers without being seen. The pool could also not be seen from the house so if we behaved we were never bothered by the owners. It was only when noise levels rose as they will with a bunch of girls and boys playing together, that an adult would appear from the house.

And that's what happened. Thankfully I was not present on that occasion and to be honest I don't think I'd have been involved. Naughty as I could be, I did appreciate the Fitzjohn's generosity in letting us use the pool and knew any misbehaviour would filter back to my parents and I'd be for the high jump.

But that Whitsun week Monika and I went a few times to knock at the door and ask permission and on each occasion we were allowed a couple of hours.

At the shallow end of the pool was a little round thatched changing hut; the area around the pool was laid with slabs and grass and on the far side of the pool at the bottom of an embankment ran the stream that came down through the village from Turleigh Trows and the old Mill pool.

I believe the stream being a natural chalk underground water source actually fed the pool through a valved pipe. The stream continues on down through the same field in which we camped to watch the badgers, under the Avoncliff road and into the river.

The one thing that drove us all crazy were the horse flies. The small fields surrounding the pool were also owned by the Fitzjohn's in which they kept horses. Whether this was the reason for the number of flies I wouldn't know; possibly it was just coincidental. But the flies were there in abundance and boy if they stung you you'd know it. Whenever a fly came hovering over we'd shout 'flies, flies, flies!' then dive or jump shrieking into the pool. It seemed as if the flies were attracted by the chlorine in the water.

It was the loveliest week that ended all too soon.

Sunday came and we returned Monika to Heathrow for her flight home. She had Pat's number and would call as soon as her father had collected her at the other end. Once again we promised each other to keep in touch by Post; I was saying goodbye once more to a very special friend and it would be Easter 1973 when we would next meet.

The second half of term flew by and before we knew it the summer holidays were with us again; with the holidays came our big move to North Bradley.

Mum and dad had arranged for Peter to go and have a holiday with Oma in Mulheim. This was for two weeks during the move. I would stay at home and help and if necessary stay at night with gran up at nineteen.

Vic Turner was the farm owner and of course our 'Landlord'; he was a really nice chap but like all farmers he was not likely to spend money unnecessarily. He decided the work that needed doing to both the interior and exterior of the farm house could be done by the happy-go-lucky Nobby Bent.

Nobby was young, in his early twenties and pretty slap-dash and irresponsible. Or at least that was my parents view not mine; I thought he was a great guy; he let me drive the tractor, go shooting with his 12 bore and encouraged me to skive school and work with him on the farm; an all-round cool bloke. Probably my parent's assessment of Nobby was the more accurate.

So the work which was mainly on the outside, leaks from guttering, replacing roof tiles, etc, had been bodged up by Nobby and in time would need to be redone by dad. However in the summer of 1970 the house was clean and liveable.

Over the months since Easter mum and dad had wallpapered, painted, cleaned and scrubbed. New carpets had gone down and Lino in the kitchen and dairy. You wonder what I mean when I say dairy; well let me explain the layout of the house and farm.

'The Rank,' the lane leading off the Bradley - Southwick road ran for a half mile, at the end of this lane and directly in front of your approach was the farm house with a metal double gate leading onto a wide path to the front door. The lawned area with a drive in the middle was the width of the house around 45 feet. On both sides of the lawn were two hedges; behind the hedge on the right hand side was a large paddock which wrapped right round the back of the house, and on the left a vegetable garden. Down the side of the veggie patch stood the farm proper.

coming in through the front door the stairs were slightly off to the left going up to three big bedrooms one over the sitting room, this was mum and dad's, one directly in front of you, this was to be the spare room, and one to the right over the dining room which was mine and Pete's room. Beside the door to our room a small balcony went back over the staircase to an open area which we used as a cloak room. The bedroom at the back of the house, bedroom number three was a newish addition and was very cold.

Upstairs heating consisted of an open fire in both main bedrooms and that was it, no heating in the third back bedroom.

At the bottom of the stairs to the left of the front door was a very big sitting room and to the right, the hallway leading to a fairly big room that had been used when the house was first built for making cheese and butter;

this is the reason it was called the dairy. Before entering the dairy a door to the right led to the dining room; a room we never used because again the only heating was from an open fire. Leading off the dairy to the right a door led down two steps to a massive bathroom; this was also an addition to the old building from its initial build.

The bathroom was approximately ten feet by eighteen and had a separate room within it we called the workshop. There was no heating in the bathroom; washing and bathing in the winter was pure misery until dad eventually fixed up an electric heater.

Two years earlier at Poston Way, dad had installed our Parkray solid fuel central heating; my parents had this installed at their own expense and of course when we moved we had to leave it behind. The coming winter we would really notice the difference and miss the warmth of the Parkray.

The dairy was a lovely room; it had a big solid fuel AGA cooker which would remain alight from October to April. In this room we also had a large Welsh dresser and a corner bench seat and chairs brought from Germany. The walls were covered up to waist height by dad in a wood panelling. Then it was through another door into the kitchen with a walk in larder and the door out to the garden. All the rooms had sash windows, they were so ill fitting the wind howled through the gaps, in the winter we jammed paper down each side of the running frames to stop the draught.

But when we moved in that summer the house was lovely. It smelled of fresh paint, wall paper paste, and new carpets; outside the sun was shining and with the earthy smell of a country farm it was wonderful.

The move started; dad recruited his mates from Marcos. Most had tow-bars on their cars and owned trailers, he also borrowed the company van and over the first weekend they moved us in. I went round saying cheerio's to my mates and also rode up to see and say goodbye to Mrs Lavington who had been very kind and generous to me over the years I'd worked for her.

Pete had also done his bit; yes he was supposed to be in Germany but after a few days got so homesick Oma had to put him back on the plane... my brother to this day has not really embraced his German side.

We thought we were very grand when we sat down to our first meal. Dad was already making plans. Chop wood for the winter and top soil, seed, and fence in the section of land behind the house as a back garden.

When we moved in the back garden was open, it was a strip of rough land joining the farmyard on the left hand side of the house to the paddock on the right; looking out of the kitchen and dairy window you viewed a huge Cesspit where all the cow-crap from the farm yard was squeegeed and left to fester. Nobby then picked up this muck with the tractor bucket and tipped it into the muck-spreader. We knew mum would not be happy staring out onto that muck pile for very long so a fence was a priority.

After our evening meal we went as a family for a walk.

Our front gate may have been the end of the tarmac'd lane but it wasn't the end of the lane completely; from the farm entrance next to our kitchen garden the lane became a bridleway going on between the fields for another quarter mile before coming to a 'T' junction at which point the bridleway went off to the left and right. To the right it led over half a mile to the Bradley Road. This was the route I would use going to school and for my paper round on my bike. To the left it cut through fields for over a mile before coming out in Southwick. Pete and I had explored this a few weeks before when we came over to help dad, but our parents had never walked these lanes.

It was a lovely evening walk with the dogs; we now had two, as dad had brought home another stray, a long haired German Shepherd puppy we called Rosko. He had been born in a scrap yard where the owner had two German Shepherd guard dogs.

I remember dad saying that most of the litter had died because the mother had no proper birthing kennel or a warm dry place to rear her pups.

Rosko was the lucky one. Although he was afflicted with 'Rickets' in his back legs we would look after him and give him the right medication. In the few short weeks he'd been with us he looked a different puppy, the joints in his rear legs strengthened by bone-meal, clear eyes, and a black shiny coat. We also had a cat, another unwanted stray that found its way to our house. Grey with black rings we called him Ringo and he was a top ratter, of which he had plenty to choose from around the farm.

As we walked up the track from the farm we passed on the right hand side, an old dilapidated cottage set in a large orchard paddock. Beneath the trees were tethered half a dozen goats chewing the grass and fallen apples. They were all bleating while an old lady who must have been at least seventy years old sat on a stool milking one of them. She was mumbling, grumbling, and shouting at the goats.

We were captivated by this carry-on and stood by the gate watching. When she looked up and saw us she went berserk, screaming and shouting at us.

Picking up a wood-axe lying next to the stool she made to come in our direction; well we were off like a shot up the lane. She was leaning over the gate still ranting on when we were hundred yards away. The four of us were actually running away from this old girl; we stopped, laughing and panting.

'What on earth was that all about?' We joked.

We discussed the lady during our walk, and the lovely old cottage. It was only a stone's throw from our kitchen window but prior to the move we'd not bothered to investigate who it belonged to or who lived there.

Dad would ask Vic Turner when he next got to see him, probably in the morning.

We went home, watched some telly and went to bed.

In our bedroom Pete and I had two new single beds. My bed was nearest to the window with Pete's bed next to mine inside the door. It was a big room measuring the same as the dining room below.

A few years before we had brought a fold-down single bed on the roof of the car from Germany; this had been my bed at Poston Way. This bed was now parked against the wall in the spare back bedroom for visiting guests.

A calamity happened during the first night which could have easily seen the end of my brother.

In our previous two houses the bathroom and toilet had been upstairs; so going to the loo in the night was no real hassle. However, now the toilet was downstairs in an unfamiliar house. A trip to the bathroom meant you had to negotiate the staircase, the step from the hall into the dairy and then two steps down into the freezing bathroom. Also from the three bedroom doors at the top of the stairs a single step led onto a mini landing. To explain this; when you got to the top of the stairs the three rooms and the cloak area led off a small rectangle roughly four feet by six feet. Each required you to take one step up. I suppose that's just the reverse of what I had first written... but you get the idea, I'm sure.

Pete needed the loo in the night. He was eleven years old, not a child that needed assistance to go to the toilet. However almost fully asleep he got out of bed, opened the door and failed to negotiate the step down onto the mini-landing; he effectively stepped into nothing and stumbling forward went head first down the stairs.

I came awake with his scream, heard mum and dad bound out of bed. I also jumped out of bed and found mum and dad consoling my very distressed brother at the bottom of the stairs.

It was unbelievable that he hadn't killed himself; in fact, except for shock he was completely unharmed. It was a blessing he was almost sleepwalking; his relaxed body actually protected him. Poor kid, a steep learning curve but I'm sure in the future he wouldn't forget where those steps were whether asleep or awake.

Eventually the panic was over; mum and dad were satisfied Pete was ok and no bones were broken. We all went back to bed.

We awoke Sunday morning with mum standing over us with a cup of tea and biscuits. After the 'did you sleep wells' she said 'come and look out of the window.'

We both bounced out from under our quilts and looked. There, tethered on our two front lawns were six goats, three on each side.

'Where did they come from?' We asked mum. She didn't know.

'They were there this morning when your father and I woke up,' she said.

'The old woman put them there,' we laughed. 'She couldn't get us with the axe so she's put her goats on our lawn.' Pete and I thought this was hilarious.

'Well,' said mum, 'this isn't the first time the goats have been here. Your father noticed the droppings yesterday while we were unloading the car. We'll wait and see what happens.'

As much as I loved Winsley I thought what a great place we'd ended up in.

Sunday would see us all chipping in to help with unpacking and arranging things in the house. We got up, had breakfast and started sorting out the many boxes and bags we had piled in the dining room and spare bedroom.

The last road out of North Bradley.
The Rank and the fields beyond.

Earlier we had heard all the noise from the farm yard, the cows being brought in for milking and the continual lowing as they waited their turn to go through the parlour. Now the farm was quiet again. Nobby had gone home; he did this at weekends when the farm schedule allowed, he was only required to be on the farm twice during Saturday and Sunday for the morning and evening milking. I was looking forward to the afternoon when I hoped I would be allowed to go with him to round up the cows and help in the parlour; this was not unfamiliar to me I had helped to do this on both Mr Beale's and Ross Daniels' farms.

It was around 11am when Vic Turner turned up to ask how we were settling in. Mum made coffee and we sat in the sun out on the lawn and drank it. We asked Vic about the old lady and pointed out the goats.

'I noticed you had visitors,' he laughed. 'The goats belong to an old chap called Sammy Paradise. The lady who cussed and chased you last night is his wife. She's half round the bend; however there are times when she can be quite normal. If you see her pushing the old pram to the shop she's quite approachable, but if she's around the house or garden it's best to tread warily. She chases everyone with the axe, as yet nobody has been killed, or for that matter harmed, but that's more a case of good luck, because she hasn't caught anyone. Best not to be the first,' he said smiling around at us.

We were a bit subdued by this.

'Well,' we all piped-up, 'she did give chase to us yesterday evening, with the axe!'

'Don't worry,' he said. 'In time she'll get used to you and settle down a bit. She's known me all my life and I still get it off her, even now. 'Sammy and his wife are both around seventy five years old,' he said. 'Sammy came to work on the farm for my father after the Great War right up to his retirement. Then my father gave him life tenancy on the cottage. He is a nice old chap and as well as his goats he keeps ferrets which keep the rabbits under control. First thing in the morning he'll go out and peg his goats all over the village, then in the evening take them home for Ivy to milk. This house has been empty for years so Sammy pegged the goats here to keep the grass down for me and also because it's close to his own house. If you'd rather not have them on the lawn I'll ask him to take them away. What if I tell him he can tether them in the paddock?'

It was the behaviour of our dogs mum and dad were concerned about, they didn't want the dogs to kill the goats.

'Don't worry,' said Vic; 'goats aren't like sheep. The dogs will go near them once and that will be it. They'll get a butt and won't ever return, believe me I've seen it.'

'Ok,' said dad. 'But I need to secure the garden for the dogs anyway, so I'll fence off between the paddock and the house, the dogs will then have the run of the front lawn and the vegetable garden, I don't want any harm to come to either the dogs or the goats.'

'Good idea' said Vic, 'I'll pass that on to Sammy, he'll be pleased and you'll find a couple of pints of fresh goat milk on the step once or twice a week; if you've never tried it you should, it's lovely to drink cold from the fridge, also I'll get Nobby to drop off a pint or two from the parlour every morning; how does that sound?'

'That sounds wonderful Mr Turner, thank you so much,' said mum.

We were grinning at each other, fresh milk on our Cornflakes straight from the cow, or goat; what a great start to the day.

The closing off of the paddock and vegetable garden would need to be one of the first jobs we carried out, along with fencing off the area outside the back door; we needed a gate between the coal house and the two brick buildings facing the farm house backing onto the farmyard. Plus a second gate from the all that ran across the bottom of the veggie garden to the front corner of the house. This is where the dogs would spend the day while our family was at work and school.

Dad with Ringo, Gina sitting and our pup the rat killer Rosko.

One of the brick buildings was a big open fronted lean-to which would be our winter wood store; the dogs were well housed underneath in baskets in the dry.

During the afternoon Des Gingell, Alan Cooper, Martin Edmunds, and Pugsley Lewis, cycled down to see me. Terrible nickname I know but his Christian name escapes me. He was so named after Pugsley in the kids TV program 'The Adams Family'. Pugsley was only a year in front of my brother, he would be going back in year two; he had an elder brother John at Trowbridge High.

I introduced them to mum, dad and Pete. I also told them that Pete had just finished at Winsley Juniors and that he would be starting at our school when we returned in September.

It was great that Pete had met my school mates, the lads said we should come up the village and look around, hang out, and meet some more of the local kids.

Des had a sister at Trowbridge High; Teresa, I had seen her some days walking through our school grounds as a short cut to the 'High', or to meet her brother. She stood out in her green uniform... a smart looking lass.

The following day mum and dad were going back to work and it was planned that Daisy and gran would come over in Daisy's Morris 1000 and take Peter and I to Winsley for the week. Our parents were worried about us kicking-our-heels unattended all day at home.

I asked mum; what's the point? Either we stayed at gran's all the holidays or we stayed alone at our house in North Bradley. At some point in time the latter would have to apply, it may as well be now.

After mulling it over my parents could see that practically I was right; however arrangements had been made so for this week at least we would be at gran's. Next week we would be on our own on the farm.

It was around five when I heard movement over in the farm yard. Nobby had turned up to fetch the cows in for milking. Dad said it was ok for me to go over and ask Nobby if I could go with him.

I went through the gate that separated our back yard from the farm yard and walked across to the milking parlour.

'Hello Nobby,' I shouted.

'Who is it?' He replied.

'It's me, Steve from the farm house.'

'Come on in, I'm in the dairy.'

Nobby was comical... he had this wild black curly hair which was totally unruly it looked like a magpie nest on his head. He was carefree and came across as being totally irresponsible especially when he was driving the tractor; but with me, or when he was out with the shotgun he was a good mentor, least I thought so.

Nobby was married to Elizabeth, Lizzie as everybody called her; she was young, lovely and very bubbly and we became good friends.

If I had time in the morning I would stop-off during my paper round for a cup of tea and a biscuit. One morning Liz introduced me to her friend Sam; a young married woman, well girl really, who would, as the weeks went by, put a wide worldly grin on my face. Oh happy days!

This thrilling carry-on would continue quite regularly until the Burt family upped sticks and headed for relocation to Norfolk in July 1971.

Anyway getting back on track...

Nobby welcomed me and asked all the usual questions about our move and the house.

I told him Pete and I were spending the rest of the working week with gran in Winsley but next week we would be left to our own devices here in North Bradley.

We walked up the track to fetch the cows, me reciting the story of Ivy and the axe along the way.

On our slow return mum called me to come in for supper. Saying cheerio to Nobby I left him to get on with the milking. I had noticed in passing that the goats were back in Sammy's paddock. He must have collected them from our front lawn for milking.

That night we all slept well and Pete managed to negotiate the stairs by foot rather than on his head.

The following morning Pete and I heard mum and dad get up to prepare for work. This Monday would be the start of a much reduced journey for both of them. They both had only three miles to travel, although heading in different directions; dad toward Westbury and mum along the Bradley Road past the rear entrance to Nelson Haden and on across Trowbridge.

When school started again in September, on days we couldn't walk or cycle we would be heading in to school in the black Ford Anglia.

Mum came in to wake Pete and me; she wanted us up, ready and packed for gran& Daisy's arrival.

I went downstairs poured myself a cup of tea from the pot and sat in the dairy. Dad left the house, he started at eight. Mum then gave me a key to the kitchen door and asked me to cancel the milk delivery from Nobby for the short term and not to forget to lock-up on leaving; I was also tasked with making sure both Pete and I had breakfast and packed clothes to last till Friday. Mum left the house at 8.30 for work.

We had a telephone, a green one; the first time ever. This was a very special piece of household equipment held in reverence by mum and dad... It sat like a shrine on a shelf at the front door; Pete and I had been told in no uncertain terms that we could answer it but had to seek permission for every call made. Call costs were high. We only had this phone because the line and number was already in place, a party-line -no one today unless they lived in the Hebrides or Faroe Islands would know what a party-line is; it's when you pick up the phone and someone halfway up the lane is already having a conversation and you put the phone down and wait till they finish, basically a shared line.

Shared line, private line, any type of line, our dad would never have paid the huge cost involved in getting a phone installed.

Also, get this... the telephone itself had to be rented from the Post Office who at that time ran the telephone service. This rental was a monthly charge added to the bill. I'm surprised dad didn't also split this bill between Pete, mum and me; he was obsessed by the telephone bill.

This obsession revolving round telephone charges would remain with both my parents for years. When I returned from the army and lived again at home for a few years during the early eighties my parents bought a strange gadget that sat under the phone, a code had to be dialed-in prior to the number. This code was highlighted on the 'call charges' so both Pete and my calls could be added up and charged by our parents to us; defies belief doesn't it!

We both washed, got dressed and I made us both some toast. Then we kicked our heels until elevenish when the two old dears appeared driving at a snail's pace down The Rank, the nominal 20mph, Daisy's top speed.

They came in fussing around us both.

Gran had been over to the farm before, but this was the first time for Daisy, so Pete and I showed her round both the outside and the inside of the farm and house.

They would drive us back the following Saturday morning, at which point mum and dad would be there to chat to them.

I locked up, made sure the dogs were secure and off we went... at 20mph.

Pete and I loved being at gran's we always had a great time, discipline didn't exist and we weren't nagged or made to wash or dry the dishes.

She had played a major part in our growing up and loved us dearly. Me especially, the rebel; whenever I got into trouble at home I would run to gran's and refuse to return. Many times one of my parents had to walk up to nineteen and fetch me. Gran would be mediator in disputes between my parents and me and would not release me back into their care unless they promised not to smack me.

When I was little I would pretend to run away from home; I had a small suitcase and I would put some clothes inside and my favourite toys and walk out the house, tell my parents I was leaving.

I wrote London on the case with my mum's lipstick in pink (Pink! What on earth was I thinking about).

When I wrote it I had the handle of the case facing me so when I picked it up 'London' was upside down and the wrong way round.

Mum has that little case to this very day, it's on top of the book case in her front room; it still has 'London' on the front and contains the remnants of Pete and my Lego bricks.

I would take my case, inform my parents I was off to London and go to gran's...

Gran and I remained incredibly close I loved her very much and I would visit her as often as I could right up to her passing in 1982. When that day eventually came I was devastated and it took me a long time to get over it.

But on this Monday in July we headed, if somewhat sedately, toward Winsley and a week of parental freedom.

Once settled in we wandered round to Jeff's to see what was happening in the village and what our friends were up to.

Jeff had a plan; we were going to make a raft and float it on the pond up the lane near Freddie Burton's farm.

This pond was a regular place of play; the main pastime being 'newting'. The pond was home to thousands; well it seemed like thousands of newts. Now a protected species I don't think this was the case at the time.

We had a typical little boy's fascination with frogs, toads, tadpoles, and newts, and would go with jam jars to collect them. After keeping them at home for a few days our parents inevitably told us to get rid of them. We knew where all the ponds were in the village and I don't mean wild country ponds, I mean ponds in peoples back or front  gardens. We would go with our jam jars and sneak into the garden and unload our amphibians into the person's pond. The biggest garden pond was Mrs Lavington's pond at 'The Chase'; over a few years we must have sneaked thirty or more newts into this pond. Sometimes we would smuggle them in when we went to work in the evening or on a Saturday morning. Other times we would steal in through the bottom field and dash from tree to tree up the long front garden till we got to the pond. We never got caught, and if we were seen no one said anything.

However Mrs Lavington did say one morning that she had strange creatures in her pond. We looked innocently astounded. She walked us over to the pond which was a good fifteen foot by eight foot with water lilies and other aquatic plants. As we stood still a newt appeared and she pointed it out.

'They are newts,' we intellectually told her.

'Well how did they get in my pond?' She asked.

'They walk across land as well Mrs Lavington, they get everywhere where there is water, you're lucky to have them.'

'Will they harm my fish? Perhaps I should get them removed?' She said.

'No,' we said. 'They're ok; they'll live with the fish and leave when they want to.'

'Oh well, I suppose that's alright then,' she said. And with a parting shot of 'Well I really don't want any more,' she left us.

She had of course seen us, or somebody had and told her. We got the hint. No more newts in Mrs Lavington's pond.

Another reptile orientated pastime we indulged in when we were at Winsley Juniors was slow-worm and lizard hunting. In the summer these would be in abundance lying in the sun on the dry stone walls of the local lanes. We would pick them up off the walls on the way to school and keep them in our pockets.

Then, when we got to school put then in the girls' desks or better still ask the girls to put their hand in your pocket. This would bring forth a scream and generally only worked the once whereas the desk prank could be repeated again and again. It was great to hear the shrieks when a girl opened her desk and found an eighteen inch slow-worm or a lizard looking up at them. Great fun!

Anyway getting back to the raft...

Jeff and gang had already collected the planks and baling twine that we needed to tie it all together. The only other item missing, which was probably the most important were the floats. After some debate we decided to go and ask Mr Little at the garage if he had any drums.

When we got up there he had piles of them, five gallon, with screw tops; Castrol oil drums, Aladdin Pink Paraffin, and antifreeze drums.

'Take as many as you want,' he said; Environmental considerations unheard of at the time.

We would take six; carrying one each, the gang of us retreated back to Jeff's to construct the raft.

We lay the cans in two rows of three and wound the baling twine over the planks and under the drums keeping it as tight as possible. The binding material which was the hardest thing to get hold of had fallen off the back of a trailer loaded with straw bales. A huge reel of it, there must have over two hundred yards of the stuff.

We wrapped the twine round and round working on the quantity not quality principle and that the water would provide stability.

Job done it was time to get the raft to the launch site a mile and a half away. The only way to do this was to carry it.

So with one of us on each corner and taking it in turns we headed for the pond.

After much grumbling and arguing about who was, and who was not pulling their weight and along with numerous rest stops we got there.

Along with the raft, which after the journey was now looking somewhat worse for wear, we had brought two short pieces of wood to act as paddles.

We dropped the raft, surveyed the scene and decided where to launch.

Tying a length of twine to one of the corners for retrieval purposes we slid the raft into the water. It floated but looked dubiously unstable.

We had no life jackets, we had no way to call for help, and the majority of parents didn't even know where their child happened to be; but safety didn't play a part in any of our activities, this one was no exception. We were out to create and conquer, we were Winsley kids and invincible.

Who would be first? There were two choices; Kevin or Gibbo. As you may have noticed Kevin always seemed to draw the short straw and get soft-talked into doing the most outrageous things.

The darts through the pram, the Guy Fawkes in the pram... it was always Kev.

If we tried to force Gibbo he would just run home. Kev would give in and do as the crowd of us had persuaded him to do.

Gingerly Kev crawled on the raft to the point where he was spread-eagled across the planks. It remained afloat but rocked precariously from corner to corner.

'Well done Kev!' We were all shouting.

'Stand up and row!' We shouted.

'I can't, I can't, it'll tip over!' Shouted back Kev.

'Pull me in, pull me in!'

'No, we're going to float you over the other side.' We were laughing with glee.

'No, no, I can't swim!' Screamed Kev. 'Pull me back!'

But no, we got a fallen branch and pushed Kev further out into the pond. The poor kid was rigid with fear and by now howling his eyes out.

'You piggy buggers!' He screamed at us.

'Piggy buggers' was Kev's favourite choice of expletive when angry, or letting rip at his siblings and peers. When Kev started shouting 'piggy buggers' we knew he was on the ropes.

However this done nothing to help him, or bestow the rest of us with any sympathy.

'Oh the lines come off!' We shouted. 'You need to row... row Kev, ROW!'

'I can't move, I can't... It'll tip over, I'll drown!' He howled. 'Get me back, get me back!'

Of course we still had the line attached and we could have easily pulled him back but we opted for another half hour of gaiety.

'We'll wash you to the other side,' we shouted. 'We'll make waves!'

'Nooo'... howled Kev. 'It'll tip over, I can't swim!' A bit late to be telling us that?

And we weren't listening. We'd picked up big clods of earth from the field and were hurling them into the pond next to the raft; water spouts were soaking poor Kev.

By now he was just lying still.

Silence...

'Kev are you ok?' We called. We could just hear sobbing coming from the raft.

We pulled him back into the bank and helped him off. He was traumatised.

But once on Terra Firma he went berserk screaming and shouting and picking up lumps of earth and throwing them at all of us, while we ran around avoiding the shell fire.

Eventually he tired and walked off to the gate and the lane home; poor kid.

'Who's next?' Was the general question...

None of us was daft enough to volunteer.

We could be brutal with each other.

We spent another few minutes bombing the raft, tied the string to a tree and ambled home.

By the next morning all was forgotten. There we were, Jeff and Burn, Pete, Kev, Gibbo, Peter Orchard, Sticky and me all sitting on the green wondering what to get up to today.

The raft was forgotten and would remain so, possibly for all summer, unless one of us decided it would be fun to go and see if it was still there and floating.

I wanted to go swimming; Jeff didn't. Sticky wanted to go fishing, nobody else did.

We talked about walking to Bradford and playing in the Trowbridge Road 'Rec' (recreation ground or playing field).

The 'Rec' on the Trowbridge Road was a good one with loads of fun equipment. (Gone now and built over with housing).But we were all worried, although we didn't admit to it, about being caught by the kids from the Trowbridge Road estate. They lived over in Downavon and Culver Road. Sometimes if there were only one or two of us they were ok and didn't kick us off, but if we went down in a big group there would be a good chance a fight would break out and they would gang-up to throw us off their patch.

This kind of territorial behaviour was not uncommon between villages and in different areas of the local towns. You tended to stick to your own patch unless invited in.

Us Winsley kids wouldn't consider going over to Westwood to muck about no more than the kids from Westwood would come to Winsley. We also had to be careful going to the annual travelling fair which was held a couple of hundred yards further down the Trowbridge Road in the field just before the canal bridge. Even there, as a group of outsider kids you sometimes had to make a speedy exit from the locals; although this was never an issue when the fair came to Bradford Leigh on the other side of town. That fairground was always more fun and you didn't need to be so on-your-guard; possibly because there were no housing estates in the area; it was less of a territorial issue.

There was no Sky TV, no Video or DVD. In fact there was no day time TV at all. There was no possibility of just crashing on the couch and watching a movie or playing computer games. Our parents didn't want us hanging around the house in the holidays so we were obliged to occupy ourselves.

Jeff and I were fourteen years old now, Sticky was fifteen; we had outgrown playing armies in the woods, climbing trees, or playing in Simon Beale's barn. We had got to the age of sitting in the bus shelter chatting, drinking Coke, and eating crisps. We had reached the age where as teenagers if we had no fixed agenda we just lounged around or got the bus to Bath where we would go into Duck son & Pinker at the end of Bridge Street; a shop that had sold just about everything to do with music since the mid eighteen hundreds - drum kits guitars, pianos, sheet music and modern day records. The shop had listening booths where you could ask the assistant behind the counter to play you a record prior to buying it. Depending on the assistant you could get away with listening to five or six records before they got fed up with you and asked you to leave the shop. This was always a good place to go on a rainy day or if you found yourself in Bath at a loose end.

My parents had told me to get my hair cut while at gran's. I wasn't particular about doing this but at the same time it had its advantages... When we were kids mum would take us to the village to a bloke called Scadden who would cut kids hair for a shilling in a greenhouse in the garden. It was horrible beyond belief! Why our parents sent us there God only knows; you could have picked any person at random from a crowd and they would have done a better job. There was no style involved. Scadden I've been told was an ex-army barber; that fact wouldn't surprise me in the slightest. He would put a basin on your head and shave around the edge; the idea of the basin was to get a straight line; it was horrendous! We hated going to Scadden. To top it off we didn't like the bloke either, it wasn't as if he was a decent type of bloke you could talk to. We had to knock on the back door of his cottage in the old part of the village, the door

In a street caf'e in Germany, I enjoy a left handed drink while admiring my brothers 'Mr Scadden' haircut.

would be opened either by him or his wife and you would say, 'mums sent me for a haircut,' holding your shilling out-stretched in your hand. He would march you to the greenhouse, sit you on a box and it took him about three minutes to shave your head below the basin rim. Anyone with a basin and a set of clippers could have done it blindfold.

By the time I was ten I refused point blank to go there. My refusal was total, I would create merry hell about going to Scadden; so much so that in the end my parents had to give in.

If they had not, the only way they would get me there was to physically tie me up and carry me. I don't think any other issue during my growing up years was as contentious as that of going to Scadden.

Eventually from around ten years old with the support of gran I won the day and had my haircut in Bradford by a Polish chap, a Mr Polwski or something like that. He had his little shop next to Greens Cycle Shop half way up Market Street.

The amazing and enlightening discovery I made on first going to this barbers was in the pile of magazines stacked on the end of the waiting bench. Along with the run of the mill local rags were... wait for it... dirty magazines!

Yes dirty magazines, it was term used to describe very light pornography; Knave, Parade, and H&E (Health & Efficiency).

Knave and Parade were just 'mags' for the lads; girls with no clothes on; lots of tits and bums but very little else. But for ten year olds this was utter Magic with a capital 'M'.

H&E on the other hand was the naturist magazine and showed the lot. Both men and women, old and young, running and jumping around on beaches and tennis courts or relaxing in caravan parks; playing netball or lazing by the swimming pool, all totally starker's. Gross!

Come and join a naturist group today; the magazine sang the benefits of getting naked showing lists of clubs and activities.

We boys would sit in the corner of the shop ogling the pictures and comparing form.

Mr Polwski would be clipping away not taking a blind bit of notice.

If we got to the shop and there were no customers we would go away and come back later. It was no advantage to go in and sit straight in the chair. We wanted five or ten minutes with the magazines first; it was all part of the hairdressing experience.

When we eventually left, heated debate would continue over the girls, their shapes, how much they got paid... all sorts.

Or we would discuss the naturist angle and question each other as to whether we would be brave enough to be so uninhibited.

It was here that we first heard the expression 'Something for the weekend sir?'

Mr Polwski would say this to all the blokes but not to the kids... we couldn't make it out, until one day a customer said 'yes please' and Polwski went to a box, asked the man how many and took out the requested number of small white sachets. We were baffled as to what it was, until bravely one day I asked him what was in the box and he laughingly told me what they were and what they were used for; condoms of course.

Along with paying Miss X a tanner for a look, Mr Polwski's barber shop was a milestone on the road to our sex education.

I left my brother on the green and nipped back to gran's to get some money and tell her we were going into town; then on my return we wandered down through Turleigh and Belcombe into Bradford. While Pete and I took turns to have a haircut; the others waited on the bench absorbed in the tits and bums. Haircut and further sex education completed we ambled home.

Later while having our evening meal gran told me our aunt Ada had called from Swindon. She was coming down the following day with Chrissie and Rob our cousins.

'Swindon' as they were collectively known had appeared regularly on Sundays over the years.

Family though my English grandfather's side, 'Swindon' were a happy, loud bunch, that would descend on us, or gran in a great big black American car with running boards on the sides at least once a month. It was like seeing the Keystone cops coming; with heads poking out of all the windows, it only needed the policeman's helmet to round off the scene.

Pete and I got on really well with Rob and Chris. Rob was Pete's age and Chris slightly older than me. They also had a sister Sue who was four years older. She came down sometimes, but had kind of grown out of our type of play.

Chris was a wild child. Chris would take over during her brief visits; even Jeff took a step back from his role as natural leader when she appeared, she was indeed Swindon's modern day answer to a fifteen year old Boudicca.

Whether the whole clan appeared in the car, or whether it was just Ada and kids on the train, the effect would be the same.

Two lots of parents screaming at us kids to, 'settle down!'

After their departure from either Poston Way or nineteen I'm sure gran, mum and dad thanked their lucky stars they had Pete and I and not Chris and Rob as children and grandchildren.

I remember vividly mum returning Ada, Robbie and Chris to Bath station one afternoon. Pete and I asked if we could come along for the ride; we were told in no uncertain terms we were under the penalty of death if we misbehaved.

We went up to the platform to see them off and Pete and I had to sit next to mum without moving while Rob and Chrissie ran riot up and down the platform.

'Come here Robert! Come here Chrissie! Sit down Robert! Sit down

Chrissie! Will you behave!' Ranted Ada.

The kids took not a blind bit of notice and never did. Oh how Pete and I wanted to join in...

So we were well chuffed to know they were coming the following day.

After tea the gang of us went up the bus shelter to drink Coke and eat crisps with pickled eggs and just chill out. A packet of crisps with a pickled egg dropped in, a strange combination I know, but don't knock it till you've tried it.

I told the others Rob and Chris were coming and we made a plan for the following day. We would go down the canal and muck about in the punt.

The canal had been drained around the mid-sixties but restoration had begun by the volunteer Kennet and Avon Canal Trust. The Limpley Stoke section had never been in bad repair but did require relining with clay. This was called 'Puddling'. Water had to be allowed into the bottom of the canal to prevent the clay from drying out; for this reason the section from Bath through to Winsley Hill bridge contained a small amount of water. The volunteer group kept their equipment in the old warehouse on the quay side at Dundas, the terminus of the Somerset Coal Canal where it meets the Kennet and Avon, Fred Sartain's place of work sixty years before.

The 'Trust' also had a punt which they chained up on the quay next to the warehouse. Occasionally it would be left unlocked and if we were lucky enough to get hold of it on such a day we would have great fun punting the flat bottomed boat from Dundas to Winsley Hill bridge.

So the plan was made. Chrissie and Rob arrived on the bus from Bath around 10am and after a couple of minutes conversation with my aunt, the 'how's the new house? How's your mum and dad?' Type stuff, we were off down the canal.

Up Vinegar Path and across the field below Bowles bottom farm to the road near the top of Winsley Hill.

At the top of Winsley Hill a driveway leads off to the left into the grounds of the Winsley Chest Hospital; on the right the lane meanders for over a mile past the beautiful Conkwell Grange to Conkwell village and Inwoods. All the land on the Limpley Stoke side of the lane sloping steeply downhill to the canal was owned by the Grange.

In the mid-sixties an elderly chap had been employed by the owners to build a sandstone wall from the Grange all the way along the side of the lane to the top of Winsley Hill, round the corner and down as far as the Murhill turning where it finished; this I presume was the end of the land owned by the Grange.

The wall, still there to this day must be in the region of a mile and a half long and in places built in two tiers almost twelve foot high, higher if you include the embankment it stands on.

Built from Sandstone, intricately locked together with a cement cap on the top with ridge stones placed vertically side by side; the chap who built it was the ultimate craftsman and his finished product is to this day a work of art. I seem to remember him taking two or three years to complete the wall.

The wall fascinated me, and if he were working on it anytime we kids were passing I would stop and talk to him. I was only young but the practical nature of country skills held a fascination for me, hedge-laying, thatching, and dry stone walling; I loved the hard outdoor kind of work and on my return to school in September I would join the Kennet and Avon Trust and spend Wednesday afternoons working on the restoration project at the bridge in Bradford on Avon.

On our way to the canal we would balance along the on top of the wall. When we got to Conkwell lane we would climb up onto the cap and cautiously balance the quarter mile down the hill to its end opposite the Murhill turning.

The Great Wall of Winsley Hill.
Photo taken at the top of the hill
at the junction to Conkwell and Conkwell Grange

We had to be really careful; the stones were not uniform and in places the wall on the high embankment was a good fifteen feet above the pavement. If you fell... well none of us thankfully ever fell.

Jumping down at the end we had another very steep half mile drop to go to the canal bridge, then another mile along the canal to Dundas.

As we came round the corner by the (then derelict) lock cottage we'd keep our fingers crossed the punt was tied up on the wharf and there were no adults around.

There it was, the battered looking flat bottom wooden boat with yellow water sloshing about in the lumps of clay laying in the bottom.

Yippee! And not locked; well at least not locked properly. The lock was an old one and at some point the person wishing to use the punt had forgotten their key; they'd clouted the lock with a hammer and bent the latch inside the lock. When you push the hasp into the lock it catches, you can rattle it and even pull the lock and it will remain closed, but a tap with a stone or a good sharp pull on the lock and it opens; we kids all knew that trick.

We unchained the boat and left the chain with the lock closed. The previous user would get a telling-off for not locking it up.

Grabbing an old tin can from the bottom of the boat we bailed out as much water as we could then everyone piled aboard for our trip down the canal. There was no one about, there rarely was. The only people to witness our mischief were the people who lived in the cottage at the entrance to the Somerset Coal Canal.

At that time the SCC had all but disappeared; canal enthusiasts still attempted to follow the route from Dundas to Frome and in places, relics of the old canal still remained but most of it had gone. The cottage at Dundas had the first lock in their front garden filled-in of course but with the outline of the concrete basin and lock gates still visible. During the eighties the owners of the cottage had the old basin cleared along with approximately two hundred yards of the old waterway; this is now used for moorings, canoe and trip boat hire and a restaurant.

Dundas Wharf Showing my great grandfathers crane and the warehouse.

Off we went and similar to our rafting exploits on the Monday, not a life jacket in sight. Taking it in turns to punt, or should I say attempt to punt, we bounced from bank to bank over the aqueduct. We didn't have a care in the world.

Who would stop us? No one; there was no one about and if there were they would just be tow-path walkers heading either to Bath or Bradford. We laughed and joked and mucked about and had a grand time. When we got back to the Winsley Hill bridge we just abandoned the punt and made our way home. We'd had our fun for the day. One of the volunteers would find the boat and take it back to Dundas.

We turned off at Murhill and made our way back through the woods.

It's a good half mile slog from the canal bridge at the bottom of Winsley Hill to the Murhill turning. We puffed and panted our way up, stopping often to catch our breath through our chattering. Just inside the Murhill road on the left is (was) an orchard where we paused to grab a few apples and pears. This orchard was very unkempt and was probably owned in the past by the Sanatorium.

Munching on the fruit we wandered back through the overgrown pathways of the upper wood till we arrived at the bottom of the hill leading back up to Winsley.

We got home just at the time gran was producing sandwiches. Tired and hungry we tucked in answering questions from my aunt who could honestly talk for England when she got going. Our aunt and cousins were going to catch the 6.40pm bus back to Bath for the train to Swindon; Gran, Pete and I walked to the bus stop with them to see them off. Aunt Ada made me promise to tell mum and dad she had asked after them and they would be down to see the new house in a week or two.

The Seven Stars 1969 showing the wooden seat where we teenagers would sit and eat crisps and drink coke.

Pete and I had a final evening with our friends sitting on the wood bench seat outside the Stars, drinking Coke and eating peanuts and crisps; the next morning Daisy was coming and we would be delivered back to North Bradley.

Prior to Daisy's arrival the next morning Jeff and Bern came round to gran's and we sat in the kitchen laughing and joking. Gran's was always a popular place with our friends. We sat eating biscuits and drinking tea. Jeff and Bern waiting in anticipation for Pete and I to climb into the back of Daisy's Morris 1000;they would be standing in the road in hoots of laughter as we slowly climbed at 20mph up King Alfred's Way and down round Dane Rise. The rotten sods would then run like crazy down Poston Way to the garages to point and laugh again as we slowly made our way past them and on down Dane Rise to the cross roads. The humiliation of it!

Daisy turned up, we said our goodbyes to our mates and like a car in a funeral procession made our way slowly home.

Mum and dad had enjoyed a quiet week on their own while Pete and I had been at gran's but nonetheless they were glad to see us. We unpacked and had a salad lunch with mum, dad, and the two elderly ladies.

After lunch Pete and I decided to take our bikes up to the playing field and see if anyone was about.

The recreation ground in North Bradley was big with a cricket field in the middle and a selection of swings, slides, etc, off to one side backing onto the houses lining Church Road; this was the old part of the village where we hung around during the long summer evenings. Over the other side of the cricket field in the far corner stood an old two storey building; an old brick and tile structure hidden away among trees and ivy. This was the winter hang-out being dry inside we would take candles and sit and smoke, chat, and drink cider on dark winter evenings.

I needed a part time job and desperately wanted to ask Vic Turner if he would employ me on the farm; however mum and dad were dubious about me as fourteen year old working with Nobby who had already shown himself to be a bit too devil-may-care, for the want of a better expression; so the answer to that request was no.

Dad told me that the shop at the top of 'The Rank' was looking for a morning paper delivery boy so this is where I ended up.

I hated the place. It was run by a Mr Taylor and his wife and the shop stunk to high heaven; I felt sick every time I went in there and of course it was worse first thing in the morning when the shop had been locked up all night.

I started the job but hated it. I only lasted about two weeks and then I jacked it in; from here I went up Bradley Road to deliver papers for Mr Parr who had 'The Bradley Road' stores opposite the 'Unigate Social Club'. Which is now a retail park.

Mr Parr was ruthless;(I hasten to add, he had every right to be with us lot) he had around six paper delivery kids working for him and paid next to nothing. Consequently we all robbed him blind. The lads and lassies leaving the shop with their paper bags in the morning would grab whatever they could to sell on at school; mainly I might add this was tobacco or cigarettes. He cottoned on to this after a while and caught a few of us red handed; but we all said the stuff had been planted by someone else and as he could prove no different, he had to leave it at that.

I needed a decent pair of boots for my paper round and for generally mucking about. I kept on at mum till she bought me a pair and brought them home, but I had not been consulted on make or colour and told her I didn't like them. The colour was Ox-blood, a kind of deep red; I created such a stink that mum took them back with me in-tow to exchange them for a pair I liked.

I knew what I wanted. They were a pair of tan coloured boots made by 'Clarkes' and they were called 'TUFF'. These were my boots of choice and what I ended up with; I was well chuffed.

However dad was angry that I had got my own way through argument and reprimanded me for being ungrateful, and mum for giving in to me; but I kept the boots and the whole hullabaloo passed over.

A few weeks later I went off at 6am to do the paper round and it was chucking it down with rain. When I got back I was soaked to the skin. I took the boots off and put them in the AGA cooker to dry out; I forgot they were in there and they dried out like iron and shrunk.

Dad went ballistic. 'All that carry-on about a pair of boots and then you go and ruin them in the oven'; he was hopping mad and made me soak them in water and wear them wet until they expanded again to fit my feet. It was bloody agony but eventually, a couple of hours and a few blisters later, they fitted; a useful trick to know, and I used the same method to soften my boots when I went in the army a year later.

It was amazing what you saw doing an early morning paper round. Let's say I became pretty complacent with the female form and knew exactly the time some young mums decided to get dressed in the morning. The paper lads would discuss these antics together while sorting papers prior to heading out on the rounds. We all agreed that in most cases this exposure was deliberate.

A couple of lads even claimed they'd been invited in for nookie but had to decline because they would be late for school. I viewed this with some skepticism until it happened to me.

I took the opportunity with both hands (literally) and continued expanding my knowledge of human biology, or in the old fashioned term finding out about the Birds and the Bee's with this young married lady even after the paper round ended.

The job ended for me one autumn morning when I failed to get out of bed and Parr drove over to our house, stood outside the gate and started shouting at the top of his voice; 'papers, papers, papers!'

My dad couldn't believe it, he was furious. He bolted out of the house and told him to f--k off in no uncertain terms (which came as a shock as dad never used the 'F' word) and that was the end of my paper round profession.

However this was the start of my working on the farm and being paid for it; it was far more enjoyable and financially productive.

The Rank farm house became home and our family settled in.

Pete and I had good friends in the village and mum and dad also changed their lifestyle, becoming far more outgoing and sociable.

In Winsley they had rarely gone out, other than to have a Friday or Saturday night over the road with Pat and Maurice playing cards. However mum had made many new young friends at VW and a Saturday night out was becoming a regular thing for my parents.

They saw Pete and me as old enough to look after ourselves and not requiring a baby sitter. After all I was fourteen years old and I'd carried out a great deal of responsible chores for my parents while at Poston Way, including getting Pete ready for school in the mornings and lighting the fire when I got home from school... at least until the 'Parkray' had been installed; that chore had started again now we lived on the farm with no central heating.

So my parents would clear off for an evening with friends without worrying about having someone come in to look after their sons.

This was a big mistake.

A few years earlier dad and mum had taken up the hobby of wine making. They really got into it and made wine from just about anything that came to hand and was free; Elderberry, Rosehip, and even tea leaf wine made from the left over tea leaves in the pot. Of course the tea wine had to be made from leaf tea rather than tea bags but in 1970 leaf tea in a tea pot was the norm.

There were a few failures initially but the art had been perfected by the time we got to North Bradley. Mum and dad had gallons of the stuff; as well as homemade wine dad had also bought beer kits and experimented with the beer home brew. The beer was not so good but the wine was really quite acceptable and both were very potent. For a bunch of adolescents it was really top drawer stuff.

After the move, and having a huge walk in larder in the farmhouse, mum and dad were churning out alcohol like a brewery. There were so many bottles in our larder that a few bottles disappearing every week went unnoticed.

Pete and I would sit like angels in front of the TV while mum and dad got ready to go out. They would come down and go through the rigmarole of telling us where they were going, how long it would take to get there, the phone number of the people they were visiting… all the information Pete and I required to know prior to the blast we were about to hold when our parents left the house.

Mum and dad would leave giving instructions as to locking the door and placing a guard in front of the fire should we decide to go to bed, and on, and on, and on… as we gently eased them out of the house.

Our friends were waiting around the corner by the farm gate and no sooner had the tail lights of the car disappeared up The Rank in they would come for a few hours of merriment. We would drink, smoke and listen to music for a few hours and then they would drift home.

Pete and I would clear up, Teresa and Sue Wiltshire, a friend of ours who had already left school and was working in the office at Bowyers, would stay behind to help us, we would leave the doors open to get rid of the cigarette smell, fill the empty wine bottles with normal cold tea and put them right at the back of the larder and everything would be exactly as it should be when our parents got home around midnight. The idea of filling the empties with cold tea was a precautionary measure just in case the bottles had been counted prior to mum and dad going out. After a few days Pete or I would empty them again and dispose of the glassware.

We really were too sharp for our own good.

Only once did we come close to getting caught when our parents came home early. Fortunately it had not been the rowdiest of nights. One of us saw the car lights coming down The Rank, shouted a warning, and all the kids, taking bottles and fags with them, piled out the kitchen door and across into the farm.

Mum and dad were suspicious but nothing too incriminating was left lying around. I said a couple of mates stopped by earlier.

The North Bradley gang consisted of Pete and I, Des and Teresa Gingell, Alan Cooper, Martin Edmunds, Susan Wiltshire who was slightly older than us and had already left school with a job in the office at Bowyers, Pugsley Lewis and on occasion Martin Giles.

Most of us smoked and we all drank. Cigarettes came from whatever source was at hand; nicked from our parents, bought from other kids at school or nicked from a shop, otherwise known as shoplifting.

I had started smoking almost as soon as starting at Nelson Haden but not to any great extent because at that time my only source of supply was from mum or dad's packet at home.

While living in Winsley I would perhaps have one fag during the day at school, never in the evening. However in North Bradley we would openly smoke while we were out in the evening, even if we only had one or two we'd share them between us. Unlike Winsley, my mum and dad knew no one in the village so the likelihood of word getting back was remote.

Alcohol either came from my mum and dad's supply or we stole from behind the pub. Scrumpy cider mainly, which was stored in a big barrel out the back. We would sneak round to the rear and fill empty beer bottles to take to our hut at the top of the playing field. Here we would lie back smoking, drinking, necking with girlfriends, and talking like some hardened gang of crooks hiding up from the law.

The summer holiday slowly drifted by; order had been restored following the move and once again our family set out on the annual pilgrimage to Mulheim for a two week holiday with Oma.

A rushed trip to Germany it will be this year but a great bit of news preceded our leaving. Marlene, Gerhart and the children will once again be making the journey up from Geltendorf; it was eighteen months since we'd last seen them in the winter of 1968.

It would be a packed house at my Oma's, but I looked forward to seeing all my cousins together again and Horst will now be two years old.

I haven't mentioned much of my two other cousins Gaby and Brigitte; daughters of my uncle Dieter and auntie Doris. Dieter was the sensible elder of the two brothers and he along with Doris and the girls lived in a flat in Duisburg.

Brigitte was actually my step cousin, although I didn't know this till I was much older and sadly neither had she been told. She grew up believing that Dieter was her natural father and when she did find out in her late teens it really came as a great shock. I never liked her much as a kid, Gaby was my favorite out of the two sisters; possibly I had a stronger unconscious bond with her because she was a Hopp and looked like a Hopp? Who knows...

Anyway we would visit them often over the years on our trips to Mulheim, and also meet up with them at my auntie Mia's house in Rurberg in the German Eifel.

Dieter and Doris had a top floor flat with a lovely long balcony. I loved going out on the balcony and looking out over the city. When I was younger I'd lifted Pete up to peer over and on one occasion encouraged my brother to drop his Corgi Cars from the balcony onto the cars parked in the street below. The repercussions of that incident stayed with me for quite some time.

This summer my cousin Gaby would almost see an end to me with a golf club. If you look closely at me in the photo you'll see a mark on the bridge of my nose.

I'd taken my two cousins and Pete to the park to play crazy golf. Gaby at the time would have been around seven or eight years old; neither Pete nor Brigitte needed any help with the golf but Gaby needed to be helped out.

But excitement got the better of her, when it was her turn to putt, and as

Pete on the left, me holding Horst, Brigitte, Gaby and Elke.
Oma's house in Mulheim. Summer 1970.

I placed the ball in a good position for her to hit it, she never gave me the chance to get out of the way. Swinging the club as hard as she could she completely missed the ball but hit me squarely across the bridge of my nose.

I went down like a pole-axed steer; it's a miracle she never killed or severely damaged me. My nose never broke but I was out cold and when I came round a crowd of people surrounded me lying there in the park. Brigitte had run home for my mum.

It hurt like hell, the skin broke, it bled and swelled to a horrendous size, but fortunately only for a couple of days and with constant ice packs it went down leaving little bruising and a scab. Once again my guardian angel was looking after me.

My poor little cousin was very upset and was still apologising when we went back a year later.

Later in the holiday when the Weitkamps arrived from Geltendorf a photo was taken of all of us kids together. This is the only photo ever taken of all of us

Sadly this photo can never be reproduced. Brigitte died in the mid-eighties. Between the holiday in 1971 and her death I only ever saw her one time. That was in 1978 when she visited us in England with her boyfriend. She was lovely, a pleasure to have around and we got on really well. The years had changed her and we did loads of stuff together while she was with us, much to the annoyance of her boyfriend who I must admit I found slightly peculiar. I'm sad this was the last time I was to see her and I'm sad she's no longer with us. I'd love to once again get all my cousins together for a photo.

On our return to England Pete and I spent time exploring the area on our bikes or with the dogs. The countryside around North Bradley was not quite so exciting as Winsley but lovely all the same. We could ride to Westbury White Horse, Longleat, or Brockerswood, or closer to home take the dogs to the River Biss in the valley below Church Lane. At the top of Church Lane where the road swings round to meet the Southwick Road a short lane led through a gate into a sloping field. A few hundred yards down the field you would come to the river, a beautiful little river running through meadowland to Yarnbrook village a mile way. Ancient willow trees grew along the banks of the river with thick branches cascading from one side to the other. Our dogs loved this walk and would clamber onto the branches balancing from one side to the other and jumping into the river below. I haven't been back to this spot in forty years, but I have fond memories and would hate to go back and find the fields were now a housing estate. I'll keep away and remember the area how it was in 1970.

Our summer break over Pete and I returned to school. Pete would be in his first year and I would go back as a fourth year, a year where I needed to make some big decisions on my future career.

In the few short weeks we had lived in North Bradley I had become very friendly with Teresa Gingell. By the time we went back to school she was my girlfriend and a very attractive girl she was too. She would finish at Trowbridge High and walk through Nelson Haden to meet me and together we would walk along the Bradley Road home.

Evenings we would all hang around together and when it was time to go home I would walk her to her house at the bottom of Church road and take ages snogging goodnight before heading off on my bike.

As summer turned to autumn and the weather changed more time was spent lying in the hut talking, or going down to the farm and laying on top of the hay bales at the back of the barn, or when the occasion presented itself taking advantage of someone's house, if their parents had gone out for the evening.

It was mainly Sue's house; I can't remember if we went there while her parents were home, or if they were just people that went out a great deal. What I do have is fond memories of lying on the couch in her parents' front room squeezed up next to Teresa while we watched the TV; oh happy days...

Sue's parents also had a back room where we would go with a so-called Ouija board (weeji board) and hold séances in the dark; frightening each other to death.

Working on the farm part time brought me the opportunity to drive the tractor. Nobby didn't care about my age, he taught me by taking me out in the middle of the field and letting me work it out for myself. I was on the tractor at every opportunity until one day Vic caught me and gave both me and Nobby a prize bollocking. I was not old enough to drive it and I should keep off it. I was desperate to drive anything at any opportunity, the tractor on the farm, which I could handle with no problem at all was the stepping stone.

In the mornings before school I would reverse mum's car out into the road for her; I had a natural ability when it came to driving, and this was not lost on dad who heard through work that Longleat safari park were going to renew many of their old vehicles. Dad bought me a truck. It was an old one ton Humber military vehicle that had been purchased by the park years before and had reached the end of its useful life... well in an everyday hard use capacity anyway.

Dad got it for next to nothing and brought it home on a trailer borrowed from Marcos.

Used in the private confines of the safari park it had no MOT or road tax so couldn't be driven on the highway. But at home in the paddock or around the fields of our farm vehicle tax was also not a problem.

The truck was a great hit with my mates; painted white with black streaks it looked totally the business and us kids would roar around in it pretending we were in the African TV series 'Daktari' out on a big game reserve. Sadly it didn't last long, something went bang in the engine and it ended up being towed by Nobby to the side of the paddock where it stayed for a few months until the scrapper came from Southwick to take it away. Oh well it was fun while it lasted and there was a whole heap of other stuff to keep me interested, such as single girls, married women and the facts of life; which were about to come my way in abundance.

This was never intended to be a smutty story; however growing up is growing up and to some it comes earlier than others. I class myself as being lucky in having my eyes open to the 'facts of life' at a pretty young age and knowing what it was all about before leaving for Dover as a boy soldier.

At 8pm on a Monday evenings a new series started on the TV, 'Alias Smith and Jones'.

This was a 'Wild West' series about two bank robbers who had been granted a secret amnesty from the law; the opening credits informed us - 'Hannibal Hayes and Kid Curry, the two most notorious outlaws in the west. Of all the banks and trains they ever robbed they never killed no one; this made them very popular with everyone but the railroads and the banks'... and so on...

It ran along the lines of Butch Cassidy and the Sundance Kid and was immediately very popular and talked about at school.

However it was shown on BBC2 and because of the choice of channel I couldn't watch this at home; we never had a BBC2 antenna on the roof, a separate antenna was needed at that time to get BBC2.

Enter stage right - Lizzie's friend Samantha.

Sam was around the same age as Lizzie, eighteen, nineteen, and worked from home as a hairdresser; she lived a couple of doors down Church Lane and was also married to a farm hand who worked on a farm in Yarnbrook a mile down the road toward Westbury.

Sam would often appear in the kitchen when I was at Lizzie's and together the two girls would laugh and joke with me. They would ask me about what we kids had got up to around the village, and as time went by the questions would get more flirtatious; they got an obvious kick out of getting me embarrassed, the questions leading back to girlfriends the 'have you got a girlfriend? How far does she let you go? Plus other flirty kind of questions and ribbing.

All very funny and light hearted leg pulling, but I would find my heart pounding as I watched Lizzie and Sam secretly smiling at each other... It wasn't long before Sam's house rather than Lizzies became my paper round cup of tea stopping off point.

One Saturday afternoon I'd stopped off at Lizzie's and was sitting chatting to both the girls, I mentioned that our TV couldn't receive BBC 2 and I was missing the western series all my mates were talking about at school.

The two girls like co-conspirators then suggested I watch the series at Sam's house.

She and her husband went out on a Monday evening and they had just bought a puppy a small black Labrador only about 10 weeks old. I could watch the telly and babysit the puppy.

So the scene was set, I would bike round to Sam's and watch 'Kid Curry and Hannibal Hayes' and babysit the dog while the two of them went out.

My affair started gradually with Sam; it began with her coming home a bit tipsy one Monday night, and while her husband was up the garden seeing to the chickens she slumped over on top of me on the couch. Giggling and rubbing the inside of my thigh she asked me to help her upright; while doing so she planted a huge wet smacker on my lips.

That was the first of many kisses... then things moved on.

One morning Sam informed me I needed a haircut; 'come round on Saturday afternoon,' she said, 'I'll give you one... and she did...

The whole thing with Sam was thrilling. Although Teresa was my girlfriend and we'd do the school boy, school girl stuff, Sam was on a different level entirely.

I knew this was wrong both morally and legally but I loved it and the direction it was going. Spill the beans? Drop Sam in it? You got to be joking! This was the stuff that adolescent boys' dreams were made of and for me they were coming true.

We made an appointment for me to have the haircut, a Saturday late in the afternoon... milking time on the farm.

I won't elaborate what happened but after her knee gently rubbing its way up the inside of my thigh a couple of times while I sat on a chair with a towel round my neck, Virgin Airways was up and away. Practice makes perfect and Sam wanted perfection; I would practice regularly even during my paper round in the morning. When that came to an end I had to work it in with my trip home from school because there were two free hours before her husband got home from milking.

My affair with Sam continued on right up to the day we left for Norfolk.

I asked her one day where they went every Monday evening. She told me she went with a group of likeminded people to watch 'Blue Films' in a house in Melksham. She explained what they were and often out of curiosity I would ask for more in depth detail of the latest film. But Sam refused to go into detail; maybe she considered that just a step to far...

Well I didn't really care did I? I was one happy boy.

For me, the fourth year at school was 'make your mind up' year.
Do I stay on an extra year and study for my 'O' levels or do I find a job and leave?

I hated school; I really couldn't come to terms with staying on another term and tried desperately to avoid the subject with my parents.

Fortunately other more pressing issues were occupying the thoughts of my mum and dad.

Marcos Cars were in trouble. A collection of events had stretched the company financially and things did not look good for the long term future of the company and the car.

The move to a metal chassis, the attempted break into the American market with all the expense that came with it, and the move to the new factory; just too much heavy financial outlay within a short space of time.

Car sales, although not going badly had not increased to provide the coffers with more income to cover the extra expense and things really had to look up by Christmas or the worst could happen.

While my parents discussed the worst case scenario, I continued going on career visits; Bowyers, Avon Tires, Ushers Brewery, and others, trying to be inspired as to a career path.

The blunt truth was that I didn't have a clue.

The turning point came when we had our careers day.

Once or twice a year both the boys and girls school halls were taken over for the day by local industries and the military and civil services.

Fourth year pupils from both schools were given time off from lessons to walk around the halls and discuss a career at whatever stand or profession took their fancy. It was seen by some, me included, as a bit of a jolly; just time away from the classroom, but as it happened it ignited a spark of interest which would eventually lead me into the Junior Service of the Army.

While living at Poston Way mum and dad had tried to get me interested in the Merchant Navy.

Whether this was to get me away from Winsley, give me a purpose and direction in life, or basically put me in a situation where my energies would be channelled for the positive I really don't know.

However my parents applied for a grant to send me as a boarder student to the Merchant Naval College, 'Conway' in Anglesey.

I was very keen to do this; the papers arrived, I had to sit an entrance exam which was carried out at Nelson Haden, and I had to complete a physical training test including swimming, which was also carried out by my school. To my utter surprise I passed the lot with no problem. It goes to show that when I wanted to, I could achieve academically. However it never came to pass and I never went. I believe the monetary grant mum and dad applied for was a council education grant (as this was a fee paying academy)and it was refused.

I was bitterly disappointed, I'd kind of made up my mind that I would be going, to the extent that I had borrowed naval books from the library to read.

So I had to tell my school that the plans had fallen through and that it looked very likely I would be at Nelson Haden until the bitter end.

So my friends and I were walking round visiting the various stands displayed in the halls and I stopped to talk to a young lad on the army stand. It turned out he was a Junior Soldier, a member of the Junior Parachute Regiment based in Aldershot.

He told us he had joined the Junior Service straight from his last year at school at just over fifteen years old. He was in his fourth term at Aldershot and had already made his first parachute jumps. I was astounded; it was just like a flashlight going off in my head. Yes, the Junior Army, this was it, this was the life for me.

That evening when we had eaten I told my parents I did not intend to stay on at school; I was going to join the Junior Service of the Army.

They looked at me stunned.

'Well this is a turn up for the book,' dad said. 'One minute you haven't got a clue the next minute your future's done and dusted.'

'Well you're not going,' challenged mum. 'I'm not having a son of mine going off to war.'

Now, there wasn't exactly a war going on at this time; but the year previously the troubles had kicked-off in Northern Ireland and by the autumn of 1970 the papers were full of news of British troops on the streets of Londonderry and Belfast being shot at and stoned. This was what my mother was referring too.

'There's no war mum,' I said. 'It's just civil disturbance and it'll be over in no time.' (Little did we all know...)

'Look,' I said. 'Two years ago you actively encouraged me to join the Navy. That didn't happen but you were prepared to let me go away and board in North Wales at thirteen years old! (*This said in a raised voice*)I don't want to stay on at school, I hate it. The Junior Service is like a school; we had a careers day today and there was a Junior Soldier on the Army stand; he told me all about it. It's just like being in boarding school except you're in the army; you carry on your education alongside military skills. I'm more likely to get my 'O' levels there then staying on at Nelson Haden.'

My parents without doubt had been taken aback. I was certainly no mammy's boy. I was very independent and leaving home at fifteen and a bit was not really an issue for me; in fact it seemed a great idea to be away from my parents; however it was not quite that simple to my mum and dad.

I could see the cogs turning in my dad's head. He was seeing this as an opportunity for me to establish myself on a secure route in life and alleviate the worries he had of me taking the wrong route in the future or making another grave mistake outside the law.

Although I hadn't been in trouble with the police since the episode with the toilet roll at Swindon, my dad was unconvinced that another bout of police trouble would not land on his door step.

Mum spoke first.

'I thought you had ambitions of becoming a farmer? You know Mr Turner is very impressed with what you do on the farm; he's even discussed the possibility of sponsoring you through agricultural college.'

'Well this is the first I've heard of it mum, when did this happen? You never mentioned it before.'

Dad chipped in....

'Calm down son. It was an option, your mum and I saw how happy you were working on the farm, (*was it the farm making me happy or the farmer's wife?*) we were talking to Vic, and it came up in conversation. You should consider it. Mr Turner would be making a very generous offer.'

So here I am, within a day I go from having no clue as to what I want to do, and no options, to having two totally different ones; stay on at school for a year then train in farm management with the backing of a very decent and fair farmer, or finish school at the end of the fourth year and join (if they'll have me) the Junior Service of the army.

'So,' said my farther. 'What exactly had you in mind if you join the army?'

'What do you mean dad?' I asked.

'Well, what branch of the army? You must have some idea of what you want to do, what do you want to specialise in; do you want to be a cook? An electrician? What..?'

Well, I hadn't given it much thought. A soldier was a soldier as far as I was concerned; I came out with the first thing that entered my head.

'A paratrooper,' I said.

241

My mum looked aghast,

My dad looked at me with some serious scepticism.

'We may reluctantly agree to this at some point in the future,' he said. 'But if you think for one minute your mother and I are going to let you go off to become a common Infantry Soldier with no background trade other than knowing how to fire a gun or jump out of an airplane you're very much mistaken. No my lad, if this is the route you eventually choose to go down then you'll be going into a regiment that can teach you a trade and give you a future when you leave the army.'

My mum was not really saying anything, she was finding this turn of events difficult to take in; it had all been very sudden for her.

'Leave it with your mother and I to discuss together,' dad said.

'After we've talked together we'll resume the conversation with you.'

Discussion had ended; the seed had been planted and I could tell dad was not opposed to it, providing it was looked into fully and held a future for me.

I went back to school the next day feeling very positive. A few other lads in my year and also in my class had been interested, Hedley Brooks and Chris Ruddling to name but two of them.

I asked them if they had spoken to their parents, they had and received much the same reaction as me. I told them my parents' reaction to my wanting to join the Junior Para's, they laughed and asked if my parents had agreed.

I told them that I was awaiting the second round of negotiations. We would keep each other informed. We didn't need to commit to staying at school the extra year unit the final term, Easter to summer, and that was still ages away.

On return to school after the summer break the fourth and fifth years had been offered a further activity on a Wednesday afternoon. As well as the different sport options we could opt to work with the Kennet and Avon Canal Restoration Group at Bradford-on-Avon helping to clean up, repair, and refurbish the canal.

I jumped at the chance as it had numerous advantages.

Firstly, on the Wednesday I would be excused school uniform. Secondly, as soon as the lunch bell went I could leave the school premises and head off in whatever direction I choose and thirdly it simply gave an opportunity of freedom.

I signed up and after the first week found I enjoyed it very much.

Talking to gran about the canal and its history I found out that our Wiltshire family had strong ties with the waterway. Fred Sartain's work at Dundas and Rosie Hosey having married a Badder had become a bargee on the Kennet and Avon and other canals of southern England.

For me this restoration work would be the start of a life time interest in the canal and I would work on it again later in the decade as well as walking the whole length with a girlfriend in 1982.

However this freedom from school prompted me to start skiving, or to call it by its proper name to 'Play Truant'.

It started slowly and I found I was getting away with it.

So I would skive-off more regularly and encourage Martin Edwards, Alan Cooper and Des to do the same. Teresa skived from Trowbridge High and wrote sick notes signed supposedly by my dad, for my brother to take and give to my form master. Even Susan Wiltshire started skiving from her job in Bowyers. It got so bad that at one point there would be a house full of kids down at mine for days at a time.

I would leave the house in the morning on my bike and when Pete and mum had gone past me in the car I'd just turn round and go home.

By the time I got there half a dozen others would be waiting outside the gate.

I let everyone in and the fun would begin. This went on and off for weeks but of course it could not continue as there were so many kids off school from the same village, it was bound to go bust.

The shit hit the fan big time when Bowyers rang Sue's mum to enquire after her health.

Alarm bells rang; Sue was confronted and confessed all. Her mum rang Nelson Haden, who rung Martin's mum who came round and caught us all red handed in my house.

She then came back in the evening and confronted my parents accusing me of being the ring leader. *As if!*

Of course Nobby was well aware of what had been going on because as well as playing in our house and garden we had spent time playing on the bales in the barn with him egging us on.

At school we had our names read out in assembly and all had to parade for the cane. It was a notorious episode in Nelson Haden skiving history; a bit like busting a drugs ring or some other major vice ring and low and behold the leader was again yours truly.

My little brother was very lucky; it never got out, or back to the school or our parents that he was the 'sick note courier', or he too could have been in serious trouble.

This could have been the time when my dad made up his mind about me going in the army.

Steven needed discipline and direction. Neither my parents nor my school were able to keep me in line. It would be better for me to utilise my energies doing something worthwhile i.e. defending Queen and Country.

Arrangements were made for us to visit the army information office in Bath to discuss my entry to the army as a boy soldier and take the 'Queen's Shilling'.

The family descended on the poor unsuspecting recruiting Sergeant one Saturday morning and heated debate took place; I was still determined to jump out of planes and my parents were equally determined I should do something useful, where I was less likely to be shot, like join the Royal Army Medical Corps or the Pay Corps...Where they thought I got the intelligence to join these regiments of intellect heaven only knew.

In the end my practical abilities and grasp of all things mechanical shone through and I was guided towards becoming a member of the Royal Engineers. I would aim at being Plant Operator or Operator Mechanic and begin my service as a Junior Leader with placement, depending of course on my passing all the entry levels, at Old Park Barracks, Whitfield, Dover, in the lovely county of Kent. My start date would be September 1971; I would be just over fifteen years old. The die was cast.

My privilege of working on the farm had been withdrawn; both dad and mum were furious at my skiving episode and this was a good method of punishment. They knew how much I loved being out there with Nobby.

Instead I was working with dad who could keep a close watch on me.

Winter was coming and cords of timber needed to be sawn and chopped for our open fire, this was a chore that took place every weekend. Dad, Pete and I working like Trojans to prepare enough wood to see us through.

Another privilege withdrawn was our being left alone while mum and dad went out on a Friday night. I was horrified to be told we would be subjected to a babysitter...aaaah!

No more raves, no more hitting the homemade wine and beer, no more blaring music. Fourteen and a baby sitter! The indignity of it.

But the question was...who would it be?

As it happened I had no complaints at all; mum worked with a stunning twenty year old called Roz. Roz was a Picture with a capital 'P'; I would walk to VW at Canal Road and drop in on mum after school just to get a look at and a few words with Roz.

Roz had volunteered to babysit Pete and me on nights our parents went out and I didn't mind at all. In fact both mum and dad looked at my passive acceptance of Roz coming over with an element of suspicion.

Roz I knew had a soft spot for me; whenever she came over to ours' or when I went to the depot at Canal Road she was always pleased to see me and would give me a lovely hug. She could tuck me in and kiss me goodnight any night of the week.

Earlier that summer VW UK had organised a big open day for all employees at their head office in Hampshire; one of the attractions of the day was an employee (female of course) beauty competition, which Roz entered on behalf of VW Trowbridge.

We had to leave early in the morning on the Saturday, so Roz after visiting the hairdresser in Trowbridge on the Friday evening, stayed over at ours. I remember thinking what a stunner she was and how she couldn't fail to win. With her sixties style 'Beehive' hairdo and yellow mini-dress up to her you-know-what my adolescent imagination ran riot. I'm glad there was no truth in the story of hand coordinated blindness, because I would have been seriously afflicted.

The day was boiling; we had a 2ltr Triumph Vittesse convertible at the time and due to Roz's hairdo had to keep the roof up and the windows closed all the way. It was a sweltering two hour trip but we got there at last and had a great day. Roz came second in the beauty pageant, no justice thought I.

Before half term a call came from the army recruitment centre. I would be called for a simple test which would take place at the information office. Then I would go for a weekend to Corsham to do selection and fitness training. If all went well I would then be called in to swear allegiance; basically to sign on; but that would be months ahead and a great deal closer to my possible intake date the following September.

I went to school and told my mates of the monumental step I had taken.

We were moving into winter. It was getting colder and the winter of 1970/71 would be a hard one. The farm house was freezing, the fire being lit by me as soon as I got home from school and banked up high all evening. The AGA was kept continually alight in the dairy both day and night and our family would use this room to get undressed for bed and to get dressed in the morning. All unused rooms had the doors permanently closed with newspaper pushed around the 'Door-jams' and beneath to prevent any heat escaping. We now knew why Nobby & Lizzie had elected to live in a council house in the village.

At night thick frost would cover the inside of our bedroom windows and condensation would freeze the windows shut.

During those weekends following my grounding dad and I had sawn, chopped and prepared logs for the winter by the hundred and we were thankful we had. Dad had made a saw horse and with him and me on the long cross-cut saw and Pete holding the log steady in the horse we had spent hours preparing the winter fuel.

It was too cold to hang out in the village. Susan's mum had put a restriction on her seeing me, or me going into her house. The same applied at Martin Edmunds. The wounds from the skiving episode were taking time to heal. I spent more weekends over my gran's in Winsley. This of course meant I saw less of Teresa.

Eventually mum and dad relented and allowed me to back to work on the farm. This change of heart was brought on by intervention from Vic Turner, who at this time had not been made aware of my choice of career path.

It was a Saturday and I was out in the shed cleaning out my rabbits when Vic came through and asked if he could phone Nobby at home.

I said sure, mum and dad were out but using the phone to phone up the village was no problem. I asked if there was a problem on the farm, as it was Saturday and Nobby was not at work.

Winter was a slow time in dairy farming and Nobby claimed back some of those long hours he worked in the summer.

'My truck is stuck up the top field,' said Vic. 'I need Nobby to come down and pull me out.'

I could do that, I knew I could do that; he knew I could do that too, but I suppose after telling me I was not allowed to drive the tractor he couldn't really go back on his own words. I was biting my tongue to ask.

I could hear the phone ringing and ringing at the other end... no answer.

Vic put down the phone. 'Bugger, he's not there,' he said.

'I'll pull you out Mr Turner,' I said. 'I can do it, you know I can; you've seen me driving mum's car and my truck before it blew up.'

'Yes I know you can Steven, but you know what I said, you're too young to be driving the tractor.'

'Yes but Mr Turner most farmer's kids drive the tractor; I'm good at it; I can pull you out, if I don't you may be here for hours.'

'When is your dad home?' He asked.

'Ages,' I said. I had no idea really; in fact it wouldn't be long. My parents had only gone briefly into Trowbridge.

Vic stood looking at me rubbing his chin.

'Ok then, let's go.'

I was grinning from ear to ear as we walked into the farm yard.

Vic opened the shed door where we kept the Zetor and reversed it out. I climbed up on the side plate beside the seat and we were set to go.

'Hold on,' said Vic.

Oh no not a change of mind surely.

'What's up,' I asked.

'You drive,' he said. 'I can see how you get on.'

We swapped places and I very professionally and sedately drove the tractor up to the top field.

'That business of you skipping school Steven... your dad spoke to me about it. He blamed Nobby for encouraging you and for not telling them what was happening in the house. I had a word with Nobby, I wasn't pleased with him, but I feel enough time has gone past now and it's time to move on, I'll have word with your dad, ask him to let you come back. How's that sound?'

'Would you? That's great Mr Turner; thanks so much. '*What a nice bloke.*

We arrived at his truck which was just inside the gate of the field, well and truly up to the axles.

We secured the tow strop with a shackle to the eye on the front of the truck and to the bar on the tractor.

'Take up the slack very slowly Steven,' said Vic.

'Then when I give you the thumbs up move off gradually in a wide circle and back out through the gate; don't on any account turn too sharply.'

'That's ok Mr Turner, Don't worry, I've been with my dad doing this loads of times.'

Vic climbed in the truck and I mounted the tractor; slowly I took up the slack and watched Vic's reaction; he stuck up his thumb and we were moving.

I increased the revs of the tractor and we began to move, the truck coming out of the mud. Around I went in a long arc until we went back through the gate and onto the track leading down to the farm. I pulled up to release the tow rope.

I felt really chuffed and Vic was smiling at me.

'Well done and thanks,' he said as he climbed out of the cab.

We chucked the tow rope in the back of the truck and he said let's go and get the tractor into the shed. I drove it sensibly back to the yard with Vic following. We locked it up and walked through the small gate to the back door; mum and dad were home.

Vic said 'let me do the talking Steven.'

I opened the door and called for my dad who was sitting with mum drinking tea in the dairy. Dad came through and Vic said hello.

'John I wonder if I could have a quick word.'

'Please come on through and have a cup of tea Mr Turner,' my mum called.

While Vic kicked of his boots on the step, I thought I would disappear. I went into the shed to carry on feeding and cleaning out my rabbits.

Only a few minutes later I heard my mum shout for me to come in and have a cup of tea, I kicked my boots off and went inside.

The adults were still sitting at the table talking.

Dad told me my going on the farm ban had been lifted. He also said that he had told Vic about my decision to join the army.

'I think it's a good choice for you Steven,' said Vic.

'You got what it takes, you've the sharp mind and quick wittedness the army needs; you'll do ok, I'd guarantee it. Anyway as nice as farming is you'd see very little of the world, you hardly get a holiday in this game. You work on the farm till the time comes and then start something fresh and exciting.

And now I'm taking the gun across the field for an hour or so how do you fancy coming with me? I hear you're a pretty good shot?'

I was; I'd been shooting with Nobby's 12 bore quite a few times and pigeons or rabbits stood no chance with me.

'That would be great Mr Turner thanks.'

'Oh and its 'Vic' Steven, no more Mr Turner ok?'

'Yes Vic, I'll remember.'

It would be dusk shortly and within the hour Nobby would be down to do the milking. The cows at this time of year were in the barn on straw;

they were fed from hay and silage baled and stacked during the summer. The silage heap was up against the barn. Fresh grass from our pastures was cut in the late summer; some baled as hay, the rest laid down and driven over by the tractor to compact it. Then with a sheet over the top it would rot internally for a different type of feed.

Vic and I went off over the fields. The 12 bore was given to me and a couple of cartridges. Vic watched as I broke the gun and inserted the two cartridges in the barrels.

I had been shooting with Nobby quite a few times and he'd sold me the cartridges. They were 9d each, and if I scored a hit I could sell the pigeon or a rabbit for a shilling to Sammy, he would feed this dead bird or rabbit to his ferrets. This small income would pay for the cartridge with a few pennies left over. It paid to score a kill, not to miss.

Nobby for all his irresponsibility had been very serious in the use of the weapon and had told me the gun should always be carried broken across the crook of the arm with empty barrels, unless you were actually stalking; then the gun is carried with the barrels pointing upward and across the body; the gun was a classic twin hammer, so the hammers are back with finger laying alongside the trigger guard. Anyone with you should walk a few paces behind. After firing the weapon should be made safe before retrieving the kill or reloading.

The penny dropped... my mum and dad had asked Vic to take me and see if I was responsible, hence the reason I, not he, was holding the shotgun.

Ok then I was fine with that; I'd proved myself once today, now I'd show him I was equally responsible when in charge of a loaded gun.

'Walk behind me Vic,' I told him.

'What are you going to beware of, Steven,' he said.

'People Vic; there shouldn't be, but could be members of the public with their pets, out in the fields; I don't want to pepper some innocent dog walker or their dog.'

'Well done, that was exactly the answer I was looking for; now let's see how good you are.'

We walked on; two magpies flew from a tree but I didn't react.

'You should have banged them,' said Vic.

'Really? I didn't know magpies could be shot.' *I did really, Nobby had told me they were classed as flying vermin, but I hadn't necessarily believed him so thought it best to play safe.*

'Yes you can shoot them, Nobby should have told you, they're vermin, and they're fair game.'

'Ok,' I said.

Two pigeons flew from the lower branches of a tree, I wasn't concentrating but the gun was up. Too late, it would have been a waste of two cartridges; but the birds had flown into a tree further down the field. Next time I'll have them.

We gingerly stalked down the side of the ditch...

As we crept closer to the tree I knew the birds were in I mounted the gun to my shoulder anticipating the moment of flight - and away they went. I let go both barrels within milliseconds of each other and to my great satisfaction saw both birds stumble and crash into the field. One was still flapping but the other was still. Vic picked up the wounded bird and handed it to me.

'What are you going to do with that then, you can't let it suffer,' said Vic.

On my other foray's Nobby did the deed but that wasn't going to happen with Vic; I had to take responsibility for finishing off my wounded prey.

'Here, I'll show you this time,' said Vic and holding the bird by the base of the neck pulled the head back with a snap.

The neck was broken.

'Here feel this,' Vic said.

I ran my fingers down the length of the bird's neck until I came to a soft gap.

'Feel the gap?' Said Vic, 'That's the gap in the spinal column, broken neck, about as painless as quick death could be. Think you can do that? If not you shouldn't be out shooting, you're never guaranteed an instant kill regardless of what you shoot or how good you are; rabbit, fox or pigeon. You've got to be able to dispatch the wounded. I recommend you have a sharp knife with you.'

He didn't enlarge on what I was supposed to do with the sharp knife. But there was no need really, it was obvious to me.

'Good shooting Steven, I trust you with the gun; come on let's go home it's getting dark and bloody cold.'

As we approached the farm I could hear the pumps going in the milking parlour and see the steam rising of the cows in the yard; those waiting to go through and those released back into the barn.

It was lovely, the evening sun setting red in the sky, the chill of the winter evening and the smell of the farm and country.

It was such a lovely place to be and what a great life.

The Christmas school holidays arrived and Pete and I were on holiday for two weeks. During this time we could spend some time with gran and our friends at Winsley which we were both looking forward to.

My parents however were not in such a good frame of mind. Things were getting no better at Marcos and a few days before Christmas dad came home from work and told mum that half a dozen men had been made redundant and would not be returning to work after the break. One was a good friend of dad's, who had suspected for some time he may be given his cards and had already been searching for alternative employment; to date he hadn't been lucky.

The whole issue was causing long debates between my parents. Should dad stick it out or should he to start looking for another job.

For Pete and I on the sidelines it seemed strange, dad was good at his job, he was highly thought of by Jem March and he was a foreman who was very inventive; surely he'd not lose his job.

But for mum and dad it seemed difficult to know what to do.

My parents decided for the first time ever that we would go out for Christmas lunch. This was unheard off. Dad was a home bird and mum was a great cook. The idea of going out and actually paying for someone else to produce and serve up our Christmas lunch was beyond belief. Pete and I were flabbergasted, but nevertheless we thought it a great idea.

The seed for this monumental move from tradition was planted by two friends of my parents; Danny and Angela.

Angela had worked with mum ever since her arrival at VW. Then mum had been asked by her if there were any vacancies at Marcos and dad had found a job for Danny. So in a nutshell both Danny and Angela worked with my parents and socialised with them on Friday or Saturday nights.

My parents booked our lunch at a restaurant just outside Bath owned by two famous comedians of the time, Arthur Askey and Jimmy Jewel.

As entertainers they were well known as the funny men of the post war period, more of my parents era than mine but I had seen them both on TV and Pete and I thought it pretty cool that we would be eating lunch with television celebrities. (No one told us that they didn't live there and that they would probably be at home having Christmas lunch with their own families not serving roast spuds at a venue just outside Bath).

Mum bought very little food in for Christmas. The whole Christmas thing was far less commercial in 1970 than it is today. Apart from a selection of salad and pastries that mum bought or made for a Christmas Eve buffet and the lunch itself, not a great deal more was purchased in the way of extras.

However as luck would have it mum did buy in a chicken for cooking and eating cold over the Christmas weekend; I'll get to the luck bit in a mo...

Also this year we would have Christmas Eve evening at gran's. Although mum would contribute with salads and suchlike, gran would provide the pickles rolls and nibbles.

So, tree and decorations aside, apart from the normal stuff that you'd find in the larder most days of the week not a great deal was different in the food or (due to excessive supplies of home brew) the drink department.

Christmas Day was a Friday; I can't remember when our school broke up for the holidays but Pete and I had a couple of days with gran earlier in the week so I'm pretty sure we must have finished school the previous Friday.

We had a lovely evening at gran's and prior to the evening meal uncle Bert and auntie Dot walked down and when they went home the four of us walked down to spend half an hour at Pat & Maurice's. We got home late and went to bed. The weather forecast had predicted snow during the last week of the year; Pete and I hoped we may get some of it.

The following morning the family stuck with tradition, mum going downstairs first and putting a match to the fire and making sure all was well. Then the little bell rang and we all trooped downstairs.

Presents were given out and breakfast was eaten.

My prize present from mum and dad was a bolt action 410 shotgun, a lovely gun with a built in magazine holding three cartridges with one in the chamber, dad had bought it second hand from a mate at Marcos; I was over the moon with this show of trust. I no longer had to beg the 12 bore from Nobby, I had my own gun and only had to ask permission from Vic to use it across the fields.

Not to be left-out Pete had also been given a gun, a 'Gnat' air pistol to use in the garden.

After 'brekkie' when normally the lunch would immediately be prepared we were at a loose end.

But mum and dad had a plan; we would go for a long walk to Brokerswood the other side of Southwick.

Brokerswood Country Park had first opened a couple of years before with a site for caravans and lovely walks through eighty acres of ancient woodland. We had been there a few times as a family and also as a gang of kids on our bikes in the summer.

We got dressed in our warm clothes and with the dogs, piled into the car.

When we arrived the site was almost empty, a couple of cars in the car park with likeminded people getting some fresh air and working up an appetite.

As we walked, scattered snow flurries fell, it was never going to turn into a serious fall but it was lovely and added to the Christmas feeling.

Our lunch was booked for 2pm; we had agreed to meet Danny and Angela at the restaurant so we weren't pushed for time.

Driving out of 'The Rank' the house looked warm and 'homely; our Christmas tree looked lovely in the front room window. We'd never had such a big tree, mainly because we never before had such a big front room.

When we got home the dogs were put out the back and there was a mad dash for who was going to be first in the bathroom.

Dad had rigged up an electric bathroom heater as the weather had got colder which was a blessing and raised the temperature slightly in the freezing room.

We were all in our best clothes with both the fire and the AGA banked up and out the front door by one-o-clock.

The restaurant was in Colerne near Bath; when we got there the car park was packed absolutely full to bursting.

We went through the door - just; I could barely move.

The bar was packed with people calling for drinks; people were standing round with nowhere to sit and hardly room to lift a glass. I could immediately see the look of disappointment come over dad's face. This was not for him. (*And now forty five years on I'm just the same; I hate crowds, I hate packed eating places and I hate having to wait for a table*).

We squeezed into a corner while dad went to the bar. Danny and Angela had not yet arrived; I wondered just how the restaurant was going to cope.

Dad went to the bar, mum told Pete and I to stay where we were and she would enquire about our table.

Dad returned with drinks and I told him where mum had gone.

It was already 2pm; by rights we should be seated. Mum returned and was in the process of telling dad that things were running late and all the people around us were waiting for a table when a lady standing near us overheard and butted into mum's conversation with dad saying she and her husband had booked for 1pm and they were still waiting.

I could see her husband had already had three or four drinks and was not looking that steady on his feet... he may not even make his table at the rate he was going.

Dad was getting flushed.

'Well,' mum said, 'they told us 20 minutes.'

'Yes that's what they told me an hour ago,' said the lady.

At that point Danny and Angela turned up; I saw them come through the door at the other side of the bar and told dad who raised his hand, just, and waved them over.

Hello's were made and explanations were given. Dad went to get them both a drink and Danny went to sort things out with the concierge; moments later he came back beaming; come on quickly he said we've been given a table; it was obviously a case of those making the biggest fuss getting seated first... or he'd slipped the guy a fiver. We dashed off to our table and as we left I could hear the lady who had butted into the conversation moaning to her husband that we had been seated and they had not.

However all was not roses... the tables were crammed in with hardly room to move and the fact that we actually had, and were, seated at a table was not the end of it.

We waited and waited; another round of drinks was bought but no waiter came to take an order. Once again dad demanded service but it fell on deaf ears. We were all starving by now; it had been a long time since breakfast and since then we had been for a long walk working up a serious appetite. I was beginning to feel miserable and so was Pete.

Mum and Angela went to the loo and came back looking very purposeful; the order was given, 'drink up we're going.'

Dad and Danny looked a little stunned.

'Come on,' said mum.

'Enough is enough, we have a chicken at home, potatoes, veg, Christmas pudding and cream; we'll go home and make our own Christmas dinner, I've spoken with Angela and she agrees, she and Danny will come with us. There's enough for all six of us and Angela can help me. We'll have some sandwiches to tide us over till dinner is ready. Come on lets go!' She insisted.

Mum had the bit between the teeth, she wasn't going to argue the point and rapidly shepherded us from the table while other diners looked on.

A waiter came over and tried to pacify mum but she was having none of it.

'This is a disgrace,' she said.

'This whole set-up is a disorganised shambles, and if the owner were here we would tell him so. Not only have you overbooked, you've crammed so many tables in here people can hardly move. Well we've wasted as much of our Christmas day in your restaurant that we're prepared to waste.'

Mum breezed by the lot of them holding the door open for the rest of us to leave. Her parting shot to the other man and lady who were still stood at the bar was 'There's a spare table over there. You should grab it while you can.'

In the car park it was agreed we would all return to our house where we would all chip in to making a lovely dinner. Mum and Angela would knock-up a plate of sandwiches, nuts, and crisps to tide us over.

As it happened it turned out to be a lovely afternoon and evening. It was gone 4pm when we got home and the first thing mum did was to get the chicken in the oven. Angela prepared snacks for us while Danny and dad prepared the spuds and veg.

Pete and I put our feet up in front of the fire watching TV.

We eventually had our Christmas dinner around 7pm and it was as usual a top class production from mum. In the end we all agreed we preferred having our Christmas day lunch at home. Danny and Angela stayed till late, Pete and I had already gone to bed when they left.

It would be six years before we went out for a Christmas Day meal again and then I would be home on leave from the army; it would be in the 'Aberdeen Angus' in Regent road Great Yarmouth.

Boxing Day was the Saturday and dad went early in the car and brought gran over to ours' for the day and on Sunday we went over as a family to Winsley where we met with the Swindon clan. It was a real house full and gran had done one of her great spreads. After our food we all went out for a walk around the village for a couple of hours. Rob, Chrissie, Pete and I were forbidden to get up to anything; it was Sunday and we were in our best clothes. It was just a case of walking off lunch and getting some fresh air.

Monday mum and dad went back to work and Pete and I were left on our own for a few days. It was very cold and not the weather to hang about around the village; a couple of days our friends came round during the day to play Monopoly or with our Scalextric car race track, set up in the dining room.

The skiving episode had more or less passed into history and I was no longer the bad boy of the village. It was only Martin Giles' parents who still had the anti-Burt ban in place; strange really as Martin hadn't even been involved in the skiving.

In between these lazy moments I would put in a couple of hours on the farm helping Nobby and earning pocket money. The work during the winter was hedging and ditching which was really hard labour. Nobby would be in his waders up to his knees in water in the ditch cleaning out the bottom and levelling off the sides.

Cutting back the hedgerows and in places relaying the hedge was a skill which was quite common at that time before mechanical cutting took over. A professionally laid hedge looked really lovely and even a hedge that had been trimmed and tidied looked good. Unlike the terrible ripping and destruction of the hedge that takes place today with a mechanical cutter.

We would work together, me pulling the cuttings into piles which we would eventually burn.

New Year's Day fell on the Friday and we awoke to snow; the plan was that dad would go over and get gran and she would spend the day with us. However due to the weather, which, according to the forecast was not set to get better, we decided to go over to gran after lunch and stay till the evening, saving dad the double trip and also saving gran turning out in the cold.

We phoned auntie Dot, wished her a Happy New Year and asked if she could pop down to gran's with the message; we would see her and my uncle later in the day.

After lunch we wrapped up and headed over to Winsley. It was bitterly cold with a very fine snow falling. We left the dogs in the kitchen and our cat Ringo curled up in the front room. The sitting room looked warm and inviting as we left, this was really a day to stay indoors.

However it was always lovely to see gran and we also went round the corner to look in on auntie Dot and uncle Bert; it was gone 8pm before we left for home.

By now the snow was falling quite heavily and after parking in the drive we knocked the snow off our shoes at the back door and quickly let ourselves in.

The dogs were waiting wagging their tails and Ringo was sitting on the open serving hatch between the kitchen and the front room. As we settled mum put the kettle on and dad went through to the toilet calling me to let the dogs out of the back door for a run.

I opened the door and called both dogs to go out. As I did so the biggest rat you've ever seen came shooting into the kitchen.

'A rat, a rat!' I shouted.

'Close the doors, close the doors, quick!'

The back door was still wide open, snow was blowing in and the dogs, as they were running out into the yard had seen the rat... they tried to turn back into the kitchen as the rat ran almost between their legs and both dogs had gone sprawling into the snow; their coats caked in the white stuff they hurled themselves back through the open door into the kitchen.

Chaos reigned!

Dad was in the toilet and all three doors were open, the back door, the door between the dairy and the kitchen and the door between the dairy and the hall.

I shouted at my brother.

'Close the hall door Pete! Close the hall door quick, before the bloody thing gets into the rest of the house!'

With the snow blowing through the outside door and the snow falling from the dogs the 'Lino' floor was like an ice rink. The dogs went slipping and crashing through the kitchen into the dairy.

The cat had come through the serving hatch from the front room like a bolt of lightning and joined the fun.

With the doors closed we had the thing contained. The dogs had cornered the rat under the corner seat in the dairy but the pair of them were too big to get under the bench to grab it. Mayhem!

By now dad had come out of the toilet and started to issue orders.

'Get the dogs outside,' he said. 'Leave it to the cat. (The cat was a great ratter).

'Get those dogs outside, and Peter stand by the door, the cat will chase the thing out, be ready to open the door when it comes through.'

It took all our strength to drag the dogs away and shove them out into the snow.

Pete stood waiting by the door as the cat now with no opposition chased the rat round and round the dairy. Mum through all this was standing on a chair in the kitchen shouting, 'get the thing, just get the thing!'

'Peter,' said dad, 'open the door a little, but not enough for the dogs to get back in.'

Pete opened the door about a foot and the rat, spying a route to safety made a bolt for it. Or at least that was probably the last thought that went through his or her head...Rosko was waiting outside and as the rat shot though the small gap that Pete had opened between door and frame it ran straight into the jaws of our youngest dog.

Crunch! Through all the pandemonium I'm sure I heard the bone snapping. We opened the door and there stood a very proud looking Rosko with the rat in his mouth and blood all over the snow. We all cheered and gave him a big pat.

We managed to get him to drop the thing and with a shovel chucked it way over the back fence into the slurry pit. The farm was infested with rats and it was not uncommon for our cat to return with lumps of fur missing where he had been in a serious scrap, or to come down in the morning only to find a dead rat on the door step where Ringo had dragged it to show us his prowess as a hunter-killer. But this was the first time one of our dogs had dispatched a rat... the rat community had better watch out, they now had another predator to contend with.

Panic over we washed and disinfected the floor and sat round the table in the dairy laughing and recounting the episode.

The rest of the weekend went past quietly and Monday we were back to school, the winter holidays finished.

This coming term and this year would see monumental changes in my life and in the life of my family. It would be the beginning of a life away from home, a break from my parents and a massive step into adulthood. It would be the first step into a very interesting life.

The second term of my fourth year January 1971 began in the usual way. Catching up on news from friends we had not seen during the holiday; sorting out a lesson plan and deciding what sport to pursue during the term.

At lunch time it was the usual scrabble for the head server place but this was not as severe as the mêlée that took place after the summer break.

Generally the same places, once established after summer break, stood through the remainder of the year.

During this term I could expect a letter from the army giving me a date for my two day selection at Corsham, I was really looking forward to this. I had already visited the recruiting office in Bath and taken and passed the first simple tests, now it was stage two and getting serious.

I knew others in the fourth year were interested in joining one of the services, but so far it seemed to me that I was the only one committed and the only one waiting selection.

The letter eventually came around half term. I was to report to the army selection centre in Corsham on Friday evening March 19th. I would be picked up again by my parents on the Sunday at lunch time. The weekend would consist of sport, introduction to military life and equipment plus written and physical tests. Things were really moving forward.

A letter was also given to all the fourth year students from the school inviting pupils on a week's camping trip to Jersey following the Easter break, this would be organised and supervised by our young Mr Jennings. I really hoped mum and dad would let me go; Jersey sounded great fun but could my parents afford to pay for me to go?

I also knew that for this jolly to be granted by my parents I would need to be on my best behaviour.

My brother was not yet twelve years old. But he too had started smoking - tobacco!

He had a pack of Golden Virginia, papers, and a rolling machine. He kept it hidden in the old pigeon loft on the farm.

However one day after rolling himself a sly fag he forgot to put it back, leaving his cigarette preparation kit in his blazer pocket. Mum found it five minutes before the school run.

She was horrified and questioned Pete on how he got it where he got it, where he got the money for the tobacco, how long he had smoked, etc.

Give my brother his due he never gave anything away and in taking such a hard line angered mum further to the point she said that that evening they would sit down with dad and she would get the truth out of him. This implied a spanking was forthcoming. Pete still kept quiet, very brave of him because unlike me who had calluses on my ass from the times I'd been whacked, Pete was never good at taking spankings.

I did a quick exit and got off to school on my bike.

Pete was on his own in the car with mum when an incident happened that prompted my brother to come out with a statement way beyond his eleven years.

They were driving up Bradley Road to turn left into College Road, the road leading to the school back gate. Just prior to turning left mum overtook a cyclist, but then slowed down. Had she looked in her near side mirror she would have seen that the cyclist had gained ground on the car and was again on the inside and level with her.

Mum turned left and bang; straight in the cyclist. Bike and rider went flying.

Of course by the time mum had turned, parked and ran back, a crowd had gathered to lift the poor guy to his feet. Luckily he was shaken but unhurt.

There was minor damage to his bike but thankfully not much else.

Mum asked Pete to walk the rest of the way to school while she took the man and his bike into town to sort out the damage and the cost. (Things were simple then).

With a stroke of genius my brother's parting shot to mum was...'I won't tell dad about this, if you don't tell of my cigarettes!'

Brilliant!

Mum was aghast and of course said to my brother...'Peter I can't discuss this now.'

'Oh yes you can,' said Pete...'yes or no? Do I keep this to myself or not?'

Mum was caught on the spot and in desperation said, 'ok, we'll call it quits.'

Pete of course hunted me down in the playground and told me; but dad never found out about either the smoking or the bike incident until thirty years later in the course of some story telling over a Sunday lunch. It caused a great deal of laughter. How great is that?

A very attractive blonde had appeared in the girls fourth year; I'm going to call her Clare Sylvester. She had joined Nelson Haden girls from

Melksham where she had been expelled for some kind of misbehaviour. Her aunt lived over near Beech Grove on the estate behind the school; she lodged with her aunt and attended NHGS during the week and went home to Melksham to her parents at weekends.

She was a stunner with long blonde hair and all the boys had their eye on her; a film was released in the eighties called 'Gregory's Girl' where a new girl turns up in a school in Glasgow. Clare's appearance at Nelson Haden ran in pretty much the same vein as the film; except Clare didn't play football.

Clare as I'll call her, hung out with a bunch of 'bad' girls...well I don't mean that in a nasty way, they were just the rowdy, fun girls who shouted constant embarrassing things at the boys they fancied, smoked over the back field, and had no hesitation in putting their hand down the front of your trousers.

Break times would see different groups of girls sitting on the path separating the two schools chatting with groups of boys; mainly these groups knew each other from different areas of town, had grown up on the same estate, or had gone to primary school together.

Clare befriended the group of girls who sat with our gang of seven or eight boys.

My ongoing love affair with Teresa was cooling slightly. Pugsley's elder brother John who was a couple of years older than me had started to take an interest in her. He'd stayed on at school to do his ' A' levels and like Teresa, went to Trowbridge High which was a mixed school and they could get together at break times.

John had woken up to the fact that a very attractive lass lived just around the corner from him who also went to the same school.

Also in that fourteen stroke fifteen year old age group girls tend to be attracted to older boys... sad but true, my once loyal girlfriend was beginning to show an interest elsewhere. I was beginning to fall out of favour.

Angela and I were still friends but since our move to North Bradley we had drifted apart, I was probably the one most at fault for this, after all I'd made a big deal out of Monika's visit at Whitsun and during the time she'd been with us I'd totally ignored Angie, things hadn't been the same between us since then. Sadly for me I was getting my comeuppance, Angie had moved on.

With no intention of being left high and dry I started to move in on Clare and to my surprise found her to be more than willing to go out with me. Once again I was pretty chuffed and my mates were well jealous. I started to see Clare two or three times during the school week and on Friday she would return to Melksham. Teresa and I still got together at weekends when John wasn't on the scene; and of course taking into account my clandestine ongoing relationship with the gorgeous Sam I was doing ok in the girlfriend department.

The weeks of the term moved on and the letter came from the army giving further instructions for my trip to the selection centre at Corsham.

I was, I'll admit, slightly nervous; not really nervous about being away from home, but nervous in case I never made the grade. After all I had banked all on becoming a Junior Soldier and not having to stay on at school beyond the coming July.

The letter contained a list of what to bring and the itinerary for the weekend.

Friday night check-in and a get-to-know-you social evening playing darts, pool, snooker, etc.

Reveille at 7am Saturday morning, followed by breakfast and a run.

The rest of Saturday morning outdoor or indoor team competitions, group challenges and medical.

In the afternoon the classroom doing written tests. This would be followed by our evening meal and in the evening an introduction to military equipment and kit.

Sunday morning a football match including the training staff; debriefing, and home. Of course all of us would be watched all the time and our suitability for army life assessed.

The weekend came; my mates and my teachers wished me luck and Friday evening dad took me over in the car. Corsham was a twenty minute journey from our house in North Bradley.

Kids came from all over the south of England for army selection assessment at Corsham; in the north they went to Sutton Coldfield.

Dad took me over in the car. Pete came along for the ride but mum stayed at home. With me I had a bag with overnight kit, sports gear and a change of other clothes. Dad dropped me at the guardroom where a soldier escorted me to another building which turned out to be our self-contained assessment centre consisting of four rooms containing six beds per room, a big room with trestle tables and chairs, the training room and another room containing a small shop, a snooker table, bar-billiards, darts, books, magazines with an abundance of sofa's and chairs; the leisure room.

A couple of hundred yards away was the cookhouse and canteen.

I was given some paperwork to fill in and told we would do it as a group later, also the itinerary for the weekend. I was shown a bed space, the ablutions (a new word to me which translates to washrooms in civilian terminology) and told to make myself at home.

I looked around. The bed looked comfortable enough. However it was not made up; the two sheets and three blankets were in some sort of bundle at the head of the bed with pillows on top; strange...*I would learn this was a bed pack, a chore to be done throughout my time at Dover, my future training establishment and home, every morning except Sundays.*

We had a table and a couple of chairs at the end of the room.

I took the few things I had brought with me and put them in the steel locker beside the bed I had chosen. I could see I was not the first prospective recruit to arrive. Other cases and bags were visible on and under beds. I went downstairs to meet the others.

A great sketch of a typical barrack room.

There were eight others in the lounge when I went in. Not all were in the same bedroom as me; in typical army organisation we had been allocated rooms alphabetically. The others looked up as I came in and all acknowledged me with a nod or hello. I could sense the collective anticipation in the room.

I walked around the room getting my bearings then sat down to see what happened. A few lads were chatting together and I got the impression that some either knew each other well or had met up on the way to Corsham. Slowly the room filled with lads and four girls; we had all been told to arrive as early as possible. I was probably the only one who had fitted in a full day at school. The others must have spent the day travelling to get there.

A soldier came in and called our attention.

'We're going to the cookhouse,' he said.

'I would like you to all go outside and form three ranks, that means three rows, one behind the other.'

By now there were around fifteen of us and it didn't take a

mathematician to work out that the front row needed to be five persons long... however we were like brainless sheep and it took ages to sort it out; this was to be my first taste of marching.

A couple of kids were army cadets and were used to this. They eventually took control and got the rest of us into shape. The squaddie just stood and watched. *Taking mental notes no doubt.*

The only thing he said was 'the longer you take the less likely there will be any food left over.'

When we were all in some sort of order he said, 'who doesn't know their left from their right?'

No one said a word.

'Good then when I say left turn I want you to all turn to the left together is that understood?'

Silence...

'IS THAT UNDERSTOOD?' He shouted.

Jesus Christ!

'YES,' we all shouted in return.

'Good...now, you may have noticed these two stripes on my arm, do any of you know what they are?'

'Corporal's stripes, Corp,' came a voice from the ranks.

'Correct and what's your name son?'

'Edwards, Corp.'

'Well done Edwards; however it's Corporal to you NOT CORP!... is that clear?'

'Yes Corporal,' said Edwards almost jumping out of his skin. (*serve him right the ' know-all'*).

'Is that clear to everyone?' said the Corporal.

'Yes Corporal,' we shouted in unison.

'Ok, I will say turn to the left, left turn; then and only then you will all turn in one movement to the left... think you can do that?'

'Yes Corporal,' we again shouted in unison.

'Ok we'll try it.'

'The squad will turn to the left, LEFT TURN!' He bellowed.

Pandemonium.

Some turned left, some turned right and some never moved at all!

How I was able to contain my mirth I don't know, it was hilarious. But I was pointing the right way.

The corporal pointed in the direction a few of us were heading.

'If you're not pointing in that direction turn round now.'

I could hear shuffling feet around me.

'Ok, it seems we need a bit of practice on what is left and what is right. All of you hold up your left arm now... that is the arm furthest from the pavement on which I am standing.'

I could see from the corner of my eye arms being changed over.

'Now, below that left arm is your left leg; I will say, to the cook house quick march. After I say the word march you'll move off, left foot first. You will try and keep in the three lines you are now in and do your best to keep in step. I will call out, left - left - left, right - left. Is that understood?'

'Yes Corporal!' Again we shouted.

'OK, here we go, *he was really enjoying himself...*

To the cookhouse, quickkkk MARCH!'

We had the best intentions, but unbelievably even after having it explained which leg was the left one, some still started with the right.

It doesn't work; when you're in a tight group and have to walk you really do need to move legs in union, march in step; if not you kick the person in front in the back of the leg, or bring your shoe down on the heel of the person's in front.

Within the space of a few yards our efforts had degenerated into chaos.

The corporal didn't stop.

'Left - left - left right – left'...

We struggled on with him.

Other soldiers making their way to and from the cookhouse were in fits over us.

We eventually got there.

'Stop,' he said (*not even a military command*).

'Ok, early days, follow me in. There are trays and plates at the beginning of the hotplate and irons, (*the first time I'd heard that expression for a knife fork and spoon*), at the end. Your table is reserved; I will sit with you, note where I sit and come and join me. Ok break-off and follow me in.'

We followed our man Corporal Robbie Timms, Corp of Royal Signals into the cookhouse and joined the queue. I was cool with this, it was quite fun.

We filed through getting the food ladled onto our plate. There were two choices, a fry; gammon, egg, pineapple and chips, or braised steak, boiled spuds and veg. The latter would do for me. There were also two choices of pudding. Treacle sponge and rice pud with strawberry jam.

You couldn't credit it; even after the explicit instructions he had given us some of the kids still sat at other tables.

Timms just shook his head in exasperation and then went off to round up his lost sheep.

I supposed this was what it was all about. This was sorting the wheat from the chaff. The point where moron man would show the army what he couldn't do. They would be noted and would progress no further up the military career ladder.

A couple of late comers, girls and boys, arrived and joined us.

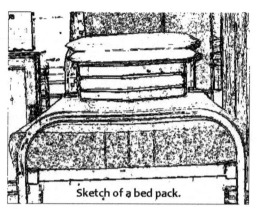
Sketch of a bed pack.

The meal was relaxed we became more settled asking Robbie questions about his life in the army and when, how and why he joined. He had also joined as a boy soldier. He had volunteered for the trainer assessor's job at Corsham as it was his home town and his mum was seriously ill. A posting almost for as long as he wanted it; it suited him, his wife and his parents.

We left the cookhouse scrapping and stacking our plates into a slops bin and dropping our irons in hot water. The march back to our block was less structured. No more trying to walk in line and no more shouted words of command. It had been a long day.

Robbie handed us over to another training NCO and disappeared home.

We were told we could get to know each other a while longer. But we would be expected to be in our pits (beds) by 2130 and lights out at 10pm - 2200. We would be woken at 0700, it was expected that we would be washed and in our gym kit by 0730 for 'brekkie' We would then return to the accommodation block and be shown how to make our beds into bed packs. *The square, blanket, sheet, blanket, configuration that was sitting at the head of our beds.*

0830 we would go for a two mile bash (road run), *peanuts to me.*

I went up to my room at 9pm, I wanted to make up my bed and get some idea how the bed pack went together. One of the lads in our room was an army cadet; full of himself I might add.

'Oh, I know how to do this we have to do it when we go to summer camp.'

I took no notice; I'd sink or swim on my own. I unraveled the bed pack noting how it was folded, I put the sheets and blankets on the bed, went for a wash and turned in.

Lying there in a room with five other kids was a real eye opener. I'd never have believed it...

The next thing I knew the lights had come on and a voice was saying, 'ok rise and shine lads; parade in front of the block in 25 minutes.'

The parting shot was...'No one better be late.'

Looking a right assorted bunch of shapes and colours we formed up loosely in the rows we'd formed the previously evening.

We had a different guy this morning. He wore a blue tracksuit with a crest on the chest. He looked mean; a female soldier stood behind him also in a blue tracksuit.

'I am Corporal Green,' he introduced himself. 'And this is Lance Corporal Jackson. You'll address us as Corporal. We are PTI's - physical training instructors. Our job is to take unfit soldiers and turn them into iron. We of the Army Physical Training Corp are not popular among the ranks of the unfit. And if you knew me long enough you would very soon learn to hate me. Fortunately for you we have a very mild two mile run after breakfast. A run I'm sure you'll all manage easily.'

Mild? I didn't believe it; nothing this bloke would do would be mild.

'Ok we'll jog to the cook house in double quick time. Turn to the left now and when I say to the cook house double march we'll move off in a rapid jog together on the word 'march' - understood?'

'Yes Corporal,' we again shouted in unison. (*We were getting good at this, well the replying anyway*).

'Ok; to the cookhouse double MARCH!'

Bodies were sprawled everywhere; some had started running some had not moved. Others had remembered the left foot forward thing others had not.

We were all over the place with at least a third of us having ended up in a pile on the floor.

'Get up, Get UP!'

We clambered to our feet.

'Right lets walk - move.'...

Looking a right rabble we made our way to the food hall.

Before entering the hall Corporal Green told us to eat and make our way back to our rooms in pairs, upright and soldierly (*what was soldierly?*)

We would form up again in front of the block at 0830 for the run.

We went through the same procedure for breakfast as we had for our meal the evening before. There was an abundance of choice; fry-up, cereals, toast, fruit, tea and coffee.

Some really pigged out... Not me; I was a runner, remember? I knew what happens if you run on an overloaded stomach.

With a lad from Bridgewater who was aiming for the Junior Infantry Regiment at Shorncliffe, also in Kent, I made my way back to the block. Along the way we discussed things so far. He like me was unruffled about the weekend, just hoping he would pass the written tests. He looked fit and played sport for his school; he was also cool about the run.

In our rooms a demonstration was given; how to make a bed pack and we were left to sort it out for ourselves. Eventually after a few attempts we got our packs to a half acceptable standard.

At 0830 we were back on the road outside our block and in three ranks. We had formed up automatically without thinking about it. *Amazing how quick a person takes on the system.*

This run was not cross country; just a short road run around the military area of Corsham.

Corporal Jackson, the female PTI was to accompany us on the run, obviously to attend to the welfare of our female contingent; as well as a young soldier wearing a tracksuit with the Royal Signals logo on the breast.

'We will jog at a brisk pace,' said PTI Green.

'You will endeavour, that means 'try' for those not familiar with the long complicated words, to keep up with me. Those of you who lag behind will form into a slower second group and jog with PTI Jackson. Those of you unable to jog at all will bring up the rear at a brisk pace with Signaller Gordon.

Signaller Gordon is not in a good frame of mind this morning. This was not his Saturday morning pastime of choice. I suggest you do not get on the wrong side of him.'

Jesus, this was enough to put anyone off joining the army full stop. They certainly weren't treating us with kid gloves.

'Is that understood?'

'Yes Corporal,' we shouted our reply.

'I suggest you do your best, your attitude and effort started to be marked from the moment you arrived.' *So now we knew.*

'Ok, turn to the right - the RIGHT I said! We're not going to the cookhouse.'

Half of us had turned automatically to the left. I hasten to add I was

268

not one of them.

'Ok space yourselves out a bit, I don't want a reoccurrence of what happened this morning.'

We shuffled ourselves over a wider area.

'On my command double march we will start jogging.'

'Squad' (*wow we're a squad now, how satisfying is that*).

'Squad....*pause*.....double march!'

We were off; *we'd managed to remain on our feet as well, that was a step in the right direction.*

PTI Green set a good pace.

Within a hundred yards we had straggled into a line with Green leading and Gordon bringing up the rear.

I was near the front along with the kiddie from Bridgewater.

So far so good, this was easy.

We'd done about half a mile when Green dropped back alongside us. There were roughly 10 of us front runners with four of us setting the pace two of which were girls. Out of the six girls (one room) four were in the top ten.

'Any of you run for your school?' Asked Green.

There was a collective, 'yes corporal.'

'Good, well done, you lot keep it up, this is all part of your assessment.'

He began to up the pace.

Looking back I could see a second group had formed and even further back some kids were already walking while Signaller Gordon shepherded them together. There was a great deal of shouting of encouragement going on.

We reached the end of the road, Park Lane I think it was, and hung a left.

Green's pace had not slackened and he was voicing encouragement to his flock.

We were hanging in there but one lad was bent over retching his brekkie up in the gutter.

'Don't worry about it, keep going,' shouted Green.

The lad recovered and battled on; he even apologised. *That will win him points I thought.*

Green had eased down slightly and together we had all picked up a good rhythm. There were still six or seven of us front runners with a couple not that far behind. We had now completely lost the other two groups.

We were heading down another long road beside the railway line on our right. I estimated we had run over a mile.

We turned left into another road; Valley Road.

To PTI Green this was a Sunday stroll. He was yakking away about what we would be doing the rest of the day.

The next thing we'd be doing was a medical? *Errrr would it not have been wise to have the medical before the run. Was this military logic at its finest I asked myself?*

One of the lads, more outspoken than me said just that.

'Ours is not to question why,' answered Green. 'We just do what we're told, we're mere squaddies.'

We laughed and continued.

But in all honesty the front group of us weren't really exerting ourselves at all; this was nothing to how I performed in cross country for my school.

The next thing I realised we were heading down the road on which our block sat. We were back.

'Ok when we come to the block we'll wind down with gentle jogging on the spot,' said Green.

The group of us stopped, a couple bending over retching with hands on hips.

'Try to control your breathing,' said Green 'jog gently on the spot, well done all of you I'm impressed.'

Others were now joining us, but as yet I could see neither Jackson nor Gordon's group.

'Ok, get yourselves inside to the leisure room, you'll find water, fruit juice, tea, coffee and biscuits. Back here at 0950 dressed as you are.'

'Dismissed and well done,' said PTI Green.

Our group wandered in to the lounge laughing and chatting among ourselves, girls as well.

We had done alright and we knew it. The eight of us would hang together, we now acknowledging ourselves as the 'A' team. We'd proved our fitness.

By 0930 all had returned, even those who had walked the course. One kiddie had vomit all down his tracksuit top and was crying. We never saw him again. He showered, packed and went home or ended up in the casserole we had at lunch time.

At 0950 we all paraded again and were jogged by Green and Jackson to the gym.

Here we were given team games and a mini indoor assault course.

Room by room we were taken for a medical.

The medical was the usual basic thing, height, weight, reflexes, flat feet, cough (*for the boys*), look down the throat, eye-sight test, and blow into a tube.

I was pronounced fit (*unofficially*).

We sat in an adjoining room waiting for everyone to go through before jogging back to the gym.

There we remained until everyone had had gone through with the medical.

We wouldn't get the results this weekend. They would be part of the assessment paperwork and also part of the pass, fail procedure. We could be unlucky and pass everything over the weekend and fail selection on the medical report. I'm quite sure that many kids did.

By midday we were finished and jogged back to our block. It had been a gruelling morning; press-ups, sit-ups, sprint runs, medicine balls as well as the mini assault course. We were all knackered.

At the entrance to the block PTI Green dismissed us.

'It's now quarter past twelve; go and shower, change into your casual clothes; sport has finished for today. This afternoon you'll be doing written tests followed by an evening of introduction to military equipment, and a film. The cookhouse is open; make your way over smartly in even numbered groups. That means for those of you with blank looks on your faces twos, fours, sixes, etc. Got it?'

'Yes Corporal!'

'Good, we will meet again in the leisure room at 1400 - dismissed.'

We peeled off and went in through the door; some made their way to the leisure room for a five minute sit down others went straight upstairs.

I went through and made myself a cup of tea, sat in one of the armchairs and drank it while contributing a few things to the conversation which mainly revolved round where a person came from and how they had arrived at Corsham. It seemed among those in the room that I lived the closest.

We also asked each other which units we were hoping to join. A mixed bag, Junior Marines, Junior Infantry, RAC, and for the girls the WRAC's - The Women's Royal Army Corp.

Later I found one other lad who was hoping to go to the Royal Engineers Junior Apprentice College at Chepstow. However he never made the grade for the trade he wished to follow; I met him a year later at Dover, he joined 'C' Squadron in the September 1971 intake the same

271

as me.

I finished my tea and went upstairs for a shower. The girls of course had separate ablutions to the boys but they still had to walk the same corridor and naturally the talk in the boys' washrooms revolved around a couple of the attractive lassies next door. 'Cor, she's alright that brunette'... and so on.

Showered and dressed with three other lads I walked smartly to the cookhouse for a very tasty and filling casserole.

At 1400 we were all where we were told to be.

Corporal Green reappeared and asked us how our morning had been. We laughed and joked with him for a few minutes. Then he explained the afternoon itinerary.

We had three tests watched over by our instructors and a young officer from the Army Education Corp who was responsible for the papers. The first was mathematics. These would be everyday addition, subtraction, multiplication and division. We would then have ten minutes for tea. This would be followed by a literacy test; a 300-500 word essay... yes, you guessed it, subject - 'why I want to join the army'. This test was followed by another break and the final test.

This final section was a weird test of placing things in boxes, shapes colour angles and sequences. Questions like 'which is the odd one out'? And 'what is the missing value'? The papers providing multiple choices answers; I think this is called isometric IQ testing. It was fun.

Each break was rowdy affair with all of us talking about the questions and comparing the answers we'd given.

At 1700 we finished and went again to the cookhouse.

The meal this evening was very light; a salad or toasty type meal as the main meal on a Saturday was at lunch time.

At 1800 we were back in the lecture room. In our absence the tables had been moved to the outside wall. Four trestles were across the front of the room, they were loaded with kit, equipment and weaponry. Wow!

We were allowed to bring a drink through with us, it was very informal and we had a great hour trying on kit and equipment, practicing breaking down the Light Machine Gun (LMG) and a Self-Loading Rifle (SLR). Of course the army cadet kids were all familiar with this stuff and tended to show off; but the instructors were used to this and soon subtly put them in their places.

Finally a projector was dragged in, a screen pulled down and a couple of training films shown.

It had been a great day, we drifted back into the lounge and had another drink, an urn of soup and bread had been brought over from the cookhouse for those who wanted supper. We were given our orders for the morning. Parade in sports kit at 0830.

We would have breakfast followed by a game of football.

Shower, debriefing talk and then, either transport to the railway station or wait for our parents to collect us.

Upstairs and lights out at 2200.

The following morning all the instructors were on parade with us. They marched with us to the cookhouse and sat among us during breakfast, chatting and asking us how we had enjoyed the weekend. As informal as this was I knew that it was all part of the selection process.

Back to the block we went.

'Return to your rooms, make up your beds and be down here at 0930,' said Corporal Green.

We then jogged off to the football field.

Divided into two teams instructors included and with a few left over on the subs bench we kicked off for a full 90 minute match. Every ten minutes or so places would be changed so everyone had a turn on the field and on the subs bench. It was great fun and at the end we were in a filthy state as well as being cold; after all it was still only March.

We went back to the block for a shower and to pack our bags.

Sundays was a brunch day in the cookhouse. This meant food was served all morning and the squaddies living on camp could go in at any time.

The food was mainly breakfast type food, toms, beans, egg and chips, bacon, sausage, etc.

We were marched for our last meal and then on return reported to the lecture room.

We were asked if we had enjoyed our weekend and picked at random to give an answer. It was very light-hearted the instructors picking up on comical events making us laugh uproariously. The staff did this deliberately to make us leave with a feel good factor about us; our final memory of the place being a happy one; all psychological.

We were told that we would be contacted by our local Army Information Office as to whether we had been successful or not. That if we had, the next step would be our formal swearing in ceremony; before receiving our orders to report.

Were there any questions?

'Ok those going to the station please go and get your case and get on the bus outside. Those waiting for family to pick them up please collect their cases and wait in the leisure room; well done all of you and good luck.'

There were three of us left behind; me, the lad from Bridgewater and a girl from Salisbury. We sat and chatted, I was the second to leave when a soldier came from the guardroom on the gate to tell me mum and dad were waiting in the car.

With the soldier I picked up my bag and went to meet my parents.

What a monumental weekend.

Dad hadn't pulled away from the parking slot before the questions started. I was swamped by them from both parents and my brother.

'Wow,' I said. 'Hang on a minute and I'll tell you the whole story.'

And that's what I did during the drive back to North Bradley.

My dad's concerns were mainly about how I performed in the tests we had been set, whereas my mum's concerns were more about how I'd like the life, the discipline, the communal living, in short my first taster of army life.

Mum's questions were extreme considering I'd only been away less than 48 hours.

I told them not to worry that all had been ok.

We got home, mum had cooked a roast for tea, we had a couple of hours TV then I went to bed knackered; I had school the following morning.

I was the first boy from the fourth year to have gone for army selection which made me a bit of a celebrity at school; not only among my peers but also the teachers.

On Monday morning after assembly we always had an hour in our form rooms with our own form teacher.

Terry Baker promptly stuck me out the front of the class to tell everyone how the weekend had unfolded. This was of great interest to a few in the class who were also contemplating the same route as me. I also answered questions from the class. It was fun and not something I minded doing; throughout my life I would never be daunted talking in front of a crowd regardless of size.

School carried on the last couple of weeks to Easter break.

We returned for the final term of our fourth year; for many, (me included if I passed my army selection), this would be the last term of what had been ten long years of school.

In July we would be setting of to work in an adult world.

However that was still a few months away and for now a whole bunch of us looked forward to the following Sunday when we would be heading for Jersey.

It would be six days under canvas in St Brelades and we would go by ship from Weymouth.

We would leave on Saturday 11th April, the day before my brothers birthday and return the following Saturday.

I was grateful to my parents for letting me go on this trip; things were far from good at Marcos. More men had been laid off and the company was in dire financial straits, dad still had grave concerns around the security of his job.

I couldn't understand this; people were still buying the cars. In fact more cars were being produced at Westbury than at Greenland Mills; so what was the problem?

Dad said it was cash flow, but didn't enlarge on this expression... I don't think he or mum knew what it meant either. But one thing was for sure they were both very worried.

The letter arrived from the army.

I had passed my assessment; I was accepted. My results had been of a high enough standard that my first choice of regiment and career could at this point be followed. My reporting date would be 16th September 1971 to the Junior Leaders Regiment, Royal Engineers, Old Park Barracks, Dover, Kent.

I just couldn't believe it.

Until that point I don't think I'd ever thought it would come-off. Of course it had all been leading to this moment, but, it had seemed so distant; now it had really come home to roost. On 16th September I would be leaving home for the army... blimey.

My parents had mixed emotions, mum especially. They wished me well in my choice, I know they admired my independence and confidence and yet they had this thing that they were casting me out, that I was too young to be leaving home. I had to remind them that a few years before they were willing to send me to boarding school in Anglesey; I'd only been around twelve or thirteen at that time. Gran was livid, because she thought mum and dad totally irresponsible and was adamantly against me going. I spent ages talking to her and telling her it was my choice; I was not being forced into anything against my will. I don't think I ever convinced her; not up to her dying day.

I would be contacted with details of my swearing in ceremony; that would take place at the army careers office in Bath.

This successful news did guarantee me a trip to Jersey with my mates in March .Yeah! Bring it on!

I passed the acceptance news on at school and was called to the teachers' staff room one break time to be congratulated by the teachers en-masse, well the teachers from the main block anyway. Then taken across the corridor into Cooky's office where I got the same celebrity treatment, along with one of his 'Well done, well done, that's the spirit, a proud moment for the school,' lectures.

Good old Cooky. You'd think I was playing centre forward for England the way he went on.

The trip to Jersey was set for a week after Easter.

Not the best time of year to go camping but I suppose it was less expensive than later in the year; also I was assured the climate in Jersey was far warmer than on the UK mainland.

One thing I never had to worry about was the camping gear; sleeping bags, outdoor clothing or camping equipment, the Burt family had the lot.

We left on the evening train from Trowbridge to Weymouth. Our parents delivered us to the station, a motley lot with an assortment of baggage, mainly suitcases. Soft bags, holdalls, and rucksacks were more or less unheard of among the masses. The suitcase was the sole means of transporting clothing and most of these were built equal in strength to a nuclear fallout shelter.

Leather riveted corners, a solid leather handle held in place by more rivets, latches and locks that would be worthy of a place on a cell door in Wormwood Scrubs and finally as a back-up should all else fail a couple of leather straps which wouldn't look out of place on a plough horse harness. It weighed a ton before you put anything in it.

I however had a rucksack... Oh yes, a real German type metal framed rucksack, as worn by those starring in German propaganda movies of the thirties or in the Sound of Music.

I'm sure the rucksack was part of a matching set bought by my mum to go with the Lederhosen. Thank god I never had to wear the Lederhosen at the same time as carrying the rucksack; I'd have been compelled to continually sing 'I love to go a wandering along the mountain track, Val-deri, Val-dera,'... and so on.

Rob waiting to be told to sit down properly and get his feet off the furniture on the ferry to Jersey.

Anyway it came in handy and relieved me of having to carry everything in my hands.

We had a whole heap of stuff to carry, sleeping bags, blankets, camp beds, etc.

Parents off-loaded their boys at the train station in Trowbridge where Bill Jennings our leader and teacher, shunted us into some form of order and gave us a mini briefing on behaviour, conduct expected of a Nelson Haden pupil, and don't let the school down type of stuff – it went in one ear and out the other.

Extra communal school camping kit was shared out for carrying, and we waited in anticipation for the train.

We looked like evacuee children leaving the smoke in 1939 the only thing missing was the name and address labels tied to our blazers. Oh! And we were all travelling in school uniform.

The train came in we said our goodbyes to our parents promising to take care, be good, and send a postcard.

Bear in mind some of these kids had been no further then Swanage or Weston-Super-Mare in their lives.

As a group, with the help of a few mums and dads we got everything aboard and we were off.

A rowdy hour later we arrived in Weymouth.

The railway station is nowhere near the ferry port; it's a good mile away.

Down Kings Street and along the Esplanade we staggered under the weight of our equipment and baggage; strung out over the mile with Jennings in the lead we looked like a bedraggled band of refugees; but eventually we all arrived at the ship. The ferry didn't leave till 11pm so we had time to explore the decks and find good recliners for the journey. Funds had not stretched to cabins.

Early in the morning we woke to the sound of the boat docking; our first stop was St Peters Port in Guernsey and we dashed on deck to watch what was happening. Cars and freight unloaded, more cars and freight loaded and we were off again to Jersey arriving an hour or so later in St Helier.

Back at sea we went to the cafeteria for breakfast and then dashed on deck to watch our entry to the island's capital with the castle overlooking the port and marina. Thousands of seagulls flew above the ship crapping on everything and everyone exposed at the rail.

Ceasaria (the name of our outbound ship) docked, we disembarked the (*posh word for leaving a ship*) into a waiting coach for our camp site in St Brelades. It was a sunny morning breezy with a chill in the air. The road followed the coast round the bay from the capital then across the headland to St Brelades with lovely scenery along the way. We were all quiet, it had been a long night and with the excitement we had not slept many hours; those few hours we had slept had been in the recliner seats, not that comfortable or undisturbed.

The tents were already erected for our arrival, we sorted out who was sleeping where and the rest of the day was spent settling in and exploring our base for the next five days.

The camp had the sad air of a place not yet ready for the coming season. The swimming pool had green moldy water in the bottom with frogs swimming around.

The few amenities on the site were also closed; but hey we were only a few hundred yards from the beach and the promenade so it was no big deal.

A big wall on the side of the car park (the outside wall of the cafeteria I think) had a big map of the world painted on it. Within no time a football appeared from somewhere and we were kicking the ball off the wall. Midafternoon it started to rain and didn't stop.

Rob hoping someone will turn up to play football with him on our camp site in Jersey. Knowing we were from Trowbridge they put our tents as far as possible from the rest of the site.

In the evening we were dished-out a packet of Vesta freeze dried meals to bring to life in boiling water. We attempted to do this on little camping cookers under the tent awnings and failed miserably. In the end Mr Jennings went into town and bought every one of us fish and chips which we ate in the toilet block which was dry and reasonably warm. This is where we all ended up sleeping the first night... Yes, in the toilet block on the floor!

The rain cleared by morning and the sun came out. Thankfully this was going to be the only rain we would experience during the week.

We soon got into the swing of the trip and during the week visited all the landmark tourist sites of the island as well as going across to Guernsey to visit the German underground hospital on the other island.

This was the one trip that really stuck out in my mind. I was well aware of the atrocities that Germany had committed during the Second World War. I had read about them; been taught about them at school, and had them thrown up at me during arguments with my peers. I had developed an ability to shrug it off. I always believed that whatever had happened during the war my German family had not been involved; sure

279

my granddad had been a soldier in the German army but he had been an Engineer.

I found the visit to the German underground hospital disturbing.

The hospital had been built by slave labour imported from Eastern European countries that Germany had overrun and occupied; thousands of these soldiers and civilians had been worked to death during its construction. The fact that it was German Military Engineers who had managed the construction did not sit comfortably with me; I was sure my grandfather had not worked on the hospital, but I knew he'd spent time on Guernsey recovering from wounds he'd sustained on the Russian front.

What made matters worse for me while we were on the visit, was listening to what my school friends said about the Germans.

Understandably they came out with nasty comments, after all they were only kids and they were horrified to read the statistics and see the exhibits.

The comments weren't directed at me personally but all the same it made me acutely aware of my part German heritage; it was also the first time that I had come face to face with the things I'd read and heard about German war crimes.

Until that point I'd not seen any television documentary programs on Auschwitz, Belsen, or any other of the German atrocities which appear daily on our TVs sixty years on from the war.

Whether they were just not on TV at that time or my parents deliberately kept me and Pete from viewing them I don't know.

Although it was an interesting visit I was glad to leave the place and to this day I remember it quite vividly. The day spent at the underground hospital remained with me for a long time I don't think I ever really got that trip out of my head.

It was an enjoyable week; we visited La Corbiere lighthouse, a Martello tower owned by Bill Jennings' uncle. We went to the zoo, the Devil's Hole and St Elizabeth castle the big castle in St Helier.

On the last night Bill Jennings took us into St Brelades for a fish and chip supper then on the way back to the site picked up a case of Mary Ann beer which he shared out between us.

Our ferry home was the Sarnia, a day ferry, we docked in Weymouth and dragged ourselves the mile back along the prom to the railway station. We arrived back in Trowbridge around 5pm where most of our parents were waiting on the station to collect us.

Mr Jennings middle front, Rob and me behind him. Jersey school trip.

Most of our week spent in Jersey I had forgotten, it's my good fortune that my mate Rob has an amazing recollection of our week under canvas and was able to more than fill in the gaps in my own memory. Also Rob must have been the only kid that brought a camera with him. The photos are also his contribution; thank you Rob.

A great deal can happen in a week and I got home to the news that gran was moving from nineteen into Mrs Weston's bungalow three doors down at number thirteen.

Mrs Weston, Jeff's gran had recently passed away and the house was waiting for a new council tenant. The bungalow was slightly smaller with less garden area than nineteen.

Gran was pleased to be able to make the move and it was a sensible thing to do as our family no longer lived within walking distance to help out around the garden on a daily basis.

The move took place during the half term holidays; mum and dad took two days off from work and Pete and I had the full week off school so together we were able to help gran with the initial move and Pete and I stayed over to help put things away and tidy up.

Over at Westbury things at Marcos were looking grimmer by the day; mum and dad were continually talking about what to do for the best; eventually they made the decision that dad should look for a new job and that would put his mind at rest. But on no account would mum let him return to the Avon.

However this project was not as easy as it first seemed. Dad spoke to a few companies but for one reason or another he never got the offer of a move, or declined a job offer for one reason or another.

The summer holidays were approaching, I received another letter from the army to say that I would be called into Bath recruiting office for my swearing in ceremony and that I was to report to Old Park Barracks Dover on Thursday 16th September. Train warrant and movement orders would be sent to me. I now had a date.

One evening out of the blue mum and dad told us we should go to gran's after school the following evening, stay with her the night and take the bus back into school the next morning. That afternoon we should go home straight from school and get ourselves some food, take care of the dogs and cat. On no account were we to go out that evening. Mum would phone at six-o-clock and let us know what time they would be home. They were going off for the day. Pete and I were intrigued and asked what was going on. Our parents would say nothing. We would know in good time. (*In good time for what...?*)

What we didn't know was mum and dad had to make an early start in the morning to go for an interview in Bedford.

A job in Norfolk had been advertised in the national press; they had seen it and decided to apply.

The job if they were successful would entail a move right across the country to Gt Yarmouth in East Anglia; to work as chicken farmers on a broiler farm for Buxted frozen foods.

Buxted had purchased a complete chicken producing company in Norfolk; twelve farms in all, with a hatchery and processing facilities in a place called Burgh Castle just outside Gt Yarmouth.

The first round of interviews were being held in Bedford. Mum and dad had applied and received a letter asking them to attend. Of this Pete and I knew nothing.

We did as instructed but of course we wanted to know where they were going, we guessed it was something to do with dad's work, but our parents would give us no details.

We were eventually told when the letter arrived offering them a second interview at the hatchery, an eight or nine hour drive away at the end of the world.

When dad and mum eventually told us I was horrified; I'd seen all I wanted to see of East Anglia on our brief trip to Wells and had no inclination to return. However I was promptly put in my place by dad who said I wouldn't be living there anyway as I was destined for Dover and the Junior Leaders. (*Didn't take too long to write me out of the family framework did it*).

Peter was a bigger concern, but mum told us they had the same schools in Norfolk as in Wiltshire and at the end of the day the importance of dad having a job overrode everything else.

I couldn't believe my father was unable to get work locally; after all, my uncle worked with dad and he seemed fine, he had no stress about job loss...Again I got the feeling, just as I had in Winsley that mum was happier the further she was away from dad's place of birth. No one had told him he was going to lose his job, he was still being paid and Marcos was still building cars.

This lovely house we had worked so hard to make habitable, to make our own, surely they weren't seriously planning on moving? But they were.

Now years on I look back and wonder if it was dad who wanted to move mum away from Trowbridge rather than the other way round. Mum was an attractive, outgoing, gregarious woman; happy, popular at work and a bit of a party person, dad was completely opposite; he would happily sit at home and watch the box. He was a home bird and I somehow feel he thought his wife was becoming too much of a party animal.

Maybe this is a bit strong as an assumption, but you get my drift. A move to a job where they worked side by side would suit dad down to the ground, rein mum in a bit... a man and wife job where he could keep an eye on her... dare I say it, constantly.

The shortlisted applicants were to be interviewed in depth at the chicken hatchery in Burgh Castle. Following the interview the applicants would be driven around farms and asked their preference on which farm they would like to live should they be offered a position.

This time we would go as a family.

Permission would be sought from the school that Pete and I miss a day and Danny and Angela would come over after work and see to our pets.

We needed to be at Burgh Castle for 11am in the morning. This meant a 2am start from North Bradley.

We joined the now completed M4 at Chippenham and continued into London on the Chiswick flyover coming off onto the north circular A405 as far as the junction with the A1.

Through Hatfield on up the A1 to Baldock, then the A505 to Royston, Newmarket, Thetford, Norwich and Gt Yarmouth.

I must admit it was a good run and we were in Gt Yarmouth by 10am. Dad's Triumph Vittesse 2000 GT just flew along.

But this was not the same as going on holiday. Pete and I said very little. I think we were both making a point of sulking and letting our parents know we were not on-side with this venture.

The country was flat and uninteresting and when we arrived in Yarmouth I thought it looked drab and uncared for. We parked on the market and went for a breakfast in a café down Market Row. I refused point blank to put a smile on my face. Pete and I took a seat in the cafe while mum and dad brought food. Pete looked at me and said, 'well Bruv, at least you won't have to live here like me.' Poor bugger...

Driving from the market place along the Southtown river road and out to Burgh Castle was slightly more interesting; well at least the river bit was with all the supply and lumber ships tied up along the two miles of quayside.

On arrival Pete and I were invited in for tea and biscuits while mum and dad had the interview. Surprisingly it was very short and we were then introduced to a bloke called John Smith who was going to escort us around the vacant farms so mum and dad could choose where, if successful, we would live. Pete and I of course prayed they would fail.

We were taken to Caister-on-Sea. Ormesby, Winterton, Martham and Sea Palling, ending up at Upton. These were the farms that were available for us to choose from. John advised we make a first, second and third choice and let them know as soon as possible should the position be offered. He then directed us to the A47 in Acle and we were on our way home.

I told my parents if they chose Winterton or worse still Sea Palling I would never come home. They may as well live on the moon. Dad was getting extremely annoyed with my attitude and told me to shut up he and mum would decide.

However we all knew that Pete's schooling had to be taken into account that would play a part in the decision.

During the drive home it was agreed they would go for Caister, Martham, Ormesby and Upton in that order. During the drive they also filled us in on the basics of the job.

The farms held sixty thousand birds. These chickens were delivered at one day old and reared in heated sheds for eleven weeks. Fed on special food they grew massive in this time; then a catching crew came in and loaded them (very cruelly I was to discover) into cages where they were taken for processing into meat for the table.

Mum and dad would be employed as a couple. Their job was to feed, vaccinate and care for the birds until collected. After the birds were caught and the sheds were empty a cleaning and fumigation gang came in to sort out the mess; after three weeks sawdust would be scattered on the floor, big heater rings hung from the roof and the whole process started again. My parents didn't have any idea just what they were letting themselves in for.

Our first home in Norfolk. The chicken farm main road Ormesby.

After a long stop for a meal we eventually got home at midnight.

We now had to wait and see if the worst happened and they were offered the job.

The following day they were phoned and offered the joint position; they accepted.

Pete and I were not happy and neither was gran. In fact gran was very, very upset. Her only son and her two grandsons were moving a long way away. I assured my gran I would spend my home leaves from the army with her. This cheered her a little, but she never got over the family moving to Norfolk. For that matter neither did I.

Dad only had to give a week's notice at Marcos but mum had to give a month. Dad decided he too would give a month's notice to Jem Marsh as it would be fairer than just the week. We also had to give notice on the farm house and find Pete a new school.

Fortunately for mum and dad their first delivery of chicks wouldn't be delivered until the end of August, this gave us some breathing space for the move and a quick week in Germany.

Pete and I would see out the term which had three weeks left to run. We would then wait until both mum and dad had served their notice before going to Germany for a quick seven days. A week after returning from Oma's we would leave finally for Norfolk.

The stage was set for the Burt family departure; the farm we would be moving to was Ormesby St Michael.

End of term came in July 1971. Some of my school friends I wouldn't see again until we held a reunion in 2007. I went round the teachers I liked and said goodbye. They wished me well. Clare had gone back to Melksham; we'd gone out together on and off during the term, she gave me a photo, a lovely picture of her in a bikini on a beach somewhere. (*This photo will feature again in book 2 when I meet a lad at Dover who lived in Melksham*).I promised to write and look her up when I came home on leave.

We had a week before we left for Germany. I spent most of it working on the farm, desperately saving some money for the trip and to tide me over, I didn't know when an earning opportunity would present itself again and the last thing I wanted was to keep asking mum and dad for money; but the final two days Pete and I spent with gran and our mates in Winsley.

The last evening once again found us all sitting outside the Stars eating crisps and drinking coke-a-cola, Jeff, Sue Mayell, who for years had a fancy for Jeff, Kev, Sticky, and also Angie who I hadn't really seen or spoken to in ages.

While the others were laughing and joking Angie looked over at me and said 'Steve can we go for a walk a few minutes?'

'Sure,' I replied.

We got up and side by side walked off toward the Bowling Green with the others ribbing us as we strolled up the road. We crossed on the corner in front of old Dr Bembridge's house and entered the Bowling Green grounds through the high black metal gates, walking to the seats on which I'd sat so many times as a youngster watching granddad play bowls.

Now, out of sight of the others Angie had hold of my hand.

We walked over to the gap between the wall and the back of the hall; here Angie stopped and turned to look at me.

'Will you write to me Steve?' She said.

I was thunderstruck... we'd not had much to do with each other at all since the family move to North Bradley and without doubt she now had another boyfriend.

'Sure' I said, 'if you want me to? I'd like that.'

'So would I,' she said. Then looking up, she leant forward and gave me a kiss. It wasn't a peck of a kiss, it wasn't a long kiss either, but it was a kiss with feeling. It was to be the last kiss I ever had from Angie.

A few seconds passed as we stood looking at each other and she said 'come on, we better get back they'll be wondering what we're up to.'

Side by side we returned to 'The Stars' to more cat-calling, sat down and continued where we left off. Around 9pm as it began to get dark we wandered back through the old village and down Vinegar path; saying goodnight to our friends Pete went into grans while I stood and watched as my mates and childhood sweetheart faded into the darkness.

The following day once more we were off across the channel to Oma's.

During the course of the school term I had got hold of a lovely flick knife. Overall it was eight inches long with a four inch blade. I'd bought it or swapped it for something, it was neat with both sides of the handle depicting a Spanish bull fighting scene. The blade came out the side not the front which made it slightly less dangerous but it was still a formidable weapon and illegal in Britain.

On our trip back from Germany we stopped for a bite to eat; mum wanted a knife for some reason and I like a rabbit out of a hat produced the flick knife. What possessed me to take it on holiday heaven only knows but that was me all over. Mum took the knife from me.

I knew she wouldn't know how to open it and sure enough she said 'how do you get the blade out Steven?'

I took the knife and with a practiced flick of the wrist shot the blade from the handle.

Immediately mum's face clouded over and she shouted for my dad to come over.

She showed him the knife and he went off on one.

'Where did you get this?' He shouted.

Other people in the lay-by could hear him bellowing and all were staring in our direction. Pete retreated to the car.

'I brought it with me from home,' I said.

That made matters worse.

'You mean to tell me you've been walking around the whole bloody holiday with this knife in your pocket?' My dad asked.

'Well, not all the time,' I innocently said. 'Sometimes I left it in my bag.'

'You young fool,' said dad. 'You know this type of knife is illegal?'

'Not this side of the channel,' I cheekily replied.

My dad looked at me lost for words.

'Don't be bloody smart with me my lad. No, not this side of the channel, but you brought it with you through Dover and you were planning on taking it back through Dover. You are a bloody fool; I doubt for one minute the army will keep you, they'll send you packing if you don't change your ways. I just look forward to the day you become their responsibility instead of mine.'

'So do I,' I shouted in return.

This was becoming a full blown row and mum was intervening.

'Stop it you two; John get rid of the knife, throw it into the bushes or something.'

'Let me think about it, Steven, Peter, get back in the car,' said dad.

We climbed in and I watched as mum and dad packed up the food box. I could see they were discussing the knife but couldn't make out what they were saying.

Pete looked at me with sympathy.

Dad was mucking about under the bonnet of the car when mum got back in.

'You are a fool Steven, this is the second time you've pulled a stunt like this, surely you remember the last time.'

'Yes mum but I was eleven years old then and it wasn't a flick knife.'

'No Steven but surely you remember the hullabaloo? Your father and I were angry enough that time?'

I shrugged and said nothing.

The previous occasion was very similar. I was at junior school then, in the final year. Jeff had got hold of a lovely Japanese paper knife, the blade slid into a matching wooden sheath with a red tassel hanging from it. Pat had told Jeff to get rid of it and Jeff had swapped something with John Phelps; then later John had swapped it with me.

Once again I'd decided to take my prize possession with me on a Sunday school outing and it had been discovered.

It was taken away from me by the person in charge of the outing and handed to my parents on our return to Winsley.

Another telling-off and the knife confiscated by dad. A couple of years later I found it in his tool box, I stole it back and I still have it to this day.

Funny how they allowed me to walk round the village with a British army Burmese jungle knife dangling from one side of my belt and a nine inch sheath knife hanging from the other and yet created merry hell over a trivial Japanese paper knife...the logic of parents eh?

The bonnet was dropped and we were on our way. I think mum had given dad a ticking off about the army comment. Mum said dad didn't mean what he said. I grunted my acknowledgement. We drove on in silence.

We went through the customs at Dover with no problem; I assumed dad had chucked the knife in the bushes. It was never discussed again until 1977 when I was rummaging through tins of odds and ends in dad's garage and there it was.

I took it into the house and said, 'hey dad what are you doing with this? It's illegal you know?'

I had been a long time in the army by then, had more than proved myself and we had a good laugh about it.

He told me that after I'd got back in the car he had hidden the knife in the bottom of the windscreen wash bottle. It had been his intension to throw it in the bushes but when he looked at the lovely markings on the handle he couldn't bring himself to throw it away. He'd dropped it in the bottle and retrieved it when we got home. He'd hidden it away in the tin in the back of the garage ever since; he'd even forgotten himself it was there.

Where is it now? Who knows; since then my mum and dad have gone through four house moves; it could be anywhere, but I'm sure it will crop up again one day.

Preparation for the move to Norfolk began. Mum and dad had finished work, Pete and I had finished school. My parents had sold our lovely caravan, why they did that I really don't know other than perhaps they needed the money.

Our parents started officially with Buxted on the 1st September. We would leave for Norfolk on the 21st August.

A school had been found for Pete; Flegg secondary school in the village of Martham; the school bus went past the house. His term began Tuesday 7th September. Our final week in Wiltshire was spent packing and saying goodbyes. Mum and dad allowed Pete and I a day and night with gran.

We were really down in the dumps when we said goodbye to her, uncle Bert, auntie Dot and our friends. Gran was in tears and made me promise to write to her every week from Dover. It was a promise I kept throughout my time in the army. She also gave me a lovely St Christopher on a chain a very sentimental keepsake that I have treasured and worn continually from that day to this.

When our parents came to collect us we drove briefly to Farleigh Wick and said goodbye to auntie Dart and the family. I can't remember seeing the family in Swindon before we left.

We had to go through the same rigmarole in North Bradley. Nobby, Lizzie, Vic Turner and my delightful seductress Samantha... that was a real blow (or not as the case maybe) and of course school friends in this village as well.

The removal lorry collected our stuff on the Friday; we departed in the car towing our small glassfibre trailer load of odds and ends on the Saturday morning after roughing it on the floor Friday night.

Vic came over in the morning to look at the house, say goodbye to us and take the key, Nobby also came round to wish us well.

Pete and I were squashed in the small back seat of the Triumph with the two dogs and the cat in his small travelling cage.

It was a very hot day and it was the most miserable trip.

Goodbye Winsley, Turleigh, and Murhill, home to generations of Hosey's, Sartain's, and Burt's. Goodbye North Bradley, and goodbye to our lovely county of Wiltshire.

Our family was heading for a new life in East Anglia.

In a couple of weeks I would be taking a huge step into manhood with my departure to train as a soldier with the Royal Engineers at Dover. I was only just approaching the midway point between my fifteenth and sixteenth birthday, really still a kid.

Looking back now it seems incredible that I had chosen to leave home at that age; to enter a profession that wasted no time in training me in the art of warfare and killing using a multitude of methods.

The step from adolescence to adulthood could not be more dramatic.

But I had to go; there was just too much testosterone in our house. Hardly a day went by without dad and I having a row about something. It was becoming damaging to the family and no matter how I tried I couldn't rein myself in. If I stayed it would only get worse.

I believe my parents knew this and accepted my decision to go.

I had to spread my wings, have firmer discipline and channel my energies into something worthwhile.

It would turn out to have been the right decision.

Dad

Reading back through these childhood memories I'm very aware that my dad doesn't feature as prominently as either my mum or my gran. The reader could get the impression that all dad ever done around the house was take a belt to my back side and it was never my intention for the story to come over this way.

Yes, I did get smacked and it happened quite often, the majority of smacking was dealt out by dad, but mum also had no qualms about dishing out the corporal punishment which in truth I mostly deserved.

The sixties were still an age where kids got smacked and nobody bothered much about it. There was no 'Childline' or anything else for a child to turn to, a kid just put up with it.

Dad did his best to keep me under control but sadly neither he nor mum had an answer to my misbehaviour and the stick, slipper or belt was the last (and accepted at the time)resort.

Pete on the other hand rarely got a spanking, why, because he was generally well behaved; it's as simple as that.

From the moment I left the family home my relationship with my dad changed beyond recognition.

We had mutual respect for each other, we became much closer as father and son and we loved each other dearly.

I left home in September 1971with a heap of knowledge about mechanics, plumbing, carpentry, etc, all learnt during my childhood and adolescent years from my dad. He was a great dad and mentor who did a great deal for both his sons; we were involved with all his projects and he was disappointed if we weren't interest enough to help.

He admired my determination to leave home and join the army and had many sleepless nights when I was away on active service.

He set me up for adulthood as a dad should and I'll be forever in his debt.

I'm just glad for ten years -five to fifteen, I had those lederhosen.

Mum

Mum came from Germany and it was only natural she wished to hold on to her German roots and her German traditions.

She had been raised, not necessarily in a strict household, but definitely within a very regimented society under a strict regime. Order and discipline were ingrained in her upbringing and it's understandable that this ingrained adherence to obedient behavior continued on after her arrival in England and also into marriage and motherhood.

Behaviour, manners, order, and discipline were watchwords in our house just as they would have been in her house as a child with her parents and in her friends' houses with their parents; it was just the way it was in Germany; her parents, my grandparents were very

Me in my Lederhosen and German rig outside 17 St Nicolas Close around 1959

good people, kind, loving and protective of their children, but strict.

Order was everything and everywhere in Germany and grew stronger still when Adolf Hitler came to power; his belief was strength through unity and discipline.

'Alles in Ordnung' (everything in order) is a very German phrase which means as much to the German people in 2014 as it always has.

Mum didn't deliberately set out to Germanize (for the want of a better word) our house, it just happened and unfortunately or fortunately depending on who's view you would have listened to at the time, I being the first child was destined to be a Germanized child. The odd thing was I did look the archetypal German boy child, just look at the photo.

What my mum was thinking about when she dressed me as a mini Bavarian doll in a small English village heaven only knows. With my Lederhosen and Tyrolean jacket I should have been auditioning for a part in the Sound of Music or Heidi. But dress me that way she did.

You would think, directly after the Second World War and being effectively still one of the enemy, mum would have tried to blend in and try to have her family blend into the little West Country village where people tend to have long memories... But no, mum done just about everything possible to stand out and remind people that she was foreign, not just foreign, but German. Did dad ever try to talk some sense into her? No I don't think he ever did, at least I'm not aware of it.

I have asked her over the years, what in God's name made her decide to marry John Burt? Not that my dad was a problem, far from it, he was conscientious, hardworking and a very good looking bloke.

But she came from a historic, cosmopolitan city; the Hopp's had a house with running water and flushing toilets, a bath and shower.

In comparison, my gran's house in Chapel Rank had a long-drop thunder-box at the top of the garden and a tin bath in front of the fire, filled with kettles of boiling water from the range. Mum was even engaged to be married to a lad with very good prospects back in Dusseldorf... still that's the way it goes I suppose.

So, mum brought her German traditions to Winsley and I grew up the German boy in the English West Country village. Does it bother me now? No.

Did it bother me then? Well, certain things yes they did and I suppose a few of my minor gripes come out in this story. But in the main they didn't and Pete and I had a lot to be thankful for in having a mum who was German. We travelled; we visited towns, cities and countries that my peers wouldn't see for 20 years if then. I had seen and done more by the time I was 12 than most grown men.

It made me self-confident, self-assured and worldly. It gave my life a foundation stone so strong that every following layer of my life was built solidly upon it.

Oh, and the answer... My mum married dad because she fell in love with him.

Epilogue

My years of growing up in Winsley and the short time I spent in North Bradley I look back on as being special; actually more than special - extraordinarily wonderful.

Winsley was a special place in which to grow up and we kids grew up in a special moment in time.

A time where we could roam far and wide, play with freedom and without restriction.

A time when kids invented their own games, planned their own play, and made their own toys.

Where we were allowed to feel our way and experiment with our own abilities and resolve our own disputes.

I wouldn't have wanted it any other way and I'm sure if you asked all my mates, the girls and boys in this book, they would say exactly the same.

I hope this book has given an insight into our special village, the surrounding countryside, the life of our family and primarily, as was the initial intention, into my own life growing up in a country village during the sixties with a German mum an English dad who loved my brother and I equally and whose hair I turned grey on an almost daily basis.

Dedications have been made in the first few pages of this book; however a special dedication is needed for a special friend whose life was taken at far too young an age. A lad who was one of the nicest people it's ever been my pleasure to call friend; Kevin Holt who died of a brain tumor in 1985.

Steve and Kevin in granny Burt's back garden, summer 1976.

CPSIA information can be obtained
at www.ICGtesting.com
Printed in the USA
LVHW031359260320
651291LV00026B/787